Riverford Farm Cook Book

Riverford Farm Cook Book

Tales from the fields, recipes from the kitchen

Guy Watson & Jane Baxter

Photographs by Sam Hofman

FOURTH ESTATE

To our early box customers, whose support, trust and love of food
allowed me to farm the way I wanted to. GW

For David and Mandy (who, for the record, are not box customers). JB

First published in Great Britain in 2008 by Fourth Estate
A division of HarperCollins Publishers
77–85 Fulham Palace Road
London W6 8JB
www.4thestate.co.uk

8

A catalogue record for this book is available from the British Library

ISBN 978-0-00-726505-3

Typeset by 'OMEDESIGN
Printed and bound in Italy by L.E.G.O. SpA – Vicenza

MIX
Paper from
responsible sources
FSC C007454

Contents

Acknowledgements

Special thanks to the team at Fourth Estate.

To Jane Middleton, recipe editor, for dealing with an erratic, stressed-out chef in such a calm manner.

To Mr 'Cherry Tomato' Julian Humphries, for making the photo shoot such a pleasure.

To Sam Hofman for not poncing around too much with the photos.

To the Field Kitchen team for being supportive and creative under pressure, especially Kelly, Russell and Popey (who was particularly brilliant in the photo shoot).

To the recipes tasters at Riverford, especially Lisa and Jenna Smith whose support was invaluable and whose comments were hilarious (if a bit too brutal!).

To Joyce Molyneux for being such an inspiration, and to Rose and Ruthie for teaching me the 'River Café' way.

To my mum, brother John and dad (who have dined out on this for months) and my new family too – you know who you are!

And lastly to Sam, my partner in crime at the Field Kitchen, for the friendship and support throughout this project – well, at least I think she's still talking to me!

Jane Baxter

Decades before any journalist was interested, and before there was even an accepted definition of what they were doing, a small band of farmers and gardeners laid the foundations of organic farming as we know it today. They were much derided for their rejection of chemical farming and for the extreme and unscientific nature of their beliefs. They were freaks on the fringe, pursuing their enthusiasms in isolation down muddy tracks while the rest of farming swept past in the opposite direction.

Likewise in the kitchen; supermarkets began to peddle exotic, convenient and increasingly processed food, and a generation turned its back on local ingredients and culinary traditions. While cooking fresh, local ingredients from scratch fell from fashion, a band of strong-minded cooks, working in the isolation of their own kitchens, continued to value what the land around them could produce in season. Their work has helped to keep some semblance of culinary tradition alive, to be picked up by today's generation.

This group of independent thinkers who bucked the trend and stuck to what they intuitively knew to be right, without regard for the currents of opinion that swept others along, are my heroes, largely unsung. They developed the skills and fostered the early interest that led to today's renaissance in food and organic farming for a local market. On the growing side there was Charles Staniland, Graham Hughes, Arthur Hollins, Gordon Strutt, Lyn Phelps and many more who offered advice and hospitality when I started out. On the cooking side it was Alice Waters who inspired me to build the Field Kitchen. Joyce Molyneux started Jane on her career. Myrtle Allen and Jane Grigson kept things ticking over and laid a foundation. Everyone should be grateful to the person who taught them to cook, so above all my acknowledgement is to my mother, Gillian Watson, who inspired all her children with a love of food prepared from what grew in her garden and on the farm.

My father John taught me that above all else I should aspire to be useful, and Andy Langford got me thinking that being truly useful should be the aim of all business.

Without the patient, skilled and well-judged editing of Louise Haines and Rachel Watson, my sister, this book would have been intolerably laboured and self-indulgent. Without their encouragement and occasional but necessary nagging, it would never have happened.

Guy Watson

About Riverford

The Riverford dynasty emerged in the post-war years out of the marriage of a fantastic cook and a determined young farmer. Fifty-five years later it is still a family business, with all five of the second generation applying the values we inherited from our parents in the search for a saner way of producing, distributing and enjoying food.

The patriarch

When the recently demobbed, idealistic and pitifully inexperienced John Watson took on the Church of England tenancy of Riverford Farm in 1951, his more traditional farming neighbours confidently predicted he wouldn't last five years. Food rationing was coming to an end and British agriculture was embarking on a new era of chemically driven intensive farming. For 25 years Riverford was at the forefront of these changes, even at one time being a demonstration farm for ICI. But by the 1970s my father was increasingly questioning the sustainability and animal welfare involved in some of the more intensive practices. By the 1980s the door was open for the next generation to take the farm in a different direction.

The matriarch

Perhaps even more significant to the shape of Riverford today was the influence of our mother, Gillian, who married John and moved to Riverford in 1952. It was her irrepressible enthusiasm for food and cooking that laid the foundations for the food businesses run by their five children today.

Their children

There was no overt pressure for us to continue in food and farming, but it was deeply instilled in us that we should do something useful with our lives, and nothing else seemed to make the grade. Over the years, those of my siblings who had gone away have drifted back to continue and broaden the farm's activities, now into a third generation.

First Ben, complete with law degree but recognising that he would be stifled in a wig, started experimenting with curing bacon in the garage. Thirty years later he has three shops and a substantial home-delivery business supplied by his own pies and preserves, butchery and bakery.

I was the next to return, after a brief spell as a management consultant in London and New York, and was responsible for setting up the vegetable box scheme and starting the Field Kitchen. Meanwhile, throughout the 1980s and 1990s, Oliver and Louise expanded the farm, developing the dairy and moving to extensive, organic production methods, complete with their own milk, yoghurt and cream business. Rachel was the last of the five to return to the farm, after a marketing career in London, and is now involved in developing the marketing of the vegetables and farm shops.

Vegetable boxes

As the vegetable business developed during the 1980s, we started looking beyond local shops. Supermarkets were just starting to stock organic produce and it was inevitable that we would eventually end up selling through them. This brought scale and forced a more professional approach, but working through such a wasteful supply chain was hugely frustrating; seeing our vegetables devalued through age, distance, excessive packaging and anonymity, while trebling in price, made me think there must be a better way. A meeting with Tim and Jan Deane, founders of the first box scheme in the UK, sowed the seed but it was the enthusiastic response of my first customers on the doorstep that really convinced me to change paths.

The first vegetable box was delivered in 1993 and since then home delivery has enabled us to break free from the clutches of the supermarkets and to relate directly to our customers. The early boxes were very basic and it soon became obvious that we would need to broaden our range and season if we were to appeal to more than a small band of hard-core local veg-heads. We put up polytunnels, experimented with new crops and eventually started trading with farmers abroad to keep the boxes interesting throughout the year. Initially my staff were sceptical. Planting and picking the small, fiddly quantities that the boxes demanded was an unwelcome complication after loading lorries with white cabbage, but the appreciative comments of customers, in contrast to a supermarket buyer's abuse, converted everyone. Like the Field Kitchen that followed, the box scheme has been the way to make the best food accessible and affordable to all, and to share our enthusiasm for food and cooking.

Why organic?

Having made myself sick spraying corn as a teenager, and seen my brother committed to hospital with paraquat poisoning, my initial motivation for farming organically was simply a personal desire to avoid handling pesticides. At the back of my mind, there was also a hunch that it offered better long-term financial prospects than adding to the lakes and mountains of overproduction that pervaded the EU in the 1980s.

During the early years there were numerous mistakes and frustrations but I came to relish the challenge of finding my own solutions to agronomic problems rather than following the prevailing belief that the answer to every difficulty lay in a chemical container. Latterly, this has evolved into a belief that we must find a more harmonious and holistic way of living within the limits of our planet. The problems faced by food and farming now have more to do with culture than with science. Organic farming, in its broadest sense (working from the underlying principles rather than just following the minimum standards for certification), provides the best framework available for finding answers to those problems.

Co-operation

By the late 1990s we were no longer regarded as freaks by our neighbours and a few were open to the idea of organic farming. In 1997 ten (now16) local farmers joined us to form the producers' co-operative, increasing production to keep pace with the expanding box scheme.

The future

Meanwhile, my father, John has stepped aside and has since devoted his time to searching for a more sustainable way of living and farming. Recreated in this role, he has become the guardian and critic of the environmental activities of his offspring. Perhaps it was partly this parental ethical audit that led me to decide that the booming vegetable box business based in Devon was big

enough. If we were going to grow any further, it would be on a local basis in co-operation with local growers in ventures on a personal scale. Over the last few years, we have been using our knowledge to set up other regional box schemes supplied by local farmers. Today that is River Nene in Peterborough, River Swale in Yorkshire and a second Riverford in Hampshire, hopefully soon to be joined by similar ventures with local farmers in Kent and the northwest. My dream is that if these ventures stay small and work together, we will have the professionalism that will allow us to offer a real and substantial, but saner, alternative to supermarkets without becoming like them.

Farming, cooking and eating habits have changed hugely over the half a century since our father milked his first cow at Riverford. The challenge for the second generation is twofold: to reduce the environmental impact of producing food and getting it to the door, while fostering the culinary knowledge and enthusiasm needed to get it on the table. Shortening the food chain and promoting the connection between producers, cooks and their tables is the best way of restoring food to its rightful position as a central part of our culture. I hope this book goes a small way towards achieving this.

About the Field Kitchen

My four siblings and I are obsessed by food. It all comes from our mother, who was a fantastic cook and, contrary to the fashion of the times, drew her inspiration from the seasonal produce grown in her garden and on the farm. Every day she served wonderful, generous lunches for the family and many of the farm staff. Looking back, I am struck by how similar the lunches we shared around a long kitchen table then are to the ones Jane serves for our guests in the Field Kitchen today. They both demonstrate a passion for simple, gutsy food, served with informal generosity, combined with an unhealthy appetite for butter and cream – but then we are principally a dairy farm.

Bolstered by occasional but erratic amateur success in the kitchen and by an unflagging enthusiasm for my vegetables, I did briefly harbour fantasies of becoming a chef whilst in my thirties. Fortunately the fantasy passed, but the seed of an idea lingered on, nourished by preparing occasional feasts at the farm for staff, customers or school groups. Meanwhile, our box scheme flourished out of an enthusiasm for sharing the farm's produce at its best, with people who wanted to know where it came from. A farm restaurant was a logical step but it took a lunch at Alice Waters' wonderful Chez Panisse restaurant in Berkeley, California, to sow the seed.

Wanting your own restaurant is an affliction common to many middle-class, middle-aged men and has been the ruin of quite a few. Anthony Bourdain, author of the wonderful *Kitchen Confidential*, puts our ailment down to a pathetic lusting after waitresses. For some, perhaps. For me, it had more to do with gluttony, and frustration at all the dreadful, overpriced meals I have been served locally, combined with a blind arrogance and naive belief that it can't be that difficult.

I was determined that we would find a way of making the kind of authentic food my mother served at those farm lunches available to a wider audience without charging the prices that, too frequently, make real food the preserve of the wealthy and childless. With a strong vision but no experience, I set about designing the building, fighting with planners, raising the cash and starting construction. But who was going to cook the food?

Chefs and their staff make up an international network, with tribal allegiances accessible only to those on the inside. Every time I met an insider, I would collar them, describe my vision and ask if they knew of a chef who might help turn it into reality.

The cook

One day the phone rang and there was Jane from Sunderland, via a string of prestigious restaurants and a Pacific atoll. After 15 years of poncy food and high-pressure urban cooking, she had slowed life down and got back to basics on a remote atoll 550km north of Samoa, where she baked bread in a stone oven, and had her son, David, along the way. Swearing that she would not go back to London, and looking for a chance to apply her skills to the best ingredients with the minimum of pretension (something all southerners are suspected of), she threw herself into making the Field Kitchen a reality. As I remember it, there was no interview; it was obvious from the outset that Jane was the perfect choice, and we just got on with talking about how we were going to make it work.

Jane has a degree in agronomy but had spent much of her time at university cooking for friends. Her break came in Cornwall, working for George Perry-Smith at the Riverside in Helford, which led to a job at the Carved Angel in Dartmouth during its heyday under Joyce Molyneux – who Jane still cites as her main influence. This was followed by a spell at the River Café in London, which gave Jane an understanding of cooking very simply with respect for top-quality ingredients. Seven years spent cooking her way around the South Pacific challenged culinary preconceptions and taught Jane to improvise with greens such as the slippery cabbage she encountered on the Solomon Islands, making anything we can throw at her seem tame in comparison.

While we were finishing building the Field Kitchen, Jane established a canteen for our staff at one end of our packing shed, then a few months later, working with the head of our local primary school, took on the contract for supplying its school dinners. Initially I was fearful that such everyday feeding of the troops would be at best boring and at worst demeaning but, true to her proclamations in favour of gutsy over poncy, Jane rose to the challenge, making these children and staff some of the best fed in the land. The Field Kitchen was opened by Hugh Fearnley-Whittingstall in May 2005 and was instantly a success with customers, if not necessarily with my accountant.

The restaurant

First-timers at the Field Kitchen can't believe the quality and generosity, given the prices, which reflect our determination to make real food accessible and affordable to all. Indeed, we did lose money for the first two years while we fine-tuned our service but it looks as if we may have made a small profit in 2007. The secret, as with our box scheme, has been to banish choice, keep things simple, cut out fussy service and make the most of what is seasonally available from the farm. With Jane's experience at the River Café and other high-end establishments, I was expecting a battle to get her interested in the humble, indigenous vegetables in our fields. I was so wrong; from the start, the ingredients around her were her inspiration, as they had been to my mother, and the menu quickly developed to reflect that week's harvest, with new vegetables appearing on it as the season progresses.

The food is brought from Jane's kitchen to the communal, refectory-style tables in bountiful quantities for guests to serve themselves and share with whoever is next to them. Occasionally there is some initial anxiety but the informal and communal atmosphere has a remarkably civilising influence, which eventually works its spell even on those cursed with a gluttonous resistance to sharing.

Getting excited about vegetables

Cooking with raw, unprocessed, seasonal ingredients requires time, commitment, and a range of skills lost to many of the current generation of cooks. I am a firm believer that the more you know about how, where and by whom your vegetables are grown, the greater will be your confidence, enthusiasm and willingness to spend time in the kitchen acquiring those skills. I hope that a walk around our fields, followed by Jane's cooking, will inspire at least some of our visitors to cook, and to make more of fresh produce. The dishes we have included in this book are our favourites from the Field Kitchen and, in most cases, make best use of local ingredients. In each chapter, Jane's recipes are preceded by information on how the vegetable is grown, when it is in season, what are the key indicators of quality, and how best to store and prepare it. Interspersed throughout the book you will find occasional rants on a diverse range of food and farming topics, which are broadly based on some of the newsletters that accompany the veg boxes each week along with a recipe from Jane.

Apples

When my father took on the tenancy of Riverford after the Second World War, he was advised that the cider would pay the rent. The tenancy combined three small Church of England farms and each had its own mill for crushing the apples and press for extracting the juice. As the nation turned to beer and then wine, the orchards surrounding the farms progressively contracted, fell into ruin and were, for the most part, grubbed out in favour of more profitable crops. As children, we earned our pocket money in autumn by gathering the apples from the remaining trees for delivery to Hills Cider, the one surviving press in the parish. Orchards were made up of dozens of different local varieties, with glorious names like Pig's Nose, Slack ma Girdle, Tommy Knight and Plympton Pippin. Most of these were 'uck and spits' – too bitter and high in tannin to be fit for anything but the press. After weeks of labour interspersed with apple fights, the hessian sacks were hauled to the cider works. While the apples were weighed and unloaded, musty-smelling men in leather aprons delighted in plying us with last year's cider in the cool semi-dark of the barns, surrounded by rows of the 120-gallon wooden barrels used to mature the cider.

Today even Hills has gone. The cider works have been converted into dwellings that financed the emigration of the last of the Hills family cidermakers to Australia. There is a renaissance of cider and juice-making amongst a new breed of enthusiasts, alongside the boosting of mainstream cider brands by some clever marketing as 'over ice' drinks. There has even been some replanting of orchards in Somerset to meet this new demand. Growing cider apples is relatively easy because you are not constrained by specifications of size and cosmetic perfection; the odd bug and blemish all go to make up the brew. Producing dessert fruit is another matter.

The southwest of England, with its mild, damp, maritime climate, has never been a good area for table fruit; the persistent humidity makes the trees susceptible to fungal diseases that sap vigour and hence yield. The main production areas in the UK are in the southeast: Kent, Sussex, Suffolk and, to a lesser extent, Hereford and Worcester.

Even in these areas it is very difficult to produce an economically viable yield of fruit that is acceptable to a buying public whose eyes have been trained by supermarket displays of cosmetic perfection. Despite numerous attempts to develop more holistic, less intrusive approaches, even most organic growers resort to regular sprays of sulphur and sometimes copper oxychloride

(allowed under organic rules) to control fungal disease. As Paul Ward, our most successful UK apple grower says, 'It's a flawed system, but a good bit less flawed than the non-organic one.' Even Jeremy Saunders, perhaps our most determinedly idealistic supplier, growing on a sunny southern slope in the most favoured part of Devon and combining fruit with chickens ranging underneath, has found that he cannot make a living without regular spraying. As things stand at the moment it is either pragmatic compromise or imports, so we go with the compromise.

Despite the nation's professed enthusiasm for heritage varieties and local food, the stark reality for most commercial producers is that if it is not nigh on perfect in appearance, it will not sell. Pile a fruit bowl with a mixture of fruit of different grades and I guarantee that, unless your household is starving, or made up of hardcore eco-warriors, any blemished specimens will be left to wither at the bottom. That is why there are so few orchards left in the UK and why the huge majority of our fruit, organic or not, is imported. Pears, being early flowering and hence susceptible to frosts, are possibly even more difficult to grow commercially in the UK than apples. Plums and damsons fare a little better but are still going the same way as apples. Our native varieties, many of which produce plums of great flavour but poor shelf life, are again being slowly forced out by the more reliable, huge plums on steroids, mainly from Spain that have a longer shelf life.

The apple varieties that combine eating quality with a reasonable degree of disease resistance and suitability to our climate are (in rough order of maturity): Discovery, Early Windsor, Red Windsor, Worcester, Falstaff, some Russets, Cox (probably the most difficult to grow), Red Pippin and Spartan. The Dutch do well with Elstar, which tastes very similar to Cox and is a good keeper but much easier to grow. The only hope of growing quality fruit without copper and sulphur (the Holy Grail for all committed top fruit producers) is through using modern varieties, and there are now some very promising ones coming from Eastern Europe (Evita and Colina), France (Cox Royal – a Cox cross) and the USA (Crimson Crisp).

Apples vary hugely in their keeping qualities. Some late-cropping varieties such as Russets will improve in store and can be kept successfully in ambient conditions until Christmas, but generally the commercial practice is to keep fruit in cold storage at 1°C and high humidity. Fruit stored beyond January will normally also have the benefit of controlled or modified atmosphere storage. This means the apples are kept in a sealed store, where the oxygen levels are reduced and CO2 levels rise as the fruit respires. The idea is to put them to sleep without killing them and, just like anaesthesia, it requires careful monitoring and control to avoid disaster. If all goes well, the reduction in the respiration rate of the fruit can double or even treble shelf life. It is even possible to hold some varieties in reasonable condition right through to the start of the next season.

Horrified at this 'unnatural' and prolonged storage? Don't be Luddite; as most affluent people view a 52-week supply of crunchy apples as a prerequisite of acceptable life, and as all apples in the northern hemisphere are picked between July and October, the only alternative is shipping fruit from the southern hemisphere (normally Argentina, Chile, New Zealand and South Africa), where it is harvested in March and April. Intelligent use of controlled-atmosphere technology is far more energy efficient. It can even save energy compared to straight refrigeration because the fruit can sometimes be kept at a higher temperature. And don't be taken in by spurious research sponsored by southern-hemisphere fruit growers; there are almost no circumstances where shipping long distance is environmentally less damaging than storage.

Storage and preparation

Ripening starts on the tree and continues at a rate determined by temperature and atmosphere (particularly concentrations of oxygen, carbon dioxide and the natural ripening agent, ethylene, which is produced by the fruit itself). The aim of storage for the producer should be to deliver fruit that reaches perfection in your fruit bowl. Once you get the fruit home there is, unfortunately, no doubt that long-stored apples will deteriorate faster and have a shorter window of perfection in your fruit bowl than freshly harvested ones. Some of the early-season varieties of apple, particularly Discovery, are at their best for only about a week. As with all fruit, smell is a good indicator of flavour and ripeness. For the main varieties, ripening is all about the conversion of starch to sugar; they get sweeter up to a point, then the texture dives and they lose moisture, becoming soft and woolly. I suspect that apples, and particularly pears, are more often than not eaten well before their optimum ripeness.

Unless your fruit is becoming overripe, or you are not planning to eat it for a week or more, it is best to keep it in a fruit bowl at room temperature; you will lose much of the flavour and virtually all the perfume if you eat it straight from the fridge. Check the smell and firmness from time to time and try to eat the apples while they are at their best.

Apple and Amaretti Tart

This contribution came from Sarah Pope, who works in the kitchen. It's lovely – which has been said about Sarah herself!

Serves 8

700g Bramley apples, peeled, cored and sliced
1 tablespoon melted butter
2 tablespoons caster sugar
½ teaspoon ground cinnamon

For the base:
100g plain flour
50g butter
50g caster sugar
40g amaretti biscuits

To make the base, put all the ingredients in a food processor and process to a fine breadcrumb consistency. Press into a 23cm loose-bottomed tart tin. Arrange the apples in an attractive pattern on top. Brush them with the melted butter and sprinkle with the sugar and cinnamon. Place in an oven preheated to 200°C/Gas Mark 6 and bake for 30–40 minutes, until the apples are golden brown. Serve at room temperature.

Apple, Potato and Cheese Casserole

This recipe was given to us by Sharman, who works front of house at the Field Kitchen and takes a lot of stick for being the token veggie on the staff. We suggest serving it with some lovely pork sausages.

Serves 4

500g potatoes (any type), peeled and thinly sliced
2 onions, thinly sliced
350g apples (eating and cooking apples both work well),
    peeled, cored and thinly sliced
150g strong Cheddar cheese, grated
2 teaspoons sugar
200ml vegetable stock
1 teaspoon tomato purée
½ teaspoon Marmite
sea salt and freshly ground black pepper

Layer the potatoes, onions, apples and cheese in a greased ovenproof dish, seasoning as you go and lightly sprinkling each layer of apples with sugar. Finish with a layer of cheese. Heat the stock to boiling point and stir in the tomato purée and Marmite. Pour the stock over the layered potatoes and apples and cook in an oven preheated to 180°C/Gas Mark 4 for about 1 hour, until the potatoes are tender.

Apple, Orange and Dried Apricot Crumble

This little twist on a classic crumble makes a welcome change. Apple and banana also works well.

Serves 6–8

8 dessert apples, peeled, cored and cut into 1cm dice
1 orange, peeled and divided into segments (or diced)
juice and grated zest of 1 orange
100g dried apricots, roughly chopped
60g dates, roughly chopped
60g light soft brown sugar

For the crumble topping:
175g plain flour
125g butter
100g caster sugar
60g rolled oats

To make the topping, put the flour and butter in a food processor and whiz until the mixture has a fine consistency. Remove and place in a bowl. Add the sugar and oats and rub together with your fingertips so the mixture is slightly lumpy and not dry.

Mix the apples and orange with all the remaining ingredients and place in an ovenproof dish. Top with the crumble mixture and then bake in an oven preheated to 150°C/Gas Mark 2 for 45 minutes, until the fruit is tender and the topping golden brown.

Caramel Apple Pavlova with Pomona

This was devised when the soft fruit had finished and we were all feeling a little finished too, but it ticks all the boxes – especially if the caramel apples are still warm when they mix with the cream on the pavlova. If they are too hot, the pavlova will be a mess – but delicious! Peaches and nectarines can be used in the same way.

Serves 10

6 apples (any type will do)
200g caster sugar
1 tablespoon water
50g butter
2 tablespoons Somerset Pomona (or Calvados)
225ml double cream

For the meringue:
4 egg whites
250g caster sugar
3 drops of vanilla extract
1 teaspoon wine vinegar
1 teaspoon cornflour

First make the meringue. Whisk the egg whites until just stiff, then gradually add the sugar, a tablespoon at a time, whisking after each addition until stiff peaks are formed. Fold in the rest of the ingredients.

Line a baking sheet with baking parchment. Shape the meringue into a large circle on the parchment, about 25cm in diameter. Place in an oven preheated to 120°C/Gas Mark ¼ and leave for 1½ hours, until the meringue is firm to the touch. Turn the oven off and leave the meringue in it for 30 minutes, then remove from the oven and cool completely.

For the topping, peel and core the apples and cut each one into segments about 1cm thick. Heat a large, heavy-based frying pan, add the sugar and water and leave over a high heat, without stirring, until the sugar turns to a golden brown caramel (tilt the pan occasionally so it colours evenly). At this point, turn the heat down and stir in the butter. Add the apples and mix well. Turn up the heat and pour in the Pomona. Stir until the caramel and Pomona are blended (the caramel may form lumps but these will dissolve back into the sauce). Cook for 5 minutes or until the apples are tender, then add a table-spoon of the cream and blend well. Allow to cool a little.

Lightly whip the remaining cream and spread on top of the meringue. Top with the warm caramelised apples and their juices.

Easy ideas for apples

✦ Core and halve some apples, sprinkle with a little sugar, then place in a baking dish and roast until tender. Serve as an accompaniment to roast pork.

✦ To make a curried apple soup, sauté 1 chopped onion in butter, then add ½ teaspoon each of turmeric, ground cumin, ground coriander and mustard powder, plus a pinch each of cinnamon and cayenne pepper. Add 3 tart apples, peeled, cored and roughly chopped, cover with chicken stock and simmer for about 15 minutes, until the apples are soft. Blend to a purée and season well, adding the juice of ½ lemon.

✦ For stuffed apples, soak 4 tablespoons of raisins in 4 tablespoons of warm port, then mix with 4 tablespoons of chopped walnuts, 4 tablespoons of light brown sugar and a teaspoon of ground cinnamon. Core 4–6 large apples. Fill the cavities with the mixture, then place the apples in a baking dish containing a splash of water. Sprinkle with lemon juice and bake at 180°C/Gas Mark 4 for 40 minutes.

See also:
Celeriac and Apple Mash (page 114)
Asian Coleslaw with Peanuts and Chilli (page 79)
Braised Red Cabbage (page 83)
Waldorf Salad (page 121)
Warm Runner Bean Salad with Fennel, Apple and Walnut Dressing (page 169)
Kohlrabi, Apple and Walnut Salad (page 236)

An ode to dirt

When I was at college, the soil scientists tended to be wildly eccentric recluses who worked from labs in the cellar, occasionally emerging, bemused and mole-like, to gather samples and bemoan the world's pitiful ignorance and lack of interest in their subject. The problem with soil is that, to the casual observer, it is an inert, uninteresting inconvenience that sticks to your shoes and threatens to pollute and infect your food. Few appreciate that this is where terrestrial life begins, that it supports myriad organisms, that it is being destroyed by modern farming and that it needs our stewardship every bit as much as the giant panda.

A key principle of organic farming is to understand nature and find ways of working with it rather than seeking to dominate and replace it. This applies as much below ground as above but the ecology is even more complex and poorly understood. It is an unfortunate aspect of human nature that we distrust what we do not understand and will frequently try to control or destroy it rather than taking the time to understand and appreciate its virtues. Soil sterilisation, as practised in greenhouses and strawberry growing, is one of the most hideous abuses of modern farming, virtually akin to Nazi book burnings in its reflection of the narrow-minded ignorance of its perpetrators.

Good organic farmers, and a few conventional ones, are acutely protective of their soil, treating it with the commitment, concern and empathy normally reserved for close family members. I have seen organic farmers sniffing and even tasting their soil, and describing its virtues with familiarity and affection. A handful of healthy soil can contain millions of life forms from tens of thousands of different species, almost all benign or beneficial to us and our crops. Not only do they recycle organic matter, making nutrients available to plant roots, they also out-compete and even attack pathogenic bacteria, fungi, eelworms and slugs. Pesticides, fertilisers, animal wormers, excessive and poorly timed cultivation, compaction and poor drainage can all drastically reduce these populations, not by just a few per cent but by 10 or even 100 per cent. Imagine the outcry from WWF if anyone could see the carnage.

So if you can't see the fungi, bacteria and invertebrates and you don't feel inclined or qualified to taste your soil, how do you know it is healthy? Earthworms are a wonderful indicator. If you can find plenty of fat, juicy worms, you can be sure you have healthy soil; I would expect to find two to five per spadeful in our soil but I have seen soils that have grown continuous cereals for decades where you can dig for a long time without finding one. It is an uncomfortable truth that the soil would be much happier if we did not cultivate it at all and went back to being hunter-gatherers. You will find the best soils, supporting the most life, where we have been denied access: in the base of an old hedgerow, for example, the debris is naturally incorporated into the soil, and the gradation from leaf litter through fungal decay and the action of invertebrates into the soil below is seamless. The structure of the soil is invariably perfectly friable, breaking easily into fine crumbs that make me, as a grower, itch to sow seeds. Our heavy machinery, and in particular the compaction that it simultaneously rectifies and causes, is a clumsy luxury afforded by cheap oil. It is notable that during my farming career the cultivations have got deeper and deeper but the soil structure has almost invariably deteriorated. The skill of a good farmer lies in being able to get a decent crop with minimum detriment to the soil in its natural state. That requires experience, sensitivity, and occasionally listening to those moles in the basement.

Asparagus

Asparagus is the ultimate challenge for an organic grower. After two failures, I am saving it for a retirement project. All perennial crops (i.e. ones that come back year after year rather than being planted annually) are difficult, but the likes of rhubarb and globe artichokes at least stay where you put them, coming up in more or less the same place each year. They have the additional advantage of casting a dense foliage, which helps to suppress weeds, unlike the thin, feathery foliage of asparagus.

A weedy annual crop can be ploughed in and quickly forgotten but a good asparagus bed will keep down for eight to ten years. During that time, it will need almost constant labour to control weeds. Mechanical, inter-row cultivation is rendered impossible by the rampant root system and spreading nature of the plant, combined with the random emergence of spears. In the non-organic crop, weeds can be controlled with selective herbicides during the summer, followed by a dose of blanket, kill-it-all glyphosate once the asparagus foliage has died back in the winter. In the organic system, mulches and ground covers may help but in the end there is usually no alternative to getting down on your hands and knees.

After a few half-hearted attempts, I am ashamed to say that much of the asparagus we sell is imported from Andalusia. Two farmers in our co-op, undeterred by my gloomy predictions, have recently planted substantial acreages, so I hope that they are going to prove me wrong; mind you, I have met many organic growers who reckon they have cracked it, but when I return a few years later their beds are invariably submerged in weeds. I am tempted to say that if you want in-season, UK-grown organic asparagus, you can grow it yourself. Leave the courgettes and runner beans to us and go for a real challenge. Truly fresh asparagus justifies all the hard work, but unless you grow it yourself you are going to have to be prepared to pay through the nose for it.

Asparagus is easiest to grow in low-rainfall areas and on sandy soils, so clay loams like ours in the damp west of England are always going to be difficult. Slugs can be a problem, especially for young crowns, but at least rabbits normally give up after an initial graze, allegedly because it makes their pee smell weird (I'm not sure who worked that out).

Depending on the area, the year and the variety, picking starts in early May and runs through to mid or late June, when the crowns must be left to ensure that the plant can grow enough foliage to put energy back into the roots for the following year.

Storage and preparation

Asparagus should always be kept in the fridge and, like so many things, is best when fresh. Standing it upright in a little water will help to preserve its life. The flavour is normally most intense in the tip, becoming sweeter lower down. Smaller spears tend to be produced at the beginning and end of the season and can be slightly tougher than their fatter cousins. White asparagus is normally grown on very sandy soils by cutting the spears well below ground level once the tip breaks the surface. It is less fibrous and often sweeter.

The base of the asparagus stalk is tough, and you generally need to cut off the bottom inch or so; the point at which the stalk snaps cleanly is a good guide to where to trim. The trimmings are good for making stock, to be used in an asparagus soup or risotto.

We like asparagus best sprinkled with salt and olive oil and maybe a few thyme leaves, then roasted in a hot oven (200°C/Gas Mark 6) for about 5–7 minutes. This seems to intensify the flavour. You can also steam it, but if you don't have a steamer, chuck the trimmed asparagus into a deep pan of boiling salted water for 2–3 minutes (more for really chunky spears), ideally with the stems in the water and the heads in the steam above. They really don't need much more than salt, and maybe some butter and lemon, or hollandaise sauce. A real treat with a poached egg, (see page 20), or dipped in a soft-boiled egg.

Asparagus Carbonara

A vegetarian alternative to the classic dish – although it has to be said that a little shredded prosciutto added with the egg lifts it to a different level. This is a good way of stretching a single bunch of asparagus to feed 4.

Serves 4

1 bunch of asparagus
350g spaghetti or linguine
4 eggs
50g Parmesan cheese, freshly grated, plus extra to serve
1 tablespoon chopped chives, basil or tarragon
sea salt and freshly ground black pepper

Prepare the asparagus by breaking off the end of each woody stalk and chopping the rest into 1.5cm pieces.

Cook the pasta in a large pan of boiling salted water until al dente, adding the asparagus 3 minutes before it is done. In the meantime, beat the eggs together well. Drain the pasta and asparagus, transfer immediately to a large warmed bowl and add the eggs, Parmesan and some salt and pepper. Mix well. The heat from the pasta will cook the eggs. Sprinkle with the herbs and serve immediately, with extra Parmesan.

Stir-fried Asparagus

Other vegetables in season could be added to bulk out this simple stir-fry – try sugarsnap peas, broccoli or spinach. Serve with grilled fish or chicken and rice.

Serves 4 as an accompaniment

1 bunch of asparagus
1 tablespoon sunflower oil
1 teaspoon brown sugar
a pinch of dried chilli flakes (optional)
1 small can of water chestnuts, drained and thinly sliced
1 garlic clove, crushed
a bunch of chives, cut into 2cm lengths, and/or some chopped wild
    garlic leaves
2 tablespoons soy sauce
sea salt

Prepare the asparagus by breaking off the end of each woody stalk and then cutting the spears in half. Heat the oil in a wok, add the asparagus, sugar and some salt and stir-fry over a moderately high heat for about 3 minutes. Add the dried chilli, if using, followed by the water chestnuts, garlic, chives and/or wild garlic leaves, plus 3 tablespoons of water, and cook for 2 more minutes, stirring constantly. Stir in the soy sauce and serve immediately.

Easy ideas for asparagus

✦ Toss asparagus spears in a little olive oil, then cook on a ridged griddle pan or barbecue until tender. Drizzle with balsamic vinegar and season lightly.

✦ Serve cooked asparagus topped with a poached egg, a couple of slices of prosciutto and a few Parmesan cheese shavings, plus a drizzle of olive oil and some freshly ground black pepper.

✦ Serve cooked asparagus with Pine Nut Salsa (see page 191).

✦ Individually wrap boiled asparagus spears in a slice of smoked salmon or good ham.

Beetroot

When I met my wife as a sassy punk rocker, I was particularly taken with her bright orange hair. It turned out that the colour was the result of dyeing it with beetroot juice. Hair is not the only thing that beetroot dyes; ensuing trips to the loo can be alarming, perhaps explaining why the culinary potential of beetroot is only recently being appreciated beyond Eastern Europe.

The first sowings of beetroot are made in February under heated glass, then planted out in April ready for picking in July. Subsequent field sowings keep us going through the summer and up until November, before the first hard frosts. The size of the beets varies enormously, determined by sowing date and density, in combination with the fertility of the field and the growing season. The beets are traditionally stored for winter use in a clamp covered with straw, to mimic life in the soil. If they are harvested carefully and at the right maturity, then stored at the right temperature, they will keep until April and still taste pretty good.

Storage and preparation

Mature beets will keep for several weeks in a cool vegetable rack, provided they have not been damaged by washing. If you are not planning to use the tops, it is best to twist them off to avoid drawing water from the beets and making them soft.

In the Field Kitchen, Jane uses beetroot pretty much all year round and has converted many a beetroot hater (though she has been defeated by the resistance of Landscove Primary School pupils, whose school dinners we provide). The summer-crop beetroot is best used in a salad or just eaten warm as a vegetable. As the winter progresses, the roots out of store lose some of their freshness of taste and can dry out a little and become soft. This is the time for a hearty soup.

Beets will bleed and lose flavour and goodness from cuts. If you are boiling them, it is best just to wash them gently and boil without trimming the root, leaving an inch or so of leaf stalk if they come bunched. Depending on size, they can take 20 minutes (golf-ball size) or up to 40 minutes or more (tennis-ball and up) to cook. The warm beets can then be easily (even pleasurably) slipped out of their skins by squeezing them under a cold running tap.

The simple alternative to boiling them is roasting: put them in a baking dish containing about 5mm water, cover with foil and roast in a moderately hot oven for about 45 minutes, until tender.

Beet tops, if fresh and free from disease, can be sweated with garlic and oil in the same way as perpetual spinach. They are a bit more 'robust' (some might say tough and bitter), requiring more cooking, but can be good.

Beetroot Gratin

Possibly one of our most popular dishes in the Field Kitchen, this is very good with roast beef or smoked fish. You could add a teaspoon of freshly grated or creamed horseradish with the cream and garlic.

Serves 6

1kg beetroot, peeled
3 garlic cloves, finely chopped
100ml double cream
2 sprigs of summer savory, chopped (or use rosemary or thyme)
sea salt and freshly ground black pepper

Thinly slice the beetroot either by hand or with the slicing attachment of a food processor; it should be about 2–3mm thick.

Mix the garlic with the cream in a small pan and bring to the boil. Remove from the heat and leave to infuse for about 10 minutes. Mix well and season with salt and pepper.

Put the sliced beetroot in a bowl and add some seasoning. Add the cream mixture and the chopped savory and mix thoroughly so the beetroot is coated with cream. Arrange in a 30cm gratin dish, cover with foil and bake in an oven preheated to 160°C/Gas Mark 3 for 40 minutes. Remove the foil and bake for a further 10 minutes or until the beetroot is tender.

Beetroot Haters' Soup

This recipe was sent to us by a box scheme customer. Who it is, we don't know, but please come forward. It's a delicious soup and very quick to make if you have some cooked beetroot to hand. If you don't have any cooked beetroot but still need a quick soup, try it with the same quantity of finely grated raw beetroot.

Serves 4

2 tablespoons olive oil
1 onion, chopped
1 potato, peeled and diced
2.5cm piece of fresh ginger, grated or finely chopped
grated zest of 1 orange, plus extra to serve (optional)
juice of 2 oranges
3 medium beetroots, cooked (see pages 21–23) and cut into small dice
1.2 litres water
sea salt and freshly ground black pepper
a little cream or yoghurt, to serve (optional)

Heat the oil in a large pan, add the onion and fry until soft but not coloured. Add the potato and ginger and fry for 3 minutes. Add the orange zest and juice, plus the beetroot and water, then bring to the boil and simmer for 20 minutes, until the potato is tender. Blend until smooth. Reheat gently and season to taste.

Serve garnished, if you like, with a swirl of cream or yoghurt and a little grated orange zest.

Warm Beetroot Salad with Orange, Bacon and Caraway

This is Jane's favourite beetroot dish. We had it on our Christmas menu with potato pancakes, smoked eel and horseradish – a lovely combination. It's also very good served simply with watercress or spinach leaves. The bacon can be omitted for vegetarians and the result will still be fine.

Serves 4

about 300g beetroot, trimmed
1 tablespoon olive oil
4 smoked streaky bacon rashers, chopped
2 teaspoons caraway seeds
1 garlic clove, crushed
5 tablespoons orange juice
1 teaspoon sugar
3 oranges, peeled and sliced
sea salt and freshly ground black pepper

Place the beets in a baking dish, add 5mm of water, then cover with foil. Place in an oven preheated to 400°F/Gas Mark 6 and roast for about 45 minutes, until tender. Skin the beetroot, trim the ends and slice into thick batons or wedges.

Heat the oil in a large frying pan, add the bacon and fry until starting to brown. Remove from the pan. Add the caraway seeds and garlic and fry for a few minutes, adding the orange juice and sugar before the garlic browns. Mix thoroughly and bring to the boil. Tip in the beetroot and stir until thoroughly coated with the hot dressing. Season well. Stir in the orange slices and then sprinkle with the bacon. Transfer to a serving dish and serve immediately.

Chocolate Beetroot Brownies

Rich, dark, moist and gorgeous – but since these brownies include healthy beetroot, you can enjoy them with a clear conscience. Another bonus is that they are wheat free.

Makes about 9

250g dark chocolate, chopped
200g unsalted butter, cut into cubes
1 tablespoon Tia Maria or other liqueur (optional)
250g beetroot, cooked (see pages 21–23)
3 eggs
a drop of vanilla extract
200g caster sugar
50g cocoa powder,
50g rice flour (ground rice)
1 teaspoon baking powder
100g ground almonds

Put the chocolate and butter in a large bowl and place it over a pan of simmering water, making sure the water doesn't touch the base of the bowl. Leave to melt, then remove from the heat and stir in the Tia Maria, if using.

Purée the cooked beetroot in a food processor. Add the eggs one at a time, followed by the vanilla and sugar, and mix until smooth.

Sift the cocoa powder, rice flour and baking powder into a bowl and stir in the ground almonds. Stir the beetroot mixture into the melted chocolate and then fold in the dry ingredients.

Use baking parchment to line a rectangular tin, roughly 28 x 18cm. Pour in the mixture and place in an oven preheated to 180°C/Gas Mark 4. Bake for 30–35 minutes, until just firm to the touch. It's important not to overcook brownies; a skewer inserted in the centre should come out slightly sticky. Leave to cool in the tin and then cut into squares.

Easy ideas for beetroot

✦ Roast 500g beetroot as described on page 23. Peel and cut into wedges, then toss with 1 tablespoon of marmalade, 50g butter and some salt and pepper. Return to a hot oven for 5 minutes or until glazed and heated through.

✦ Peel some beetroot, cut them into wedges and toss in a little olive oil and seasoning. Roast at 180°C/Gas Mark 4 for about 1 hour, until tender and slightly caramelised. Serve hot as a side dish or use in a warm salad.

✦ Grated raw beetroot works well in salads. Alternatively, cook grated beetroot in a covered pan with a knob of butter, a tablespoon of wine vinegar and some seasoning for about 10 minutes over a low heat. Serve with meat or game.

✦ Cook 200g grated beetroot as described above, then mix with an equal quantity of mashed potato, plus 2 fried diced onions, 1 tablespoon of soured cream and 1 teaspoon of creamed horseradish. Leave to cool, then shape into cakes, dust with flour and fry in butter until golden. Makes a shocking-pink alternative to bubble and squeak.

✦ To braise beetroot with their leaves, cut the leaves from the beetroot, wash well and chop coarsely. Peel the beetroot and cut them into wedges 1.5cm thick. Cook 1 chopped onion and 1 crushed garlic clove in a tablespoon of olive oil, until softened, then add the beetroot segments and enough water just to cover. Season and cook slowly for about 30 minutes, until the beetroot is tender. Add the chopped leaves (ruby chard can be added at this stage, too) and cook for 5 minutes. Season and sprinkle with lemon juice. Good served with Puy lentils and seasoned yoghurt.

✦ To make a stunningly coloured dressing, liquidise 1 cooked beetroot with 2 tablespoons of chicken stock, then whisk in 4 tablespoons of olive oil, 1 tablespoon of pink peppercorns, a pinch of caster sugar and some salt and pepper. Warm slightly and drizzle over a salad of roast pigeon breasts or sautéed chicken livers, or serve with grilled calf's liver.

✦ Deep-fry beetroot shavings (made using a vegetable peeler) in sunflower oil, then drain well and sprinkle with salt for an alternative crisp.

✦ Substitute beetroot for carrots in the cake on page 96.

See also:

Bitter Leaves

Though the members of this family resemble lettuce in the field, they are actually more closely related to the dandelion. As a child, experimenting in nastiness, I can remember delighting in squeezing drops of milky sap from a dandelion stem on to the lips of adults sleeping on the lawn. The taste, for those fortunate enough to have escaped encountering such beastly children, is intensely bitter and hard to remove from the palate. Perhaps this is not a great recommendation for a salad or vegetable but growers and cooks over the centuries have gone to extraordinary lengths to extract culinary value from this family. The Romans, Greeks and Ancient Egyptians all prized chicory and its relatives, from whence the 'bitter herbs' used at the feast of Passover were derived.

The family is so well dispersed that it is not clear where it originated, but its culinary significance is greatest around the Mediterranean. Dandelion leaves are still cultivated or collected from the wild to be cooked as a common green in Greece and Spain. The Italians are obsessive about radicchio and grow many different forms, each named after the area of its origin and supposedly essential for a particular regional dish. Further north, the Belgians have adopted the forced chicons of Witloof chicory, which is normally served wrapped in ham and smothered in a cheesy béchamel sauce. The French crown each head of endive with an opaque cap to produce the blanched heads of crisp, frilly leaves so popular in their salads.

Their difference from the weakly rooting lettuce family is obvious if you dig the plant up – all the family, and chicory in particular, have a strong, substantial tap root. This is the root that is roasted as a substitute or adulterant of coffee and is used in herbal medicine as a tonic, laxative and diuretic. The family is also slower growing, but more frost tolerant, than lettuce and thrives in the autumn under the conditions of lower light intensity, when lettuces lose their flavour and their will to live. In our mild Devon climate, it is possible to harvest a supply of leaves, particularly escarole, from a garden right through the winter.

Radicchio

Dark red leaves with white mid ribs and veins. In Italy there are many different varieties but in the UK we normally see the cannon-ball-shaped chioggia type with its tightly packed leaves, probably because it will keep for weeks in a chef's fridge. At Riverford we also grow the more upright and open form known as Treviso, which resembles a small purple or crimson Cos lettuce. Small amounts of radicchio bring another dimension of colour and flavour to salads, though in the UK, with our monochrome national palate, I suspect most is left on the side of the plate. It can also be grilled or, in one of my favourite recipes from Antonio Carluccio, used to make a wonderful risotto combining the bitterness of the leaves with the sweet richness of sausage meat.

Curly endive

Crunchy, highly indented green leaves that tend towards a white heart. The French eat huge quantities of curly endive and will often cover the heads with a cap in the field to blanch them. I'm afraid I think life is too short, so only the centre of ours will be blanched. Endive is less bitter than radicchio, especially in the heart. It is quite difficult to grow without some dead leaves, so expect to have to pick it over a little, and spare a thought for the grower before being too indignant over imperfections. The really fine-leaved varieties are particularly hard to grow to a high standard, though they are undoubtedly better to eat if you can manage it.

Escarole

Large, lettuce-like heads of smooth, slightly crunchy, bright green leaves. The central leaves tend to be paler, with more crunch and less bitterness, becoming less palatable (some of our customers have said leathery) as you progress to the outer leaves. Escarole is the least bitter of the family, being mild enough to eat on its own. Very frost hardy, and sometimes used to bulk out the cheaper salad bags sold by supermarkets.

Chicory and chicons

Chicory is grown in the field for its roots, which are harvested, packed in sand and sprouted during the winter in sheds lit only by a candle. The resulting, tightly packed, pale green chicons can be eaten raw in a mixed salad, often with boiled egg, or cooked. Confusingly, these chicons are also sometimes referred to as endives.

Storage and preparation

Don't be put off by your first taste. Bitter leaves are always milder by the time they are dressed and reach the salad bowl, and if you cook them they are completely transformed. In a nation that measures quality largely in terms of sweetness, it is a challenge to persuade people of the virtues of bitter leaves, especially when the first taste typically produces a wince and a pucker, but judiciously combined with complementary ingredients, they have great potential. When serving bitter leaves in a green salad, soften their impact by combining them with blander leaves and accompanying with a sweet dressing. Try mixing with dried fruit (cranberries are my favourite) or fresh fruit (mango, peach, grapes, pears all go well). Blue cheese and cubes or slices of roasted squash can also be good in a salad. It is normally best to dress the salad before scattering the fruit or cheese on top.

All the bitter greens have a good shelf life and should keep in the fridge as whole heads for at least a week and often two without significant deterioration. Radicchio and curly endive both have a tendency to die back from the tips if they suffer any stress in the field, requiring a fair amount of picking over at the sink.

Grilled Radicchio

Radicchio doesn't appear in the boxes more than a couple of times a year but if you do get it, try grilling it and serving with grilled fish or some creamy buffalo mozzarella.

Serves 2

1 head of radicchio
3 tablespoons olive oil
1 tablespoon balsamic vinegar
1 teaspoon sugar
1 garlic clove, crushed
1 tablespoon chopped marjoram
sea salt and freshly ground black pepper

Remove the outer leaves of the radicchio, halve it and then slice it into wedges about 1.5cm thick, keeping the leaves joined at the core in each wedge.

Whisk together all the remaining ingredients in a shallow bowl to make a dressing. Heat a ridged grill pan (or a barbecue), then grill the radicchio wedges until brown on both sides. As you remove the wedges from the griddle, place them straight in the dressing and mix well.

Salade Lyonnaise

Traditionally this hearty salad is made with curly endive but there is no reason why you shouldn't use mixed salad leaves or baby spinach.

Serves 4

½ ciabatta loaf (or baguette), cut into 1.5cm cubes
2 tablespoons olive oil
250g streaky bacon, cut into lardons (matchsticks)
1 head of curly endive
4 eggs
1 tablespoon chopped chives

For the vinaigrette:
4 tablespoons olive oil
2 tablespoons white wine vinegar
2 teaspoons Dijon mustard
1 teaspoon sugar
sea salt and freshly ground black pepper

Mix the bread cubes with the olive oil, spread them out on a baking tray and bake in an oven preheated to 200°C/Gas Mark 6 for 10 minutes, until crisp and slightly browned.

Fry the bacon lardons until the fat starts to run out and the bacon is lightly coloured. Drain on kitchen paper. Wash the curly endive and dry well.

Mix the dressing ingredients together by whisking well or shaking in a jam jar. Poach the eggs in gently simmering water for 3–4 minutes so that they are still soft.

Put the curly endive in a bowl and dress with 3–4 tablespoons of the vinaigrette, so that the leaves are lightly coated. Divide between 4 plates and sprinkle with the bacon and croûtons. Top with the poached eggs and then scatter with the chives. Drizzle with more of the vinaigrette, if you like, and serve immediately.

Escarole and Bean Soup

Don't be afraid to cook these bitter, frizzy leaves. They can be braised on their own as an accompaniment or cooked with pulses to make this great soup.

Serves 6

300g dried white beans, such as haricot or cannelloni, soaked in cold
    water overnight and then drained
1 head of garlic, cut horizontally in half
½ teaspoon dried chilli flakes
1 sprig of rosemary
3 tablespoons olive oil
1 onion, finely chopped
1 garlic clove, crushed
2 heads of escarole, chopped
sea salt and freshly ground black pepper
very good olive oil, to serve

Place the drained beans in a large pan with the garlic, chilli and rosemary, cover with fresh water and bring to the boil. Simmer for about 1 hour, adding more water if necessary so that the beans are always just covered. When the beans are tender, season well with salt and pepper and mix in 2 tablespoons of the olive oil. Leave to cool, then squeeze the garlic out into the beans, removing the skins.

In a large pan, fry the onion and crushed garlic clove in the remaining olive oil for 5 minutes, until softened. Add the chopped escarole, mix well, then cover and cook for 5 minutes, until the escarole has wilted. Stir in the beans and their cooking liqueur and heat through. Remove 2 cupfuls of the mixture and blend in a food processor, then stir back into the mixture in the pan. Add some water if necessary to adjust the consistency and season well. Serve drizzled with good olive oil.

Glazed Chicory with Orange

A classic combination, best served with duck, grilled fish or scallops.

Serves 4

1 tablespoon butter
1 onion, chopped
2 garlic cloves, crushed
4 heads of chicory, thinly sliced
50g caster sugar
200ml white wine
juice and grated zest of 2 oranges
a sprig of thyme
sea salt and freshly ground black pepper

Melt the butter in a large pan, add the onion and garlic and cook over a medium heat for a few minutes, until softened but not coloured. Add the chicory, sugar, wine, orange juice and zest and thyme and bring to the boil. Lower the heat and simmer for about 10 minutes, until the liquid has caramelised slightly and reduced enough to coat the chicory in a light glaze. Season well and serve.

Easy ideas for bitter leaves

+ Fry a little chopped pancetta and sage in a pan, then add 1 chopped garlic clove and 2 heads of finely shredded radicchio. Cook gently until wilted. Pour in 150ml double cream and cook rapidly for 5 minutes, until slightly reduced. Serve with tagliatelle, sprinkled with Parmesan.

+ Finely shred radicchio and toss with diced apple, walnuts and some vinaigrette for a winter salad.

+ Slice 4 Italian sausages into chunks, fry until browned on both sides, then remove from the pan. Add 1 sliced garlic clove and cook for 1 minute. Add a shredded half head of escarole, stir until wilted, then add a drained tin of chickpeas, 1 tablespoon of tomato purée and 100ml chicken stock. Return the sausages to the pan, cook, covered, for 15 minutes, then serve.

+ Serve chicory leaves with Bagna Cauda (see page 176) as a dressing or dip.

Beware the freaks from the fringe

I remember being taught that evolutionary progress happens on the fringes: whilst the dominant, overtly successful species (currently us) are busy thriving, dominating, specialising, multiplying and basically doing more of the same, the less successful, freakish creatures are banished to the harsher fringes, where they scratch a precarious existence and await their day. For most freaks it never comes, and they perish without a fossil or obituary to mark their struggle.

Our planet is constantly changing, and no one stays at the centre forever. The fine adaptation and specialisation that bring a species success ultimately prove its downfall. Dinosaurs dominated Earth for 160 million years until, 65 million years ago, a 10km-wide asteroid crashed into Mexico and upset the conditions in which they thrived. They couldn't adapt to the new reality and were gone in an evolutionary blink.

In so many ways, business follows the same patterns as nature: survival of the fittest is one with obvious appeal for many post-Thatcherite worshippers of the free market and globalisation. Response to change is something on which those at the centre, growing fat on the status quo, tend to be less keen.

Organic farmers were freaks from the fringe until very recently. They typically lived in isolation in the depths of Wales or Devon, where no self-respecting, tweed-clad, country-landowning Barley Baron would soil their fat, oversized Range Rover tyres. Some were even women and one or two wore sandals, woolly jumpers and beards and had the occasional dope plant hidden amongst the tomatoes. They were derided for decades. Surely it would take a massive intergalactic collision for this lot to threaten or displace mainstream farming and food retailing, which is fiercely protected by a well-heeled agribusiness and backed up by a powerful global agrichemical sector.

Change has been driven more by an asteroid shower than a single meteor: BSE, foot-and-mouth, pesticide and fertiliser pollution and contamination, global warming, 'peak oil', public concern over the excesses of food transportation, routine antibiotic misuse, the imposition of genetic manipulation, revulsion at factory farming and the normalisation of the abuses of a food industry where a chicken can quite legally be only 50 per cent chicken, the rest made up of beef gristle and water. The soft underbelly of success is complacency, and the accompanying lack of imagination and willingness to learn. Within the mainstream, there is little genuine desire to adapt to a new climate of well-founded public concern. A few groundbreaking organic brands have been bought by Cadbury, Dean Foods, Unilever and the like, and a fair amount has been spent on greenwash-inspired PR initiatives and Corporate Responsibility Indexes, but behind the smokescreen little has changed. Could we be witnessing the start of a mass extinction of global agri-food businesses? For decades, they have seemed immovable and omnipotent in their power – but then so did the dinosaurs, until the last one found itself being chased around by a bone-wielding, two-legged freak previously seen rubbing two sticks together in a cave.

Broad Beans

The best conversations I can remember having with my mother were while shelling peas and beans. Keeping the hands busy, and having a reason not to make eye contact, is a great way of taking conversation into areas that you would normally skirt around. If you need to have a potentially difficult chat with adolescent children, a pile of beans is a great way to bridge the silences and lubricate the flow.

There is something unique and wonderful about the smell of a broad bean field, particularly when in flower – added to the fact that they come early in the summer, when there is little else around, so we grow quite a few of them. We used to have an eccentric doctor who rang up every spring to buy tonnes of young beans in their pods for pressing into some sort of elixir, which he claimed cured just about anything. I have not heard from him for a few years so I suspect he has been struck off. Recently a customer assured us that rubbing warts repeatedly with the furry inside of a broad bean pod was a reliable cure (she insisted that her success had always been with organic pods).

Prior to the conquest of the Americas, broad beans were the only beans grown in Europe and, when meat wasn't available, they were a vital source of protein. They are also the only beans that are frost hardy and truly happy in our climate. As such, they can be ready to pick six weeks earlier than runner or French beans.

Our over-wintered crop, sown in the autumn, can be a bit hit and miss, depending on the severity of the winter, the hunger and determination of the local crow population and the weather at the time of pollination. As a result, the first picking in June tends to be feast or famine. The spring-sown crop is more reliable and flowers when pollinating conditions have improved, producing better-quality, well-filled pods for picking in July. It is possible to pick right through the summer but by mid July we are normally picking French beans and find that our customers' interest has waned, so we seldom sow beyond early April.

From a grower's perspective, the aphid black fly is the main problem, along with occasional voracious attacks of bean weevil. There is a certain stage, about two weeks before the first beans are ready to pick, when the leading shoot can be picked out (and stir-fried to good effect – see page 44). If you grow broad beans in your garden, you may find that this helps to delay black fly attack and encourages the upper pods to fill.

Storage and preparation

Broad beans keep well in their pods and will survive for a week in the bottom of your fridge without significant deterioration, even if the pods become a little limp. It is, however, vital to pick the beans while they are still tender. The very small, immature pods can be boiled and eaten whole but you will have to grow them yourself for this. In Italy it is common to eat the shelled beans raw with pecorino cheese while they are still only about 1cm long. Larger beans are normally shelled and boiled for 3 or 4 minutes. Larger beans can be blanched in boiling water before slipping them out of their inner skins – an enjoyable task for children. Jane always does this with larger beans in the Field Kitchen and I enjoy the results but lack the patience or dexterity to do it often myself. If the stalk attaching the bean to the pod is starting to brown, they are getting too mature, and fit only for an Andalusian donkey. If you get these from us, you should complain.

Don't be put off by the appearance of the pod; broad beans often develop chocolate spot (causing speckled browning of the pods) later in the season and, as this does not affect the eating quality of what is inside, we assume you will be fairly tolerant of it. To get a really strong bean flavour, if the pods are in reasonable condition they can be simmered to make a stock to use in a risotto or for inclusion in a béchamel sauce.

Bean tops can be pretty nasty steamed or boiled but I strongly recommend stir-frying; only use the leading shoot and make sure you use them fresh. Not everyone likes them – despite my protestations, Jane refuses to serve them in the Field Kitchen. Stir-fry the dry bean tops in olive oil with roughly chopped garlic and seasoning until they collapse. Serve immediately, perhaps with squeeze of lemon. Goes well with lamb.

Broad Bean and Courgette Soup

A quick and easy late-spring soup. Frozen peas can be added at the broad bean stage, if you like.

Serves 4

1 onion, chopped
2 garlic cloves, crushed
2 tablespoons olive oil, plus an extra splash
400g courgettes, grated
500ml vegetable stock
400g shelled broad beans
a small bunch of mint, chopped
a small bunch of basil, chopped
sea salt and freshly ground black pepper
grated Parmesan cheese, to serve

Sauté the onion and garlic in the olive oil for 10 minutes, until soft but not coloured. Add the grated courgettes, cover the pan and sweat for 10 minutes. Pour in the vegetable stock, add the broad beans and simmer for 10 minutes, until the courgettes and beans are tender. Season with salt and pepper, then add a splash of olive oil and lots of chopped mint and basil.

Take out a third of the soup, liquidise it until smooth and then stir it back into the pan. Sprinkle with Parmesan and serve warm or at room temperature.

Penne with Broad Beans, Bacon, Mint and Cream

This makes a great quick pasta dish but you could also serve the sauce on its own, as an accompaniment to grilled or roast chicken.

Serves 4

500g shelled broad beans
350g penne
100g pancetta or smoked streaky bacon, cut into fine batons
1 tablespoon butter or olive oil
1 garlic clove, crushed
200ml double cream
a small bunch of mint, roughly chopped
2 tablespoons freshly grated Parmesan cheese
sea salt and freshly ground black pepper

Cook the broad beans in boiling salted water for a few minutes, until tender. Drain and set aside.

Cook the pasta in a large pan of boiling salted water until al dente. Meanwhile, fry the bacon in the butter or oil until just beginning to brown, then add the garlic and stir for a minute without letting it colour. Stir in the cream, mint and broad beans and simmer for a few minutes. Then add the Parmesan and season to taste.

When the pasta is done, drain well, toss with the sauce and serve immediately.

Fattoush with Broad Beans

This classic Middle Eastern toasted bread salad is given a new twist with spring vegetables. The cumin in the dressing adds a bit of a kick but you can reduce the quantity if you prefer a more subtle effect. Serve with grilled fish or as part of a mezze.

Serves 4

2 pitta breads, torn into 2–3cm pieces
100g shelled broad beans
1 Cos or Little Gem lettuce, shredded
1 small cucumber, peeled, quartered lengthways, deseeded and cut into
    1–2cm chunks
4 radishes, sliced
10 cherry tomatoes, cut in half
50g feta cheese, crumbled

For the dressing:
6 mint leaves, chopped
6 tablespoons extra virgin olive oil
1½ tablespoons red wine vinegar
1 teaspoon cumin seeds, toasted in a dry frying pan and then crushed
a pinch of cayenne pepper
sea salt and freshly ground black pepper

Spread the pieces of pitta bread out on a baking sheet, place in an oven preheated to 180°C/Gas Mark 4 and toast for about 5 minutes, until just crisp. Remove from the oven and leave to cool.

Blanch the broad beans in boiling salted water for 2–4 minutes, depending on size, then drain.

Whisk together all the ingredients for the dressing. Toss the bread, broad beans, lettuce, cucumber, radishes and cherry tomatoes with the dressing, then sprinkle with the crumbled feta.

Easy ideas for broad beans

✦ Boil 300g shelled broad beans until tender, then blend in a food processor with 2 tablespoons of the cooking liquid, adding enough very good olive oil to make a thick purée. Season, spread on a serving plate and drizzle with olive oil, then garnish with finely chopped spring onions and mint. To spice this up, you could add ½ teaspoon of ground cumin and a pinch of paprika when puréeing the beans.

✦ Add cooked broad beans to Roast Artichokes and New Potatoes (see page 188).

✦ Boil a handful of shelled broad beans with a bunch of trimmed asparagus until just tender, then drain and toss with sliced spring onions, a little chopped tarragon and a light vinegar and oil dressing.

See also:
Braised Artichokes with Broad Beans and Mint (page 187)
Spring Vegetable Risotto (page 406)

Broccoli

This is a part of the vegetable world where nomenclature gets confusing. To growers in the mild, coastal areas of Devon and Cornwall, 'broccoli' means late-winter cauliflower. Traditionally, to gardeners and cooks, broccoli is an abbreviation for our wonderfully winter-hardy purple sprouting broccoli. But over the last 30 years, for most people broccoli has come to mean calabrese, the uniform, succulent, green-headed impostor from Calabria in southern Italy, and the version most commonly found on supermarket shelves.

Calabrese

This is juicier and milder in flavour than most of the brassica family and as such is one of the few vegetables that nearly all children will eat. In the fields, it can take a little frost but lacks the hardiness of our native broccolis, and needs more sunlight. The UK season conventionally runs from late June to November but the early crops are hard to keep growing without nitrogen fertiliser (which, as organic growers, we don't use), and the very late ones tend to have poor flavour, so for us the season lasts only from August to late October. Through the winter, calabrese for the UK market is trucked up from Spain in huge quantities. We may occasionally buy it in the depths of winter, but where possible I prefer to use cape broccoli and romanesco in early winter and purple sprouting through late winter and spring.

Purple sprouting broccoli

To my delight, PSB, as we know it, has enjoyed a renaissance over the last few years, as people tire of the bland predictability of hybrid calabrese. It has the great advantage of coming into season from January to May, when other home-grown greens are in short supply. At the height of the season, through March and April, we make no apologies for including it in virtually every veg box and every meal in the Field Kitchen. Supermarkets have tried to respond to this rise in popularity but have been frustrated by PSB's wild appearance and its seasonality. There is a pressure to 'tidy it up' with uniform hybrid varieties, as has been the case with calabrese, and to banish its seasonality by developing varieties for the summer and early winter – despite the fact that these out-of-season hybrids are tough and nasty to eat. Seasonality and variation are anathema to supermarkets. They keep trying to bully farmers into trimming

the individual shoots and laying them geometrically in trays so they look as if they came from a factory, regardless of the fact that the spears come in all different shapes and sizes and the discarded leaves make wonderful greens.

The harvesting of a single variety can be spread over three to six weeks, depending on the type and the time of year. Once the primary head has been harvested, the side shoots develop into secondary spears, which we pick with a rosette of leaves. If the plants are strong and the pickers sufficiently nimble, there can be a third generation to pick. The secret is to pass through the crop frequently enough to avoid the spears bursting into flower or the stems becoming tough, without spending too much time searching rather than picking.

The varieties we grow come mostly from Tozers, one of the last independent English seed producers. We start the season with Rudolf, normally in January or early February, then move on to Redhead and Red Spear. There is always a glut in late March and April, as the highest-yielding Claret comes into season. We finish the season with Cardinal, or with Tozer's 'late selection', in late April or early May. Such is the popularity of PSB with our customers that over the last few years we have been trying to breed our own late-heading variety to allow us to continue picking a little later into the spring 'hungry gap'. I would not recommend buying PSB between mid-May and December, when you will be getting the inferior modern hybrids.

We tried white sprouting broccoli but it is lower yielding, goes off quickly and normally doesn't taste as good anyway, so it has been dropped. Because it is possible to continue harvesting over a long period, right down to the small spears that would be uneconomic for a commercial grower, I would recommend PSB as a crop for any keen cook with access to a reasonable-sized garden or allotment.

If you cannot snap the spears cleanly when you receive them in your box, we have probably got a bit behind with the picking, and you may need to trim the bottoms a little to get to the tender stalks. Other than that and picking off any diseased leaves, the whole lot is edible. The stalks themselves can be very sweet, and normally don't take much cooking. If they are large, it is sometimes worth splitting them from the bottom with a knife to ensure they cook before the flower is overdone. My mother was a big fan of purple sprouting broccoli and would carry on picking a few plants well into May, when the spears were the size of matchsticks. She would bunch them with a band as she was picking and then boil them standing up in the pan, as you might asparagus, so that the flower buds did not get overcooked.

Romanesco

You cannot fail to be impressed by the bright lime green colour and mathematical perfection of a head of romanesco. Its florets have a repeating fractal pattern, making up a conical shape that reminds me of Madonna's aggressively brassiered breasts in her Boadicea phase. Romanesco's virtues extend beyond its marvellous appearance. With a crunchy texture, and a flavour somewhere between cauliflower and calabrese, it is one of the few 'novelty' vegetables that taste better than the more common relatives. It is in season through the late summer, autumn and early winter but is easily damaged by hard frosts.

Cape broccoli

Cape broccoli produces purple, calabrese-like heads in November or March, depending on the variety, when calabrese is out of season. It is fairly winter hardy but lacks the flavour of romanesco and can lose its colour when cooked, turning from a deep purple to a less appetising brown. The heads tend to be smaller than romanesco or cauliflower and looser than calabrese. The greens surrounding the heads can make good eating.

Storage and preparation

Calabrese in particular can go yellow in a matter of hours, usually as a result of stress. Whether in the field or indoors, this is usually because of a rise in temperature. So keep it cold, in which case it is usually good for about a week. It doesn't affect the flavour much if it goes a little floppy, but if you get a seaweedy whiff off it, I'm afraid this is probably because of something unattractively named 'head rot'. It may still look okay but will not taste so good.

Romanesco keeps well, longer than calabrese (more like cauliflower). Purple sprouting broccoli lasts for 4–6 days in the fridge, while cape broccoli needs eating within a few days. The stems tend to be the best bits; if they are large, peel off the outside with a potato peeler and cut them into sticks. The centre of romanesco has great flavour – it just needs slicing into similar-sized bits.

All these vegetables are best blanched for a few minutes, then finished off in various ways (see following pages). They are delicious in Asian-type dishes such as stir-fries, with ginger, soy and chilli, and also good roasted.

Broccoli, Bean and Pasta Soup

A lighter, quicker version of the Italian *pasta e fagioli*, with lots of broccoli added for freshness and colour. You will need good chicken stock for the best flavour. To make the soup more substantial, you can serve it over some toast drizzled with olive oil.

Serves 6

3 tablespoons olive oil
1 onion, chopped
6 garlic cloves, crushed
½ teaspoon dried oregano
leaves from 2 sprigs of thyme
500g broccoli, finely chopped (including the stalks)
2 x 440g cans of haricot or cannellini beans, drained
1 litre chicken stock
100g small pasta shapes (or use broken spaghetti)
2 tablespoons freshly grated Parmesan cheese
sea salt and freshly ground black pepper

Heat the olive oil in a large pan, add the onion and cook gently for about 10 minutes, until soft. Add the garlic and cook for a further 2–3 minutes. Add the herbs and broccoli and cook for 5 minutes, then stir in the beans and chicken stock. Bring to the boil and simmer for 10–15 minutes. Add the pasta and cook until it is al dente. Season well. Serve sprinkled with the Parmesan.

Warm Salad of Romanesco, Grilled Leeks and Haricots

We always wonder what to do with the alien of the broccoli family. This recipe developed out of desperation and we were all pleasantly surprised with the results.

Serves 4 as an accompaniment

4 leeks, trimmed and cut lengthways in half
1 romanesco, divided into florets
3 tablespoons cooked haricot beans (or cannellini)
1 tablespoon chopped parsley
2 teaspoons balsamic vinegar
2 tablespoons olive oil
1 tablespoon freshly grated Parmesan cheese
sea salt and freshly ground black pepper

Cook the leeks in a large pan of boiling salted water for a few minutes, until just tender, then drain and dry well. Heat a ridged grill pan, place the leeks on it and grill on both sides until ridge marks appear. Remove from the grill, cut into strips and set aside.

Cook the romanesco florets in boiling salted water until just tender. Drain well and toss with the grilled leeks, white beans, parsley, vinegar and olive oil. Season and sprinkle with the Parmesan, then serve.

Annie O'Carroll's Roast Calabrese with Chilli and Soy

This dish comes from Jane's friend, Annie, who used to run Fig restaurant, in Islington, London, but has recently emigrated to Devon. It is very quick and easy to make.

Serves 2

350g calabrese (broccoli), broken into florets,
   stalks cut into thick batons
1 tablespoon olive oil
2 garlic cloves, thinly sliced
½ red chilli, deseeded and finely chopped
½ tablespoon sesame seeds (optional)
2 tablespoons soy sauce

Toss the broccoli in the oil, spread it out on a baking tray and roast in an oven preheated to 200°C/Gas Mark 6 for 10 minutes. Add the garlic, chilli and sesame seeds, if using, and mix through. Return to the oven for 5 minutes. Remove from the oven, sprinkle immediately with the soy sauce and serve.

Braised Broccoli with Bean Curd

Jane felt we should include a recipe with bean curd because of our proximity to Totnes and its New Age lifestyle. Whether you circle dance or not, this makes a delicious vegetarian main course.

Serves 4

1½ teaspoons cornflour
150ml vegetable stock
1 tablespoon rice wine or sherry
2 tablespoons soy sauce
1 tablespoon sesame oil
2 tablespoons sunflower oil
2 garlic cloves, chopped
2cm piece of fresh ginger, grated
1 chilli, finely chopped
350g broccoli, broken into florets, stems peeled and cut into batons
1 red onion or 3 spring onions, chopped
250g firm tofu (bean curd), cut into cubes
1 teaspoon sesame seeds, toasted in a dry frying pan
sea salt and freshly ground black pepper

Mix the cornflour with 50ml of the stock, then stir in the rice wine or sherry, soy sauce and sesame oil. Set aside.

Heat the sunflower oil in a wok, then add the garlic, ginger and chilli and stir-fry for 30 seconds. Add the broccoli and onion and stir-fry for a minute. Pour in the remaining stock and season with salt and pepper. Cover and simmer for 3 minutes or until the broccoli is tender.

Remove the broccoli from the wok. Add the tofu to the wok, along with the cornflour mixture, and heat through for 1 minute. Return the broccoli to the pan, adjust the seasoning and heat through. Serve sprinkled with the sesame seeds.

Spicy Purple Sprouting Broccoli with Garlic, Olives and Toasted Breadcrumbs

This can be served as a sauce with pasta – ideally penne, conchiglie or fusilli. Alternatively serve as an accompaniment to grilled or roast poultry.

Serves 4

50g fresh breadcrumbs
75ml olive oil
600g purple sprouting broccoli, trimmed
1 tablespoon capers, soaked in cold water for 20 minutes, then squeezed dry and roughly chopped
4–6 anchovy fillets, chopped (optional)
6 garlic cloves, chopped
½ teaspoon fennel seeds
a pinch of dried chilli flakes
1 tablespoon chopped parsley
4 tablespoons chopped black olives
sea salt and freshly ground black pepper

Toss the breadcrumbs in 2 tablespoons of the olive oil and spread them out on a baking tray. Bake in an oven preheated to 200°C/Gas Mark 6 for about 5 minutes, until golden. Remove and set aside.

Break the purple sprouting broccoli into separate small heads. Warm about 2 tablespoons of the olive oil in a wide, shallow pan over a medium heat, add the broccoli and stir well. Leave to cook for about 10 minutes, until you see the edges browning slightly, then season to taste and stir gently. Add the capers, then cover and cook for about 5 minutes, until the broccoli is tender. Drizzle over the remaining olive oil and scatter with the chopped anchovies, if using, plus the garlic, fennel seeds and chilli flakes. Toss to mix in. Cook for 2 more minutes, then add the parsley and olives. Sprinkle with the toasted breadcrumbs and serve.

Purple Sprouting Broccoli with Mustard and Tarragon Hollandaise

We wanted to do something with purple sprouting broccoli at the Exeter Food Festival, but didn't want to boil it at the food stall. To make things easier, we took it up there ready blanched and just griddled it to order before smothering it with this gorgeous hollandaise or with Bagna Cauda (see page 176). It also made a great breakfast with a poached egg on top before we started work.

Serves 4

400g purple sprouting broccoli, trimmed

For the mustard and tarragon hollandaise:
250g unsalted butter
3 egg yolks
juice of 1 lemon
a pinch of cayenne pepper
2 teaspoons wholegrain mustard
1 teaspoon chopped tarragon
1 teaspoon chopped chives
salt and freshly ground black pepper

To make the sauce, melt the butter slowly in a pan, then remove from the heat. Put the egg yolks, lemon juice and cayenne in a bowl set over a pan of simmering water, making sure the water doesn't touch the base of the bowl. Using a balloon whisk, whisk until slightly thickened, then whisk in the melted butter a little at a time until it has all been incorporated. The sauce should be thick and glossy. Stir in the mustard and herbs and season with salt and pepper. The sauce will keep in a warm place for about an hour.

Cook the purple sprouting broccoli in a large pan of boiling salted water until just tender. Drain and refresh in cold water, then dry well. Heat a ridged grill pan (or a barbecue) until very hot, then place the broccoli on it. Cook, turning occasionally, until slightly charred. Arrange on a serving dish and drizzle over the hollandaise sauce.

Easy ideas for broccoli

✦ Gently cook 2 chopped garlic cloves, 1 chopped chilli, 1 crumbled dried chilli and 1 teaspoon of dried oregano in 2 tablespoons of olive oil for 2–3 minutes. Blanch romanesco or calabrese florets for 2 minutes, then drain well and toss in the flavoured oil. Sprinkle with lemon juice and serve.

✦ Roast broccoli as for Annie O'Carroll's Calabrese on page 57, and then toss with 1 tablespoon of capers, a handful of pitted black olives, 2 sliced spring onions and 2 sliced roasted red peppers.

✦ Cook 2 thinly sliced garlic cloves and ½ chopped red chilli in olive oil for 1 minute, then add 5–6 anchovy fillets. Remove from the heat and mash with a wooden spoon until the anchovies have almost completely disintegrated. Add 500g blanched purple sprouting broccoli, mix well and cook over a low heat for 10 minutes, stirring occasionally. Makes an excellent accompaniment to grilled fish or lamb.

✦ Substitute broccoli for half the cauliflower in a cauliflower cheese – you could try some of the variations on cauliflower cheese listed on page 107.

✦ Serve steamed purple sprouting broccoli with Bagna Cauda (see page 176).

Brussels Sprouts

Without the barrage of fungicides and insecticides that protect conventionally grown Brussels sprouts from germination to harvest, our organic sprouts are never quite cosmetically perfect. However, their iconic status for the annual Christmas feast, means that we are obliged to do our best. And though yields are low, these slowly grown organic sprouts do tend to taste better, rewarding the additional effort often needed at the sink to take off the dodgy outer leaves.

Seeds are sown under glass in March for planting out in May. Sprouts are heavy feeders, so a deep and fertile soil with plenty of muck is needed to give a good crop. Today the huge majority of the UK crop is grown on the deep, fertile soils of the Fens. As the crop matures, the lower leaves senesce and drop off, leaving a plant a bit like a palm tree, with just a crown of leaves at the top. The sprouts are born like mini cabbages in a dense, DNA-style double helix up the stem, one developing from each bud above each fallen leaf. As the spreading crowns join across the rows, a dense canopy is formed which traps the humidity, providing a protected breeding ground for the slugs, aphids and fungal diseases that plague the crop.

With traditional, open-pollinated varieties, the sprouts mature from the bottom up and could be picked from September right through the winter. Modern hybrids are bred for vigour and to develop sprouts synchronously and uniformly right up the stem, thus facilitating machine harvesting. As Christmas approaches, the sprout harvesters rumble across the Fens day and night with a team of workers grabbing the stalks as they are cut and feeding them into the greedy machine that strips off the sprouts and spits out the chopped leaves and stalks while delivering the perfect sprouts to a hopper.

Oh, how I envy them. Most of our sprouts are grown and picked by hand by our co-op member, Anthony Coker. He spends the summer picking courgettes and the winter picking sprouts before dispatching 400 turkeys and moving on to lambing his sheep. He used to shear sheep for a living, so he must have a very strong back, which is just as well because picking and selecting by hand to get reasonable quality is backbreaking work.

Sprouts keep well on the stalk and, provided the crop is reasonably free of disease and aphids, we will cut the whole stalk for the boxes during Christmas week. I would like everyone to know that I started doing this back in the 1980s, a full decade before any Johnny-come-lately supermarket got in on the act.

Storage and preparation

The stalks will keep for 2 or 3 weeks in a cool outside vegetable rack or in the fridge. Once the sprouts are picked off the stalk, their life is reduced to a week or so.

Peeling the outer leaves off a sprout is a tedious task but most people only do it once a year. I'm not sure if cutting a cross in the stem is worth it; it can make the sprouts go mushy. My approach is to do it to just the larger sprouts to speed up their cooking, so they are all ready at once. They take anything from 5–10 minutes to boil, according to size – try to catch them before they go soggy.

Think of sprouts as mini cabbages, so anything that goes well with cabbage tends to be a good accompaniment – caraway, bacon, nuts. And they make a good alternative to cabbage in bubble and squeak – or try Jane's Bubble and Squeak Soup on page 66.

Sprout tops

Before the days of hybrid varieties, it used to be traditional to harvest the apical bud (or growing point) of the plant in late autumn and eat it as a small cabbage. This has the effect of stopping the plant generating new sprouts and thus helps persuade it to put energy into filling the small buds higher up the stalk. An alternative approach if there was no market for the tops was to walk down between the rows with a mallet in each hand a few weeks before harvest, giving the heads a good thwack. Sprout tops can be excessively bitter and are best boiled – not a vegetable for the fainthearted. Check for colonies of mealy aphids lurking in the centre before cooking.

Bubble and Squeak Soup with Wensleydale Cheese

Jane got the idea for this smooth soup from Gary Rhodes. If you prefer it to be more rustic, just take out a cupful and blend it, then stir it back in to bring it all together. The smooth version is also very good finished with truffle oil instead of cheese.

Serves 6

1 tablespoon olive oil
1 onion, chopped
4 smoked streaky bacon rashers, chopped into small pieces
500g potatoes, peeled and cut into small dice
250g swede, peeled and cut into small dice
about 1.5 litres chicken stock
500g Brussels sprouts, finely sliced
25g Wensleydale cheese, grated
1 tablespoon chopped parsley
sea salt and freshly ground black pepper

Heat the oil in a large pan, add the onion and cook for 5 minutes, until softened. Add the bacon and cook for a further 5 minutes. Add the potatoes and swede and cook over a low heat for 10 minutes. Pour in enough stock to come about 2cm above the level of the potatoes and simmer for 10 minutes. Add the Brussels sprouts and cook for 10 minutes more, until the vegetables are tender. Blend in a food processor or liquidiser (for a really smooth finish, pass through a good food mill). Reheat gently, season to taste and serve sprinkled with the cheese and parsley.

Crisp Brussels Sprouts with Pine Nuts and Balsamic Vinegar

Instead of risking the usual soggy, overcooked boiled sprouts – and the smell that goes with them – try roasting them instead. The balsamic vinegar and honey emphasise the natural sweetness of sprouts, while the pine nuts add texture.

Serves 6 as an accompaniment

600g Brussels sprouts, trimmed
2 shallots or 1 onion, thinly sliced
4 tablespoons olive oil
1 tablespoon honey
1 tablespoon pine nuts, toasted
1 tablespoon balsamic vinegar
sea salt and freshly ground black pepper

In a bowl, mix the sprouts with the shallots or onion, olive oil, honey and some salt and pepper. Transfer to a baking tray or shallow dish, place in an oven preheated to 190°C/Gas Mark 5 and roast for 20 minutes, until the sprouts are tender and lightly browned. Sprinkle with the pine nuts and balsamic vinegar and serve.

Wok-fried Brussels Sprouts with Ginger

Sprouts are effectively mini cabbages, and can be shredded and stir-fried in the same way. Serve as part of your Christmas lunch, or on its own with rice.

Serves 4

3 tablespoons sunflower oil
2 shallots or 1 onion, finely chopped
2 garlic cloves, finely chopped
1 chilli, finely chopped
600g Brussels sprouts, finely shredded
4cm piece of fresh ginger, cut into very fine strips
4cm piece of crystallised stem ginger, cut into very fine strips
sea salt and freshly ground black pepper

Heat the oil in a wok, add the shallots or onion, plus the garlic and chilli, and fry quickly for about 2 minutes, without browning. Add the shredded sprouts and the fresh and crystallised ginger. Cook, stirring constantly, for 2 minutes. Add 3 tablespoons of water, cover and steam for 3 minutes. Season to taste and serve.

Easy ideas for Brussels sprouts

✦ Combine cooked Brussels sprouts with fried bacon lardons, then stir in cooked chestnuts (vacuum-packed ones are fine) and a little chopped parsley.

✦ Fry some chopped garlic and sage in a little olive oil, then add finely shredded raw Brussels sprouts. Cook for 5–7 minutes, until tender, then season and serve.

✦ Make some brown butter by heating 50g butter in a small pan until it just starts to brown. Add a tablespoon of flaked almonds and 350g quartered cooked Brussels sprouts. Stir rapidly, coating the sprouts in the brown butter and almonds, then season.

✦ Substitute Brussels sprouts for kale in Kale, Chorizo and Potato Hash (see page 230).

✦ Toss shredded, very fresh raw sprouts with toasted sesame seeds and soy sauce for a quick, healthy salad.

See also:
Turnips, Brussels Sprouts and Beetroot with Hazelnuts (page 386)

Enough

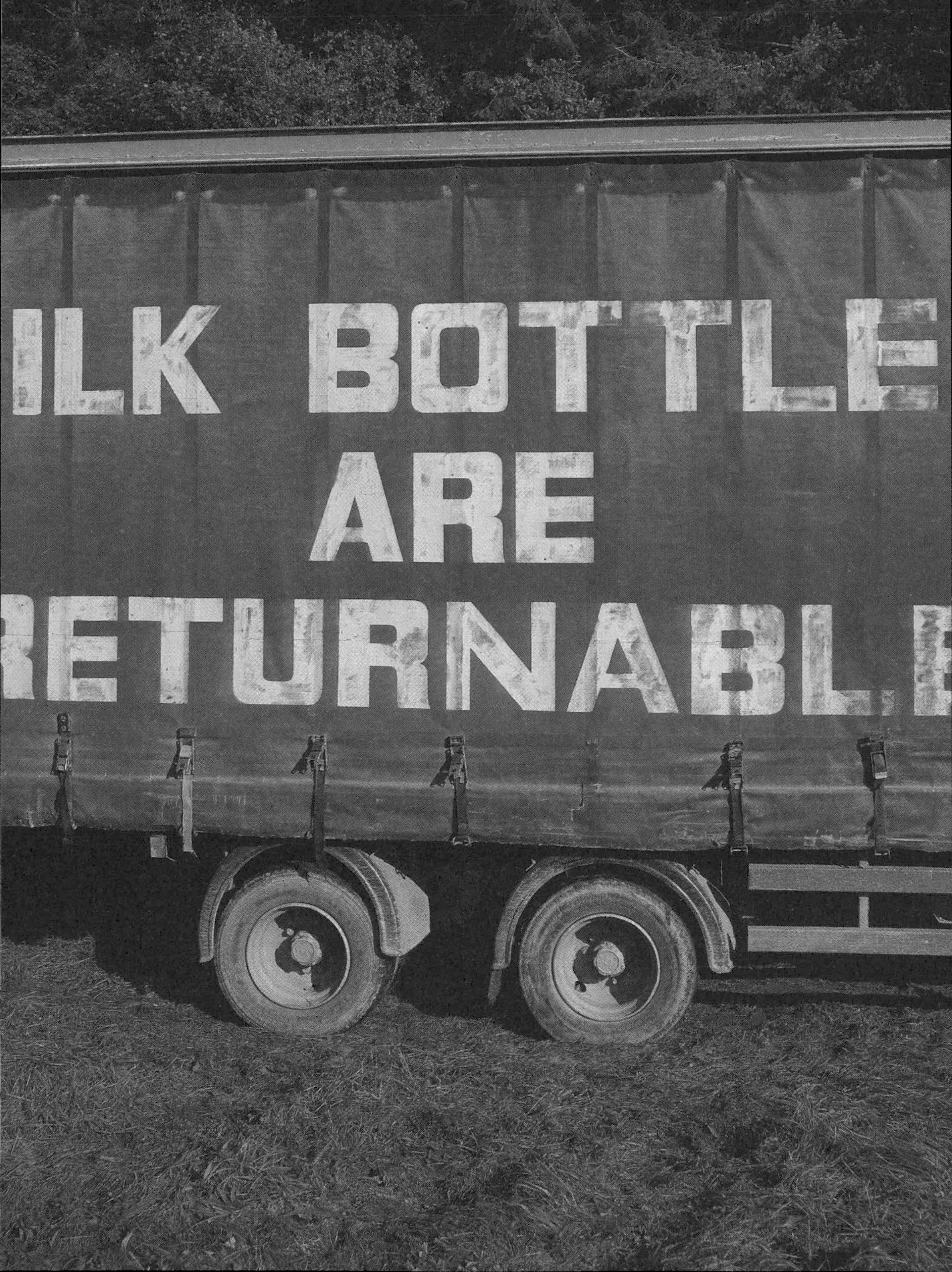
ILK BOTTLE
ARE
RETURNABLE

See the happy moron,
He doesn't give a damn.

I wish I were a moron.

My God! Perhaps I am!

Anonymous

Most of us live our lives the way my overweight Labrador eats her dinner: in a frantic rush, with little pause for consideration or appreciation and an almost paranoid resistance to sharing. She salivates at any suggestion of food and invariably wants more as soon as it is finished. For her, there is no such thing as enough. It is said that her breed lacks the satiated gene and, given the chance, would eat to obesity and ultimately death.

I watch her eat with pity. Like Pooh Bear, she is a dog of very little brain, but her appetites are fairly harmless and, between meals, provided there is no hint of a bin to raid or a child's lunch to steal, she is loyal and endearingly happy in her skin.

I like to believe that I am smarter than my dog and, though I admire her ability to live in the moment, as a higher being I have the future to think about. Surely we should be able to organise and live our lives for long-term happiness and fulfilment. Surely we should be able to balance the fleeting pleasures of short-term material gratification with the needs of our long-suffering planet. All the evidence shows that material wealth in developed countries is very poor at delivering lasting happiness, but we allow our appetite for it to outweigh all the wisdom that would recommend a more balanced life. I sometimes think we might stand a chance of attaining that wisdom if it weren't for the fiendishly clever and well-resourced marketing industry that is so adept at appealing to our base desires.

Our phenomenal technical prowess, combined with a century of cheap fossil fuel, has given us the power to consume our planet in one last supper. All the signs are that we will consume until the last drop of oil has gone or the capacity of our planet to support us has been destroyed, whichever comes sooner. The spectacle of a species hell bent on self-destructive consumption is, like our Labrador, both pathetic and tragic, but not nearly as endearing.

Cabbage

Savoy cabbage is one of my favourite vegetables, yet we dare put it in the boxes only three or four times a year as we encounter such resistance – mainly from customers who are less committed to local, seasonal food. It is a nutritional and culinary tragedy that our traditional greens have been maligned in a national capitulation to the bland, seasonless, overpriced, over-travelled broccoli, peppers and mangetout that have replaced them. The decline may have been started by over-boiled white cabbage and tasteless, uniform varieties of green cabbage but the main culprit is the same fascination with the new and exotic that brought us fondues and prawn cocktails. A couple of generations after Elizabeth David initiated our love affair with Mediterranean food, most people are more comfortable with an aubergine than a cabbage. Last year, however, for the very first time, the calls for more cabbage in the boxes outweighed the moans for less. So maybe the tide is turning. If eaten fresh and not boiled to death, green cabbage and some kales (see page 226) are fantastic vegetables. Never mind the latest exotic or wonder food. You are being taken for a mug. A Savoy or January King cabbage will help you live longer at a fraction of the price. It's just that they are so cheap, no one has the advertising budget to point this out.

Cabbages, along with kales and greens, belong to the brassica family and originate from the kale-like plants that can still be found growing wild between high tide mark and the cliffs on some of our beaches. Varieties differ in their winter hardiness, making it possible to harvest a good supply of greens for ten months of the year. April and May are the most difficult months, when we sometimes find ourselves arguing with the pigeons over the last remaining greens.

Savoy (July–March, best October–February)

The dark-green Savoys, with their heavily blistered leaves, are the slowest growing of the green cabbages and the most difficult to produce organically. They have a robust texture and strong flavour, making them ideal for inclusion in hearty peasant soups. You can substitute them for cavolo nero in most recipes – see pages 229–33.

January King (October–February)

A very pretty cabbage with tinges of red and blue in the leaves, a crunchy texture and sweet flavour. Tends to be unpredictable and can be ready any time from October to February. Along with Savoy, this is my favourite winter cabbage.

Tundra (September–March)

Boring, but the most reliable green cabbage for late winter. It is the last to plant and is often the only option for February and March when Savoy and January King have finished. Tundra is a cross between a Savoy and a white cabbage and passes the culinary acceptability test, but only just. Often a bit stalky as it gets ready to run to seed.

Celtic/Green (June–March)

This is the generic name for a host of solid green cabbages that make cannon-ball heads from July to December. They are easy to grow and high yielding – great for the farmer but dull in the kitchen – and have contributed to the culinary demise of the cabbage. Best avoided if anything better is around.

Hispi (May–November)

These pointed, crunchy, sweet-tasting cabbages are in season from late May to November but are at their best in the summer. They are relatively quick growing and are our staple summer cabbage. Good steamed, boiled and stir-fried; the more solid ones will even make coleslaw.

White cabbage (July–January, or May out of cold store)

When we grew vegetables for the supermarkets, we used to send off lorry load after lorry load of white cabbage. I was always at a loss as to who ate them all. How much coleslaw can the nation eat? Just about every other use of a white cabbage is better served by green cabbage or kale.

Red cabbage (July–December)

Red cabbage shares many lengthy growing and storage characteristics with white cabbage but has considerably more culinary potential. Depending on variety and planting date, it can be harvested fresh from the field from July to the first really hard frost, normally around Christmas. If handled carefully and harvested in good condition, it is possible to keep red cabbage in cold store for several months. The Dutch even manage to keep them right through to the start of the new season, though I would question how much nutritional value they have by then. When they are fresh and raw, the flavour is similar to white cabbage, though perhaps more earthy and less sweet. They can be included in coleslaw to good effect, giving colour and depth of flavour. Traditionally, red cabbage is braised with apples to make a wonderful accompaniment to game and roast meat.

Storage and preparation

As with all green vegetables, cabbages are best fresh but most of these cabbages will keep for a fortnight or so (a week for Hispi) in a cool vegetable rack or the fridge.

For any recipe requiring robust textures and flavours, such as stews, soups and stuffed cabbage, Savoy is usually the best choice. For quick eating – with lots of pepper and butter – January King and Hispi do well. As I have probably hinted already, I don't see a lot of virtue in Tundra, except when nothing else is available, in which case I suggest you steam it and smother in pepper and butter. The heart can sometimes be sweet and crunchy enough to use for coleslaw.

All cabbages have a tendency to bolt or run to seed if left in the field too long. For the over-wintered varieties, this tendency is accentuated by the approach of spring. When you cut a cabbage in half, you will sometimes see the stem pushing up and trying to break out. Unfortunately, unlike that of broccoli or cauliflower, this stem or central core tends to be tough and bitter and should be cut out, perhaps for use in a stock.

If you boil brassicas, use plenty of water at a rolling boil, with the lid off to help maintain the colour. I like to boil Savoys and steam the more delicate January King and Hispi. Jane often opts not to put cabbages in water at all, but to cook them briefly in butter.

Asian Coleslaw with Peanuts and Chilli

One of Jane's favourite dishes is som tam, or green papaya salad, which is from Northern Thailand and a daily staple in that region. She often tries to emulate it with the humble cabbage and carrot for staff meals here at the farm.

Serves 4

½ cabbage, finely shredded
3 carrots, coarsely grated
2 apples, grated
1 red pepper, sliced
100g beansprouts (optional)
1 tomato, chopped
2 tablespoons crushed roasted peanuts

For the dressing:
1 garlic clove, crushed
½ onion, finely sliced
1 chilli, chopped
1 tablespoon Thai fish sauce
1½ tablespoons brown sugar
3 tablespoons lemon juice
a dash of sweet chilli sauce

Combine all the dressing ingredients, either in a pestle and mortar or by whisking them together in a bowl. Set aside.

Mix together all the vegetables, toss with the dressing and pile on a serving plate. Sprinkle with the roasted peanuts.

Cabbage with Lentils, Chilli and Coriander

Joyce Molyneux, who used to own the Carved Angel in Dartmouth, recommended to Jane that she include this recipe. It's perfect as a side dish or a vegetarian main course.

Serves 4

3 tablespoons olive oil
1 large onion, chopped
2 garlic cloves, crushed
1 chilli, chopped
500g cabbage, preferably Hispi or January King, shredded
juice of ½ lemon
1 tablespoon chopped coriander
sea salt and freshly ground black pepper

For the lentils:
100g Puy lentils
2 garlic cloves, peeled
1 tablespoon olive oil

First cook the lentils. Put them in a pan with the garlic and add enough water to cover. Bring to the boil, then reduce the heat and simmer for about 30 minutes, until tender, topping up the water if necessary. Drain, then season well and mix in the olive oil.

For the cabbage, heat the olive oil in a large saucepan, add the onion, garlic and chilli, then cover and sweat for about 5 minutes, until softened. Add the shredded cabbage and season well. Cook, stirring, over a high heat, until wilted. Stir in the lemon juice, lentils and coriander and adjust the seasoning.

Gujerati Cabbage and Carrot

This is based on a recipe from Madhur Jaffrey's first cookbook. It makes a wonderful accompaniment to curries. Any type of cabbage will do but Savoy is best.

Serves 4

1 tablespoon vegetable oil
1 tablespoon black mustard seeds
1 dried chilli
½ cabbage, thinly sliced
2 carrots, coarsely grated
1 tablespoon caster sugar
juice of ½ lemon
sea salt and freshly ground black pepper

Heat the oil in a wok and add the mustard seeds and chilli. When the seeds start to pop, add the cabbage and carrots and stir-fry for 5 minutes. Add all the rest of the ingredients and cook for a minute longer. Serve immediately.

Stuffed Cabbage

We have a number of Eastern Europeans working at the farm and we occasionally try and serve dishes in the staff canteen that will remind them of home. We also once did couscous for Norddine, our sole Moroccan worker, only to discover that he hated our version. Fortunately this stuffed cabbage went down rather better.

Serves 6

1 medium Savoy cabbage
600g sauerkraut
250g minced beef
250g minced pork
50g long grain rice, cooked
1 egg
1 teaspoon salt
½ teaspoon ground black pepper
4 smoked streaky bacon rashers, cut into thin strips
2 onions, chopped
3 garlic cloves, crushed
1 tablespoon paprika
a pinch of cayenne pepper
400g can of chopped tomatoes
1½ teaspoons caraway seeds
200ml water or stock
1 teaspoon cornflour
150ml soured cream

Remove and discard the outer leaves of the cabbage. Cut off the rest of the leaves from the core and blanch them in a large pan of boiling water for 2 minutes. Drain well, refresh in cold water, then drain again. Set aside the 12 largest leaves and chop up the remaining cabbage. Spread half the sauerkraut over the base of an ovenproof dish and cover with the chopped cabbage.

Mix the beef, pork, rice, egg, salt and pepper together in a bowl. Fry the bacon in a saucepan until just beginning to brown, then remove with a slotted spoon. Add 1 onion and the garlic to the pan and cook them in the bacon fat for 5 minutes over a medium heat. Mix the onion and bacon with the meat and rice mixture.

Spread out the 12 reserved cabbage leaves on a board and divide the meat mixture between them. Fold in the sides of each leaf and then roll it up around the filling. Place the cabbage rolls on top of the sauerkraut mixture.

Put the paprika, cayenne, tomatoes, caraway seeds, water or stock and the remaining onion in a pan and bring to the boil. Add the remaining sauerkraut and then pour the mixture over the cabbage rolls. Cover the dish, place in an oven preheated to 180°C/Gas Mark 4 and bake for 1 hour.

Mix the cornflour and soured cream together. Pour the mixture over the cabbage rolls and bake for 10 more minutes.

Braised Red Cabbage

We regularly cook this basic recipe in the Field Kitchen, where we like to serve it with roast pork and game. Raw grated beetroot can be added, along with a little orange juice and honey, and cooked for a further 15 minutes.

Serves 6

1 red cabbage, finely shredded
2 dessert apples, peeled, cored and chopped
1 onion, chopped
50g butter
1½ tablespoons dark soft brown sugar
1½ tablespoons balsamic vinegar
sea salt and freshly ground black pepper

Put all the ingredients in a large, heavy-based pan and place over a high heat, stirring until well combined. When the mixture is simmering, turn the heat down low, cover the pan and leave the cabbage to cook in its own juices for about 2 hours, stirring occasionally to prevent sticking. Taste and adjust the seasoning, adding more sugar or vinegar if required.

Warm Red Cabbage Salad with Toasted Walnuts and Blue Cheese

This is based on a salad in *The Greens Cookbook* by Deborah Madison and Edward Espe Brown (Bantam Books, 1987). They used goat's cheese but we changed it slightly to work with our autumn menu.

Serves 8

75g walnut pieces
2 tablespoons walnut oil
2 crisp red apples
1 garlic clove, finely chopped
2 tablespoons balsamic vinegar
2½ tablespoons olive oil
1 red onion, quartered and thinly sliced
1 small red cabbage, shredded
100g blue cheese, crumbled (we use Devon Blue)
1 tablespoon chopped parsley
1 teaspoon chopped marjoram
sea salt and freshly ground black pepper

Toss the walnuts with the walnut oil and some black pepper. Spread them out on a baking tray and toast in an oven preheated to 180°C/Gas Mark 4 for 5–7 minutes. Remove from the oven and leave to cool.

Core the apples and cut into small pieces. Put the garlic, balsamic vinegar and olive oil in a frying pan and sauté over a medium heat for 3 minutes. Add the red onion and cook for 30 seconds, then add the cabbage and cook for a couple of minutes, until it begins to turn from red to pink. Season with salt and pepper. Finally add the cheese, apples, herbs and toasted walnuts. Toss well and serve.

Red Cabbage and Beetroot Confit

This dish is designed to go with roast duck. It comes from Bill Gunn, who owns Bistro Tatau in Apia, the capital of Samoa. Jane worked there for a while, helping to develop dishes in a country used to taro, lamb flaps and turkey tails. So if you are ever lucky enough to be in Apia, pop in.

Serves 4

1 tablespoon butter
1 large red onion, finely sliced
100ml red wine vinegar
100g light soft brown sugar
150g cranberry sauce, cranberry jelly or dark plum jam
½ small red cabbage, finely shredded
3 medium beetroot, peeled and cut into matchsticks on a mandolin, or grated
a splash of balsamic vinegar
celery salt and freshly ground black pepper

Melt the butter in a large, heavy-based saucepan, add the onion and sweat gently until soft but not coloured. Add the red wine vinegar, sugar and cranberry sauce and bring to a gentle simmer. Add the cabbage and beetroot, stir well, then cover and cook very gently for 30–40 minutes, until the vegetables are soft and the liquid has reduced to a sticky sauce. Adjust the seasoning with balsamic vinegar, celery salt and pepper.

Easy ideas for cabbage

✦ Melt some butter in a pan, sprinkle in some caraway seeds and cook for a couple of minutes. Stir in finely shredded white or green cabbage, cover and cook slowly for 10 minutes or until soft. Chopped cooked bacon can be stirred in to keep meat eaters happy.

✦ To make an anchovy coleslaw, mix chopped anchovy fillets, crushed garlic and rosemary with a basic oil and vinegar dressing, then toss with finely sliced Hispi or white cabbage.

✦ Substitute cabbage for Brussels sprouts in Bubble and Squeak Soup (see page 66).

✦ Substitute cabbage (ideally Savoy or similar) for kale in Kale, Chorizo and Potato Hash (see page 230).

✦ Make the classic Irish dish, colcannon (see Perfect Mash variations, page 288).

✦ A dish from Modena, the home of balsamic vinegar: mix very finely shredded Savoy cabbage with slivers of Parmesan and a drizzle of good aged balsamic vinegar. Serve with slices of prosciutto.

✦ Brown some partridges (or could be pigeons or pheasant) well in a little oil in a heavy casserole, add a few rashers of streaky bacon, a chopped cabbage (January King is good), a splash of red wine and enough chicken stock to come half way up the cabbage. Cover the partridge with the cabbage, then bring to a simmer, season, and cover the pan. Put in an oven preheated to 160°C/Gas Mark 3 and bake for about 30 minutes, until the partridges are cooked through.

✦ To make a red cabbage slaw, mix shredded red cabbage, grated carrot and finely chopped red onion with sliced pickled jalapeño chillies, mayonnaise and chives.

Carrots

The best-tasting carrots I ever grew were an old-fashioned, non-hybrid variety called Autumn King. We grew them on top of a hill to avoid carrot root fly, scraping what little soil there was into ridges and sowing the seed on top. They grew slowly and steadily without irrigation or fertiliser until they hit the bed rock and then pushed themselves out of the ground, so that by November they stood several inches proud of the soil. Some of the carrots were over a foot long and weighed several pounds. They were harvested by hand and we had to stand some upright in the sacks because they were too long to lie crossways. It is interesting that when carrots are grown for processing, where flavour rather than cosmetic appearance is the main determining factor, this variety, or its modern-day cousins, is still grown commercially.

The carrot industry excels at growing and selling carrots that are cheap, cosmetically perfect and consistently tasteless. Over the last 20 years the drive to reduce costs has concentrated the industry in the hands of three or four large players with land in the east of England and southern Spain, supplied with seed by two or three international seed companies and all fighting for contracts with four major supermarkets. Carrots are lifted, sifted, sorted and washed; polished, packed, cooled and distributed to shelves around the country with extraordinary speed and efficiency 52 weeks of the year.

The major casualty in this drive for cheapness and consistency has been flavour, perhaps accompanied by nutritional value. There is no place in modern systems for smaller growers, imperfect soils or a carrot that has suffered any degree of damage, is lower in yield, inconsistent in shape or lacks the robustness to withstand all the mechanical handling that is essential to reducing costs. Taste is notoriously subjective but it is quite remarkable how Nairobi, the variety that accounts for over half the UK carrot crop, consistently comes out bottom in all our trials at Riverford; at best it is tasteless and often it is nasty. I once visited a carrot variety trial (mainly attended by large, commercial growers) where I was the only person who wanted to taste the carrots. Everyone else was banging them on their wellies and bending them to test their 'robustness', or how easily they would snap. Nairobi's most noted virtue is that you could drop it out of an aeroplane without it breaking. This is an industry removed from both the living soil and the kitchen, dominated by technicians, engineers and accountants, which seems to have forgotten that it is producing food.

Variety is the main factor in flavour, but it is as noticeable with carrots and potatoes as it is with wine that the flavour of a particular variety will vary according to region and soil type. I could be prejudiced but my experience is that roots taste better if grown more slowly on a healthy, mixed, balanced soil with a minimum of irrigation, rather than at very high densities on pure sand, fed for maximum growth and maximum yield with soluble fertilisers and copious irrigation. Any clay in the soil will make harvest much more difficult, which is why most carrots are grown on virtually pure sand. Our relatively heavy soil here in Devon makes harvesting hard work but I believe it pays dividends in terms of flavour. The varieties we currently favour are Junior, which tastes wonderful but is so fragile that we hand harvest and bunch the whole crop, and Artemis, Trevor, Nerac, Narbonne and Nepal; these combine flavour with sufficient robustness to survive mechanical harvest. Sadly, the seed company is ceasing production of Junior, our favourite variety. I am tempted to go back to Autumn King but fear that our customers will judge these mammoths with their eyes before their taste buds get a chance.

Carrots are sown in the UK from January to May for harvest from late June to November. The winter and spring crop is either stored in the ground under an insulating duvet of 30cm of straw between two layers of plastic – this protects from frost and delays re-growth – or harvested in late October and November and kept in cold store. Counter-intuitively the autumn-harvested, barn-stored crop often tastes better by spring than the ones left in the soil. With either method, by April the carrots can be dodgy in terms of taste and shelf life; their natural desire is to be running to seed by now. We find that they have become such a staple of many customers' diets, however, that from May to late June, like everyone else, we have to import them from Italy and Spain to plug the 'hungry gap'. Even the organic ones are normally grown with intensive irrigation on pure sand and tend to be pretty tasteless. So we do all we can to advance the new crop using south-facing fields and crop covers, and very much look forward to the first bunches in late June.

We were once sent a bloke by Channel 4 when it was doing a series on people with phobias. His phobias were dirt and less than perfectly shaped vegetables. He was a city-dwelling vegetarian who dared not touch a vegetable and lived entirely off processed food. He was a thoroughly likeable chap who worked hard at overcoming what was obviously a very real fear. We got him as far as pulling a carrot out of the ground and eating it raw, but anything at all misshapen was a step too far and he left us with this part of his fear unresolved.

Storage and preparation

We sell our carrots unwashed and, until the spring, when they are liable to sprout, they will keep for many weeks without significant deterioration. Like potatoes, parsnips, onions, garlic etc, these organs are designed by nature for storage; we just need to leave their skins on and give them the right conditions. Most carrots are sold washed and, increasingly, 'polished', using high-pressure water jets. The virtue of polishing is that it performs a facelift, removing minor blemishes and temporarily rejuvenating a second-rate carrot. The problem is that the water jets take off the protective skin of the carrot. It's like prolonged exfoliation with sandpaper. The carrots may look red and shiny for a while but they go septic pretty fast afterwards.

If your carrots arrive muddy, washing is made easier by soaking them in water for a few minutes before scrubbing or peeling. Carrots are best stored in the bottom of your fridge if already washed or if spring is approaching. Dirty carrots should keep for several weeks in a paper bag in a cool veg rack – i.e. one in an unheated room. If your carrots come bunched, it is a good idea to twist off and discard the tops to prevent them drawing moisture from the roots. Don't immediately throw away dirty carrots that have gone a little bendy; they often taste surprisingly sweet. It can even be an indication that they have been grown more slowly, with less water.

The summer and autumn crop usually scrubs up well without the need for peeling. As winter progresses, if they have been in store, the skins become discoloured and may have a tendency to be bitter, so peeling progressively becomes the favoured option.

Carrots feature heavily on Jane's menus in the Field Kitchen. We share the view that these are a most abused vegetable – usually cut up and boiled when there is so much else you can do with them, exploiting their natural sweetness. This is intensified if they are kept away from water, and Jane tends to cook them without water (for example, roasting or cooking with a little butter). But, as children often say, why cook them at all? Really fresh carrots are best used raw in salads. The skins add hugely to the flavour, so should just be washed wherever possible. We only peel them when we get on to the older, stored ones.

Carrot Salad with Beetroot and Sesame

If you get the proportions of carrot and beetroot right here, depending on their size, you get the most amazing fluorescent pink colour – irresistible even to people who don't like beetroot. Serve as a refreshing accompaniment to Middle Eastern or Asian dishes.

Serves 6

4 carrots, coarsely grated
3 beetroot, peeled and coarsely grated
juice and grated zest of 2 oranges
2 tablespoons sesame seeds, lightly toasted in a dry frying pan
2 teaspoons honey
1 small garlic clove, crushed to a paste with a little salt
1 tablespoon olive oil
1 tablespoon chopped coriander (optional)
sea salt and freshly ground black pepper

Mix the grated carrot and beetroot together in a large bowl. Add all the remaining ingredients and mix well. Check the seasoning, adding more salt, pepper, honey or orange juice as required.

Braised Carrots and Turnips with Honey

When Jane prepares this recipe for cookery demonstrations in the Field Kitchen, people are amazed how quickly the vegetables cook with so little water added. It is important, though, to check the pans frequently, so they don't catch on the bottom.

Serves 8

For the carrots:
1kg bunched carrots, trimmed and cut lengthways in half
50g butter
1 tablespoon honey
50ml water
1 tablespoon balsamic vinegar
1 tablespoon chopped parsley
sea salt and freshly ground black pepper

For the turnips:
600g turnips, peeled and halved
50g butter
1 tablespoon honey
50ml water
1 tablespoon balsamic vinegar
1 tablespoon chopped parsley

Put all the ingredients for the carrots except the vinegar and parsley in a heavy-based pan and place over a high heat until the mixture is simmering away. Turn the heat right down, cover the pan and cook for about 10 minutes, frequently checking and stirring the carrots to make sure they don't stick and burn. When the carrots are almost cooked, uncover the pan, increase the heat slightly and stir in the balsamic vinegar. Cook for 3 minutes, then turn off the heat and stir in the parsley.

Cook the turnips in the same way – they should take a little less time than the carrots. When both carrots and turnips are done, mix them together, season to taste and serve.

Crushed Roast Carrots with Cumin and Goat's Cheese

Russell, who works in the Field Kitchen, cooked this for us when we served a Moorish-inspired menu. It went down an absolute storm and we've often done it since.

Serves 4

1 bunch of carrots (about 750g)
4 tablespoons olive oil
2 teaspoons cumin seeds, lightly toasted in a dry frying pan and then ground
2 tablespoons pine nuts, lightly toasted in a dry frying pan
75g goat's cheese, crumbled
1 tablespoon chopped mint (or oregano or marjoram)
good extra virgin olive oil, for drizzling

Scrub and trim the carrots, then cut them in half lengthways. Put them in a roasting tin and toss with the olive oil. Place in an oven preheated to 180°C/Gas Mark 4 and roast for about 50 minutes, until they are tender, slightly browned and have a caramelised appearance.

Mash the roasted carrots roughly with a fork, a masher or your hands and mix with the ground cumin. Spread the mashed carrots on a plate and sprinkle with the pine nuts, goat's cheese and herbs. Drizzle with extra virgin olive oil and serve with toasted pitta bread.

Carrot Cake

This recipe was kindly sent to us by Tina Richardson, a box scheme customer in Harrow, and has been very popular. Instead of carrot, she used beetroot, which you can substitute here – or use a mixture of both.

Serves 6–8

250g self-raising flour
2 teaspoons baking powder
150g soft brown sugar
100g sultanas
200g carrots, grated
150ml vegetable or sunflower oil
2 medium eggs, lightly beaten

Sift the flour and baking powder into a bowl and stir in the soft brown sugar. Add the sultanas and grated carrots. Beat the oil and eggs together and add to the bowl. Combine with either a wooden spoon or an electric mixer.

Spoon the mixture into a greased and lined 20cm springform cake tin and bake in an oven preheated to 160°C/Gas Mark 3 for 1–1¼ hours, until a skewer inserted in the centre comes out clean. Cool in the tin for 10 minutes, then turn out on to a wire rack to cool completely.

Chickpeas with Carrots and Swiss Chard

If you have carrots and Swiss chard in your veg box, this is the perfect dish to make. Good served with fish or lamb, or as part of a mezze.

Serves 6

150g dried chickpeas, soaked in cold water overnight and then drained
1 head of garlic, sliced horizontally in half
3 tablespoons olive oil
1 onion, finely chopped
1 garlic clove, chopped
400g carrots, cut into 1cm dice
3 tomatoes, skinned, deseeded and chopped (or use canned tomatoes)
2 teaspoons tomato purée
400g Swiss chard
1 tablespoon finely chopped mint
a little good extra virgin olive oil
sea salt and freshly ground black pepper

Place the drained chickpeas in a saucepan and cover with fresh water. Add the halved garlic head, bring to the boil, then reduce the heat and simmer, uncovered, for about 1¼ hours, until tender. Top up with more water if necessary. When the chickpeas are done, drain, season well and dress with 1 tablespoon of the olive oil. Set aside.

Heat the remaining oil in a shallow pan, add the onion and cook gently for about 15 minutes, until very soft. Add the chopped garlic and the carrots and cook slowly for 10 minutes. Stir in the tomatoes and tomato purée, turn up the heat and cook for 5 minutes or until the tomato mixture has reduced enough to coat the carrots.

Strip the leaves off the stalks of chard, discarding the stalks. Add the chard leaves and chickpeas to the pan and cook until the chard has wilted. Stir in the chopped mint, toss together and dress with a little good olive oil. Adjust the seasoning and serve with warm crusty bread.

Easy ideas for carrots

✦ Substitute young whole carrots for potatoes in New Potatoes Baked in Parchment (see page 286), using bay or tarragon instead of rosemary or thyme.

✦ Dress grated carrot with lemon juice, olive oil and coriander leaves for a simple Middle Eastern salad.

✦ Sweat very thinly sliced carrots in butter and a few tablespoons of water until just tender. Add a splash of double cream and simmer until the cream has thickened enough to coat the carrots. Season and finish with chopped chervil.

✦ Put 500g very thinly sliced carrots in a wide pan with a tablespoon of butter, a tablespoon of honey, the juice of 1 lemon and a teaspoon of grated fresh ginger. Cover and cook slowly under tender.

✦ Mash boiled carrots and swede together with plenty of butter and black pepper to make an orange mash to serve with roasts.

See also:
Asian Coleslaw with Peanuts and Chilli (page 79)
Gujerati Cabbage and Carrot (page 81)
Celery Braised with Anchovies (page 122)

Cauliflower

Cauliflower needs a makeover, especially as it is possible to grow this much-maligned vegetable virtually all year round in the UK. Perhaps it is this ubiquity, combined with memories of school dinners, that has caused it to be held in such low esteem. Elsewhere in the world, in countries such as India where it is more difficult to grow, it is much sought after. I suspect that part of the problem is the huge amount of nitrogen fertiliser applied to the conventional crop to force it on through the winter, producing sappy, rapid growth in the field but mushy, insipid curds on the plate. When grown organically, on mineral soils outside the main brassica-growing areas on the Fens (where the constant breakdown of the peat provides excessive nitrogen even without fertiliser), cauliflowers tend to be smaller and firmer, with exceptional flavour.

Summer varieties are thoroughbred sprinters with a serious nitrogen habit. Without being drip-fed the stuff with plenty of water, they will come to nothing, and consequently do not do well in an organic system. We tend not to bother with cauliflowers during the summer, when there are plenty of other vegetables around, starting the season in September or October instead. The winter and spring crop are all planted in July but different varieties produce curds in response to different combinations of day length, temperature and maturity, making it possible to harvest right through to the following May. Though our customers' enthusiasm for cauliflowers can wear thin, they are a very welcome standby in the 'hungry gap' in April and May.

From December to March, cauliflower can be reliably harvested only in certain coastal areas, where the maritime climate gives protection from frost. Traditionally these were the Isle of Thanet in East Kent, a few areas of South Devon and most famously West Cornwall. Even in these regions the supply, and consequently the price, varies wildly with the weather. Fortunes and reputations have been made and lost on the cauliflower market. Brittany Ferries was set up by a cooperative of French farmers so that they could get Brittany cauliflowers to the UK quickly when the price was high. The strip of Cornish coast from Penzance to Marazion is known locally as the Golden Mile because of the profitability of crops of early potatoes, followed by winter cauliflower, which were fertilised by seaweed dragged up from the beach below.

When a cauliflower is ready, it has to be cut regardless of the weather, which can be pretty extreme on a Devon cliff in January. All our cauliflowers are cut by hand by our 'A team', a bunch of hardened and experienced workers who can sense a cauliflower's shape and size from five paces even when it is fully wrapped in leaves. They spend all winter roaming our co-op's cauliflower fields, machete in hand, with a specially built rig on caterpillar tracks that will go anywhere in any weather, carrying up to 1,500 heads.

We tried the tractor-drawn rigs used by conventional growers but I was horrified by the ruts and soil damage left at the end of the winter. I am a frustrated engineer at heart and have always enjoyed the challenges of finding original ways to meet the particular needs of organic growing on our soil and slopes. The need to look after our treasured soil has led us to design and build a range of machinery for winter use that exerts less ground pressure than the pickers' wellies. It is also quieter, more sociable to work with, and takes at least some of the physical strain out of a very demanding job.

Storage and preparation

The striking whiteness of a perfect cauliflower has led supermarkets to be ridiculously prescriptive in their specification of acceptable quality. This leads to a huge waste of heads that are marginally off white or in any way misshapen but that otherwise share the culinary qualities of their cosmetically perfect cousins. A healthy, undamaged head is remarkably durable and will keep for a fortnight in the fridge without much loss of quality. Even on a cool vegetable rack, they are normally good for a week. We sometimes leave a fair amount of leaf on to protect the delicate curd, provided they are reasonably healthy, but most supermarkets are in the habit of trimming the leaves off and replacing this natural packaging with a plastic bag or, even more ridiculously, over-wrapping them on a tray. The leaves are the best indicator of freshness and, if still healthy, they can be very sweet, succulent and increasingly tender as you move in towards the curd. Rather than trimming them off, try cooking and serving them with the cauliflower – particularly good in cauliflower cheese.

Cauliflower can be eaten raw or lightly steamed with dips such as Bagna Cauda (see page 176). It can also be sliced and stir-fried, as well as boiled. I like it in all these ways. My main advice is not to overcook it – especially if you want to avoid the worst of those cooking smells. Break the head into even florets, then boil or steam them till they have some bite left.

Cauliflower and Potato Dal

Jane's first kitchen job was in a Gujerati restaurant in Leeds called Hansa's. They always finished their dals with a final frying in this way, which really lifts the flavours.

Serves 4

2 tablespoons sunflower oil
2 onions, finely chopped
2 celery stalks, finely sliced
4 garlic cloves, crushed
1 tablespoon finely chopped fresh ginger
1 teaspoon salt
½ teaspoon ground black pepper
1 teaspoon good-quality curry powder
¼ teaspoon grated nutmeg
250g yellow split peas, soaked in cold water overnight and then drained
750ml vegetable stock
3 potatoes, peeled and cut into 1cm cubes
1 small cauliflower, cut into florets

For the final frying:
1 tablespoon sunflower oil
1 onion or 2 shallots, thinly sliced
1 garlic clove, thinly sliced
¼ teaspoon dried chilli flakes
½ teaspoon mustard seeds
2 tablespoons lemon juice
1 tablespoon brown sugar
1 tablespoon chopped coriander

Heat the oil in a large pan, add the onions and celery and cook gently for 5 minutes. Stir in the garlic, ginger, salt, pepper, curry powder and nutmeg and cook for 1 minute. Add the split peas and vegetable stock, bring to the boil, then reduce the heat and simmer for 20 minutes, skimming off any froth from the surface. Add the potatoes and cook for 10 minutes. Finally stir in the cauliflower and cook for 10 minutes or until the potatoes and cauliflower are just tender.

To finish the dish, heat the tablespoon of sunflower oil in a frying pan until quite hot, then add the onion or shallots and cook, stirring constantly, for a minute. Quickly add the garlic, chilli and mustard seeds and cook until the seeds start to pop. Stir this mixture into the dal, followed by the lemon juice and sugar. Finish with the chopped coriander.

Cauliflower and Stilton Soup

You can purée this if you prefer a smooth soup but the cauliflower tends to break down a bit anyway, giving it an interesting texture. It's an extremely useful way of using up Stilton after Christmas if, like us, you ordered too much.

Serves 6

40g unsalted butter
1 onion, roughly chopped
4 garlic cloves, finely chopped
1 teaspoon dried oregano
1 large cauliflower, cut into florets
2 tablespoons finely chopped flat-leaf parsley
500ml chicken or vegetable stock
150g Stilton cheese, crumbled
150ml milk
2 tablespoons double cream
sea salt and freshly ground black pepper
toast spread with Stilton, to serve

Melt the butter in a heavy-based saucepan, add the onion, garlic, oregano and some salt and pepper, then cook over a medium heat for 5 minutes or until the onion is soft. Add the cauliflower and parsley and cook, stirring occasionally, for 10 minutes. Add the stock, bring to the boil and simmer for 20 minutes or until the cauliflower is tender. Reduce the heat to low, add the Stilton and stir well until combined. Add the milk and heat through gently. Taste and adjust the seasoning.

Pour the soup into bowls, top with the cream and serve with Stilton toasts on the side.

Spanish Crisp Cauliflower

Jane cooked something like this while staying in Andalusia in the house of a friend (who went on to set up Moro restaurant in London). It took her several attempts to recreate the dish here. If you can't find gram (chickpea) flour, you can use plain white flour – though it won't have the same nutty flavour.

Serves 4 as a starter or a side dish

½ cauliflower, broken into small florets
2 tablespoons gram flour
1 teaspoon paprika
sunflower oil for deep-frying
1 dessertspoon good-quality red wine vinegar
1 tablespoon capers, soaked in cold water for 20 minutes, then squeezed dry and chopped
1 tablespoon chopped parsley
sea salt and freshly ground black pepper

Cook the cauliflower florets in boiling salted water for a few minutes, until just tender. Drain the cauliflower well and, while it is still hot, put in a bowl with the flour, paprika and some salt and pepper. Mix it all together until the cauliflower is coated with flour.

Heat the sunflower oil to 190°C in a deep-fat fryer or a deep, heavy-based saucepan. Fry the cauliflower florets in batches until crisp and golden, then remove from the oil and drain on kitchen paper. Sprinkle with the vinegar, chopped capers and parsley and serve.

Penne with Cauliflower, Garlic and Anchovies

Any excuse to use anchovies. If you let them 'melt' into the oil, as in this recipe, the flavour will be mellow, and completely different from the usual overwhelming anchovy experience on pizzas.

Along with cabbage, people most frequently ask us what to do with cauliflower. This dish provides a quick and elegant solution.

Serves 4

1 cauliflower, divided into florets
350g penne
4 tablespoons olive oil
2 garlic cloves, finely chopped
5 anchovy fillets
a pinch of cayenne pepper
2 tablespoons chopped parsley
sea salt and freshly ground black pepper

Cook the cauliflower florets in boiling salted water for 5 minutes, then drain and set aside. Cook the penne in a large pan of boiling salted water until al dente.

Meanwhile, heat the oil in a separate pan, add the garlic and cook until softened but not browned. Remove from the heat, add the anchovy fillets and stir and mash them into the oil until dissolved. Add the cauliflower florets and cayenne, mix well to coat the cauliflower in the anchovy oil, then return to a low heat. Cover and cook for 5 minutes, then mash the cauliflower roughly with a fork.

Drain the pasta and mix with the cauliflower. Season to taste, sprinkle over the chopped parsley, then serve.

Easy ideas for cauliflower

✦ Cook cauliflower florets in brown butter with almonds, as for Brussels sprouts (see page 69).

✦ Use cauliflower florets as well as or instead of leeks in the lemony marinade on page 250.

+ Gently fry a chopped onion in a tablespoon of oil and a generous knob of butter until soft. Add a head of cauliflower, divided into small florets, mix well, then add 150ml milk. Cover and simmer until tender. Whiz to a purée in a food processor. At this point you can serve it as a soup: return to the pan, thin with a little more milk, season to taste and serve each bowlful with some truffle oil drizzled on top. Or serve the purée as a base for a piece of roast white fish, surrounded by cooked Puy lentils.

+ Cook cauliflower florets in boiling salted water until tender, then drain and mix with 2 tablespoons of Salsa Verde (see page 216) and 2 grated hard-boiled eggs.

+ Substitute cauliflower for broccoli in Spicy Purple Sprouting Broccoli with Garlic, Olives and Toasted Breadcrumbs (see page 59).

+ Substitute cauliflower for romanesco in the first Easy idea listed on page 62.

+ Cook 1 tablespoon of mustard seeds and 2 tablespoons of fennel seeds in 2 tablespoons of oil until they start to pop. Add 3 chopped garlic cloves, ½ teaspoon ground turmeric and 1 cauliflower, broken into florets. Mix well, add 100ml water, then cover and simmer for 8 minutes, stirring occasionally, until the cauliflower is cooked. Sprinkle with fresh herbs if you have any – coriander, mint or parsley.

+ Make cauliflower cheese in the usual way, with a cheesy béchamel sauce, but try one of the variations below:

   Substitute some of the cauliflower cooking water for half the milk in the sauce.

   Add a good dollop of mustard (Dijon and wholegrain work well) to the sauce and top the cauliflower cheese with breadcrumbs before browning in the oven.

   For a more substantial meal, mix cooked smoked fish or bacon and some chopped hardboiled eggs into the cheese sauce before pouring it over the cauliflower.

   Use cauliflower cheese to top a cottage pie mix.

Keeping the faith

Farmers are a stubbornly independent lot who tend to spend too much time in their own company. Most organic farmers are no different, so it is a bit misleading when people talk about the organic 'movement' – a word that carries connotations of an unanimous tide of opinion, or even gurus and mindless followers. Few things could be further from the truth. Organic farming boasts a host of free-thinking individuals, each with their own pet enthusiasm, often verging on obsession, that has been developed in isolation on their farms and only occasionally tempered by an audience more challenging than a flock of sheep. They can be a bit extreme, and grouping them together is like trying to herd a yardful of cats. Organic is a broad church that constantly re-evaluates itself and has its share of schisms along the way.

I feel uncomfortable about some aspects of the organic certification standards and the broader movement: I feel no allegiance to those who use organic food as a form of snobbery or those who see it simply as the latest way of maximising their short-term farm income or developing a brand. Some organically certified practices, particularly in the areas of poultry and dairy, where production is increasingly concentrated in the hands of ever-larger producers, make me uncomfortable. Given a free hand, I might use some seed treatments where a tiny quantity of chemical would massively ease the challenge of growing crops at a price that makes them accessible to everyone. I have done my share of cantankerous objecting to these things but I am still in the church and toeing the certified line.

At times I have wavered and considered simply doing it my own way according to the standards of my conscience and beliefs about food and farming – perhaps becoming the farming equivalent of Martin Bell as an independent politician. That way we would end up with 101 different standards, and customers would have to have the patience to listen to a diatribe about the subtle differences of each. On top of deciding which brand of recycled loo roll to buy or whether to offset their carbon, few people have the time. So we must all put up with an approximation to our own preferred standard. For me, being certified by the Soil Association is a shorthand way of describing more or less how I want to farm. It is close enough and allows me to be able to farm without boring everyone with the details of why I do it the way I do.

Over the years I have reached the conclusion that few people who buy organic food really understand the specifics of organic farming (why should they when the regulations extend to 400 pages?) but most do have an intuitive trust, amongst the insanities and abuses of modern food and farming, that organic farming is right for us and right for our planet. And for the most part it is. Perhaps even more importantly, by moving organic farming in the right direction we are dragging conventional farming along with it.

Celeriac

Celeriac is surely the ugliest of vegetables. I once lost several Conservative customers by unwisely comparing its appearance to Iain Duncan Smith's forehead on a bad day. It is also one of the most difficult vegetables to grow and store reliably but its many culinary possibilities and long winter season make it a favourite with most serious cooks. Used in huge quantities in northern France and Belgium, where celeriac rémoulade (see page 118) is an ubiquitous accompaniment to crudités, it has enjoyed a justifiable rise in popularity here in the UK over the last 20 years.

Celeriac's leaves look very similar to the closely related celery but are not really edible. In the UK, celeriac comes straight from the field from October to December, and then, provided it hasn't suffered too much frost and is disease free, can be put in cold storage from January to March or even April. Like carrots, parsnips, celery and parsley, celeriac is part of the *Umbelliferae* family and can harbour carrot root fly. We tend to grow it in isolated fields, where it will not act as a carry-over host for this pest.

Seeds are sown in February or March for planting out in May. They are very slow to establish and need a long growing season to produce the target one-kilo root. The plants can stand light frosts but need to be in the barn before the first hard freeze of the year, which we normally expect around Christmas. Starting in October, we harvest through November and December by hand. This is normally a wet time for us, and though the crop does best on heavier, moisture-retaining land, our staff has threatened a revolt if we ever grow it on our sticky clay soils again. The misery of working with balls of clay on your feet, handling celeriac whose weight is doubled by a coat of clinging mud, is unparalleled on the farm. We have experimented with a potato harvester but ended up with a barn full of soil, so we are back to machete-style knives in the field, trimming off the worst of the fibrous root and clinging soil as we go.

Storage and preparation

Cool and damp is best, so an outdoor, shady vegetable rack is good and the bottom of your fridge even better. Healthy celeriac should keep, unwrapped, for several weeks without any significant loss of quality. Even when cut in half, they will still keep for a week or more, though you may need to shave off a layer to refresh the surface. In this way you can use a root to flavour stocks

over several weeks. Technically speaking, they are a corm, and as such a natural starch store that would be used to produce a seed head in the second year if we gave them the chance.

Rather like Jerusalem artichokes, celeriac's uneven surface is a bit of a challenge in preparation. You need either a very good vegetable peeler or to trim back the bottom and not to worry about wasting a bit (the trimmings are good in stock).

The easiest way to use celeriac is to mash it with potato (I recommend a potato/celeriac ratio of 2:1). This produces a wonderfully smoky-flavoured mash that goes particularly well with game. You will find that the celeriac cooks faster than the potato, so either cut it in larger chunks or add it to the pan later to prevent it losing its flavour before the spuds are soft – or, for the best result, cook the two separately.

Celeriac is also good in soups, and raw in salads, which tends to emphasise its slightly aniseed taste. I don't recommend using the leaves, which can be very bitter, except for a very small quantity added to stock.

Celeriac and Apple Mash

Celeriac and apple go so well together. This is a lovely mash to serve with game or roast pork, alongside Braised Red Cabbage (see page 83).

Serves 4

1 large dessert apple, peeled, cored and finely sliced
1 large celeriac, peeled and cut into quarters
1 large potato, peeled and cut into quarters
3 tablespoons double cream
30g butter
sea salt and freshly ground black pepper

Cook the apple in a pan with about a tablespoon of water until soft and broken down. Cook the celeriac and potato in boiling salted water until tender, then drain well. Mix with the apple and pass through the finest plate of a mouli-légumes (or a potato ricer or sieve). Heat up the cream and butter in a small pan and stir them into the mash. Reheat gently, if necessary, season to taste and serve.

Celeriac and Celery Soup

Jane saw something like this on a restaurant menu in Sydney and devised her own version. With three celery flavours – celeriac, celery and celery seeds – it really packs a punch, and the Worcestershire sauce gives it an extra kick.

Serves 4–6

50g butter
1 onion, chopped
1 leek, thinly sliced (up to the dark green bit)
400–500g celeriac, peeled and finely chopped
400–500g celery, sliced (reserve the leaves)
½ teaspoon celery seeds
1 litre chicken stock
1 tablespoon double cream
1 tablespoon Worcestershire sauce
sea salt and freshly ground black pepper
chopped parsley, to serve (optional)

Heat the butter in a large saucepan, add the onion and leek and cook for 10 minutes over a medium heat. Add the celeriac, celery, celery seeds and some salt and cook, covered, for 10 minutes, without letting them brown. Add the chicken stock, bring to the boil and simmer for about 15 minutes, until the vegetables are tender.

Purée the soup in a blender and then pass through a mouli-légumes, for the best result, or a fine sieve. Reheat gently, then add the double cream and Worcestershire sauce. Season to taste. Garnish with chopped celery leaves and parsley, if liked.

Spiced Celeriac with Lemon

Celeriac is often drenched in cream and butter, but here the delicate spicing gives it a faintly Middle Eastern flavour.

Serves 6

1 large or 2 small celeriac
3 tablespoons olive oil
a pinch of smoked paprika
a pinch of cayenne pepper
a pinch of ground cinnamon
grated zest of 1 lemon
juice of 1½ lemons
sea salt and freshly ground black pepper

Peel the celeriac, cut into slices 5mm–1cm thick, then cut the slices into long, thin sticks. Heat the oil in a large pan, add the celeriac sticks and fry for about 15 minutes, until slightly browned. At this point sprinkle with the spices, lemon zest and juice and 100ml water. Simmer for about 10 minutes, until the celeriac is just tender. Season to taste, adding more lemon juice if necessary.

Celeriac Rémoulade

A classic dish. The question with rémoulade is whether to blanch the celeriac or not. It's not absolutely essential, but Jane believes it does improve the flavour and texture.

Serves 6

1 medium celeriac
juice of 1 lemon
3 tablespoons Dijon mustard
150ml good mayonnaise
1 tablespoon double cream
1 tablespoon chopped parsley
sea salt and freshly ground black pepper

Peel the celeriac and cut it into matchsticks about 3mm thick, either by hand or using a mandolin. Add them to a large pan of boiling water and cook for 1 minute, then drain well and leave to cool.

Mix the rest of the ingredients together in a large bowl. Season well and mix in the celeriac.

Easy ideas for celeriac

✦ Deep-fry celeriac shavings (made using a vegetable peeler) in sunflower oil, then drain well and sprinkle with salt for an alternative crisp.

✦ Substitute celeriac for all or half of the potato in the Basic Potato Gratin on page 284, adding a little grated apple too, if you like.

✦ Cut peeled celeriac into chunks or chips and roast in hot oil with a sprinkling of thyme, sage or rosemary.

✦ Peel and chop a celeriac and cook with a couple of peeled garlic cloves in enough milk to cover. Drain, reserving the milk, and pass through a food mill (or whiz in a food processor). Stir in a few tablespoons of the milk to loosen the consistency and season to taste. Serve with game or braised field mushrooms.

Celery

Celery was traditionally grown on the dark, fertile, moisture-retentive peat soils found in the fens of Lincolnshire and the mosses of Lancashire. By growing the crop in a trench and subsequently ridging up to bury the plants, it was possible to produce blanched and tender stalks and to afford a degree of protection from frost, allowing the crop to be harvested into the depths of winter. Traditions and fashions have changed. Almost all celery is now grown above ground and, though the seed catalogues describe it as 'self blanching', the resulting sticks are never as pale or tender as the old-style crop, though they may well have more flavour and nutritional value. All the ridging and subsequent washing was expensive compared to trucking celery up from Spain in the winter, so the trenched celery industry is history and we all now expect our celery to be green.

Green celery is in season here from July to the first frost in October, and gets easier to grow as the season progresses. Most celery for the UK market is then trucked up from southern Europe through the winter and spring. In order to produce tender stalks, celery needs to be well fed and watered to give fast, uninterrupted growth. Once checked, the plant will never recover and will produce tough, rather bitter sticks fit only for making stock. During a hot spell the crop can need watering every two or three days to prevent moisture stress and the cell death that is later revealed as rots.

You will find that the stems get progressively more tender and less bitter towards the centre. The leaves can be bitter and are generally not eaten, though they can be useful in small quantities to flavour a stock or soup.

Storage and preparation

Celery is best kept in the fridge and should last for at least a week without deterioration. If you are planning to use it in a stock, it should be good for a fortnight. Remove any damaged parts from the outside. A potato peeler can help get rid of some of the fibrous outer layer without wasting the outer sticks.

Cooking practice has yet to catch up with the switch from blanched to green celery and the associated increase in flavour and fibre. Modern green celery, and in particular organic celery, is often more suitable for cooking than eating raw, with the central stalks often the only part that is tender enough to enjoy

without cooking (very good with a strong cheese). Under organic conditions, when the plant has to work harder to find nitrogen, this tendency to produce more flavour and more fibre is accentuated by slower growth.

I was fed a lot of celery in various forms in my childhood – in soup, braised, or in a mixture of vegetables – and I have to admit that my taste for it has only developed with age. I now think it is excellent roasted or braised (chop it up and put it in a heavy pan with a bit of butter and oil, cover and cook gently for 20 minutes or so, shaking occasionally). It is also a must in stock (along with carrots and onions or leeks and perhaps the stalk or a few leaves from a cabbage).

Waldorf Salad

Who could eat this and not think of the classic *Fawlty Towers* episode? This recipe should clear up any strange ideas about what it includes.

Serves 6

85g raisins
3 tart green dessert apples
50g walnut halves, lightly toasted in a dry frying pan
4 celery stalks, peeled and thinly sliced (reserve a few celery leaves)
about 3 tablespoons good mayonnaise
1 Cos or 2 Little Gem lettuces, shredded
1 tablespoon chopped flat-leaf parsley
sea salt and freshly ground black pepper

Cover the raisins with hot water and leave to soak for 1 hour, then drain.

Peel and core the apples, then slice them thinly. Put them in a bowl with the walnuts, celery and half the raisins. Add enough mayonnaise to coat, season to taste and toss well to combine.

Arrange the shredded lettuce on a serving dish and place the salad on top. Sprinkle with the remaining raisins, plus the parsley and celery leaves.

✦ Try using grapes instead of soaked raisins and add 150g diced cooked chicken and 1 teaspoon chopped tarragon.

Celery Braised with Anchovies

This recipe came from Nigel Marriage, who's worked in some of the finest restaurants in the country, including Le Manoir aux Quat' Saisons and L'Ortolan. It's a good way to use up a glut of celery. Serve with braised beef, pheasant or roast chicken.

Serves 4

60g butter
2 tablespoons olive oil
1 onion, sliced
250g carrots, sliced
8 anchovies, mashed with a fork
1 tablespoon white wine vinegar
4 celery hearts, tied with string if not compact
800ml beef stock
2 bay leaves
1 tablespoon chopped parsley
sea salt and freshly ground black pepper

Melt the butter and oil in a wide, shallow casserole, add the onion and carrots and cook over a low heat until slightly softened. Add the anchovies and vinegar and continue cooking for 3 minutes.

Put the celery hearts on top of the other vegetables, pour in the beef stock, add the bay leaves and bring to the boil. Cover with greaseproof paper and a lid, then transfer to an oven preheated to 160°C/Gas Mark 3. Cook for 20 minutes or until the celery is tender.

Remove the celery and vegetables from the casserole and keep warm. Place the casserole back on the hob and rapidly boil the stock until reduced by half. Taste for seasoning and adjust accordingly. Pour the juices over the celery, sprinkle with the chopped parsley and serve.

Celery with Garlic and Walnut Sauce

This makes an excellent accompaniment to fish goujons, or cooked, shelled mussels that have been dipped in batter (use the one for courgettes on page 145) and deep-fried. You could substitute almonds or hazelnuts for the walnuts in the sauce, if you prefer.

Serves 4

1 head of celery
60g butter
1 tablespoon olive oil
1 tablespoon chopped parsley
sea salt and freshly ground black pepper

For the garlic and walnut sauce:
3 slices of stale bread
3 garlic cloves, crushed to a paste with a little salt
100g walnuts
2 tablespoons white wine vinegar
1 tablespoon olive oil

Peel off the strings from the celery stalks, then cut the stalks into batons about 5cm long and 5mm–1cm thick. Heat the butter and oil in a pan, add the celery, season well and stir. Cover tightly and cook over a low heat for 15 minutes, stirring occasionally, until the celery is soft. Sprinkle with the parsley.

Meanwhile, remove the crusts from the bread and soak it in water. Squeeze out the excess water and blitz the bread in a food processor with the other sauce ingredients until smooth. Serve the celery with the sauce.

Easy ideas for celery

✦ Use a few stalks of finely chopped celery as the base for any meat stew or vegetable soup, sweating them gently in butter or oil with finely chopped carrot and onion.

✦ Quarter some black figs, mix with finely shredded celery heart and dress with a hazelnut dressing (made by substituting hazelnuts for walnuts in the dressing on page 123). Crumble goat's cheese over and serve.

✦ Blanch celery stalks in boiling salted water for 10 minutes, then drain well. Cover with a cheese sauce, sprinkle some grated cheese and breadcrumbs on top and place under a hot grill for a celery gratin.

✦ Cook celery sticks in olive oil with sliced onion for 10 minutes, then add garlic, thyme and chopped tomatoes. Cook for a few more minutes, season and sprinkle with black olives.

✦ Braise or roast as described on page 122.

See also:
Celeriac and Celery Soup (page 155)

Chillies

Like all the *Solanaceae* family (potatoes, tomatoes, aubergines etc), chillies originate from the Americas, where they have been cultivated for over 6,000 years. While most spices and flavourings travelled from East to West, with fortunes being made and wars fought over their trade, chillies have moved East in a less lucrative but even more influential culinary tidal wave. Given that they probably didn't arrive in Europe in any quantity until the sixteenth century, it is remarkable how fast they have spread to become an essential part of the cuisine of virtually all tropical and temperate regions of the world.

There are thousands of varieties of chillies, of varying colour, shape and heat. Even within a variety, and indeed from the same plant, there is substantial variation in heat. As a general, but not foolproof, rule, the smaller the hotter, and red is hotter then green. They also tend to be hotter in taste during a spell of hot weather and if they are not watered. If you want to get scientific about it, the Scoville Scale (named after the chemist, Wilbur Scoville, who developed it in 1912) will give you a heat rating for each chilli (going up into the hundred thousands). The heat can be attributed to the compound capsaicin, which is repellent and ultimately toxic to most mammals (unless they have consumed vast quantities of lager). Hence capsaicin is thought to be a ruse to help select an effective dispersal agent: it protects the plant from being eaten by mammal herbivores, who are able to digest the seeds and are therefore useless as a means of dispersal. Conversely birds can eat chillies with impunity but the seeds retain viability and pass through their gut unharmed, and are thus able to colonise new areas.

John Harding, who looks after our polytunnels, is an enthusiast and has tried many chillies over the years. We have settled on just three red varieties that seem to do well in our climate and are harvested from the tunnels from July to October. None is life-threateningly hot. Cherry Bomb is the roundest, earliest, thickest-skinned and mildest, making it great for inclusion in a salsa, stir-fry or even a salad. Fresno is slightly more elongated and a bit hotter. Cayenne is the hottest we grow (but is by no means extreme) and is more suited to a chilli con carne. Because it has a thinner skin, it is good for home drying (see Storage and preparation, below). Most chillies turn red when fully ripe. As with peppers, chillies become sweeter as they ripen and, though some people will eat them in their green, bitter state, for most purposes they are better left to maturity.

Storage and preparation

Chillies will keep for 1–3 weeks in the fridge or, if you leave them out, will often slowly dehydrate rather than rot. You can dry your own chillies by tying them individually to a length of cotton with a clove hitch knot (or thread them on to the cotton using a needle) and hanging them in a dry, airy room (our open, sunny porch seems to be ideal).

It can be hard to know how much to include in a dish because it's impossible to judge the heat level of an individual chilli until you've actually tasted it. There used to be a nasty initiation ritual in our tunnels whereby an old hand would pick a chilli, bite off the tip and pass it to the new recruit to try. The tip is the mildest part, often with no discernible heat, but the heat level rises rapidly as you go up the fruit. Apart from playing nasty tricks, biting off the tip can be a useful way of gauging the heat of a chilli and assessing how much to use. My guide is that if a taste from the tip doesn't take your head off, it is pretty safe to include a whole fresh chilli in a cooked dish for my family of six without too many complaints – provided I remove all the seeds and white pith, which are the hottest parts.

Dried chillies retain all their heat, so are about ten times hotter, weight for weight, than fresh. I hope none of you would do any of these while cooking, but do be very wary of rubbing your eyes, picking your nose or touching any of the less mentionable and highly sensitive parts of the body during or after cutting up chillies; it can be very uncomfortable.

Linguine with Chilli, Parsley and Garlic

Before Jane arrived and took over doing the recipes for our weekly news-letters, my friends used to rib me that all mine started with, 'Fry some garlic and chilli in olive oil' – and to this day my favourite summer lunch is pasta tossed in this with plenty of chopped parsley. I just love the cleanness of the tastes; it is a great tonic for a jaded palate without resorting to meat and all my instincts tell me it is good for me.

Serves 4

350g linguine (or spaghetti)
2 tablespoons olive oil
2 red chillies, deseeded and finely chopped
3 garlic cloves, finely chopped
a pinch of dried chilli flakes
2–3 tablespoons chopped parsley
sea salt and freshly ground black pepper

Cook the pasta in a large pan of boiling salted water until al dente. Meanwhile, heat the olive oil in a medium pan, add the red chillies and cook gently for 3 minutes. Add the garlic and cook for 2 minutes, being careful not to let it brown. Add the dried chilli flakes and parsley and remove from the heat.

Drain the pasta and add to the chilli, parsley and garlic, mixing well over a low heat. Season to taste and serve at once.

Ceviche

This is a classic Central American dish in which the fish is 'cooked' by the action of the acid in the lime. It's important to use very fresh fish. Serve as a starter or as a light lunch with sliced avocado and salad. Jane likes to serve it in Little Gem leaves as a canapé.

Serves 4

350g very fresh lemon sole fillets or other white fish
1 teaspoon salt
juice of 4 limes (lemons will do but the result will not be as good)
2 red chillies, finely chopped (more if you like it hot)
1 garlic clove, crushed
3 tomatoes, finely chopped
½ red pepper, finely chopped
½ red onion, finely chopped
¼ cucumber, peeled, cut in half lengthways, then deseeded and finely
    chopped
1 tablespoon finely chopped coriander
1 tablespoon olive oil

Skin the lemon sole fillets and slice them finely. Place in a shallow glass or ceramic dish, sprinkle with the salt and cover with the lime juice. Leave in the fridge for 1–1½ hours, until the fish looks opaque. Remove the fish from the juices and mix gently with the rest of ingredients in a bowl. It's best served straight away but can be kept in the fridge for a few hours.

Stir-fried Chicken with Chillies and Basil

Jane based this on her favourite Thai dish, a searingly hot stir-fry made with chicken, chillies and holy basil. You could substitute fish – especially squid – or beef for the chicken.

Serves 2–3

2 tablespoons sunflower oil
2 chicken breasts, skinned and thinly sliced
2 spring onions, sliced
2 bird's eye chillies (if you like it hot) or 2 mild red chillies, deseeded
  and sliced
1 tablespoon soy sauce
1½ tablespoons Thai fish sauce
1¼ tablespoons palm sugar (or brown sugar)
leaves from a bunch of basil

Heat the oil in a wok, add the chicken and stir-fry over a high heat until it turns white. Add the spring onions and chillies and stir-fry for 1 minute. Add the sauces and sugar and toss briefly, then add the basil leaves. Serve with rice.

Braised Shoulder of Lamb Stuffed with Salsa Rossa

Salsa rossa is an amazingly versatile sauce. It can be served with grilled lamb leg steaks or with firm white fish, used as a dip or even spread on toast. Here it is mixed with couscous to provide a stuffing for a slow-cooked shoulder of lamb.

Serves 6–8

1 shoulder of lamb, boned (you could ask your butcher to do this)
100g couscous
1 tablespoon olive oil
2 onions, sliced
3 garlic cloves, sliced
200ml red wine
1 litre lamb or chicken stock
a branch of rosemary
sea salt and freshly ground black pepper

For the salsa rossa:
6 tomatoes, skinned, deseeded and diced
1 large red pepper, roasted, peeled and chopped
1 garlic clove, crushed
½ red onion, finely chopped
1 tablespoon capers, soaked in cold water for 20 minutes, then squeezed dry and finely chopped
2 anchovies, finely chopped (optional)
1 red chilli, finely chopped
1 tablespoon balsamic vinegar
1 tablespoon chopped parsley

To make the salsa, mix all the ingredients together in a bowl and season to taste.

Open out the lamb flat and lay it on a board. Mix the couscous and salsa rossa together and spread them over the lamb. Roll up the lamb and tie in several places with string.

Heat the olive oil in a large ovenproof pan, add the lamb and cook over a fairly high heat until browned all over. Remove and set aside. Turn the heat down, add the onions and garlic to the pan and cook gently for 10 minutes. Pour in the red wine and stock, bring to the boil, then return the lamb to the pan with the rosemary. Season well. Place in an oven preheated to 140°C/Gas Mark 1 and cook, covered, for about 3–4 hours, turning occasionally, until the lamb is very tender.

Remove the meat from the pan, place on a serving dish and leave to rest for about 15 minutes. Meanwhile, put the pan on the hob and boil the cooking juices until reduced to a coating consistency. Skim off the fat from the surface, strain through a fine sieve and adjust the seasoning. Serve the lamb cut into slices, accompanied by the sauce.

Easy ideas for chillies

✦ Mix 2 chopped deseeded red chillies with 1 crushed clove of garlic, 1 tablespoon of chopped parsley and 2 tablespoons of olive oil. This is a great sauce to serve with scallops, squid, fish or lamb.

✦ To make chermoula (a Moroccan spice paste), mix 4 finely chopped deseeded red chillies with the juice of 2 lemons, 2 crushed garlic cloves, 1 tablespoon of roasted and ground cumin seeds, ½ tablespoon of roasted and ground coriander, 1 tablespoon of paprika, a pinch of saffron, 100ml olive oil, 1 tablespoon of fresh coriander and some salt and pepper. Blitz to a paste in a food processor. Toss with root vegetables before roasting, or use as a marinade for fish, lamb or chicken before barbecuing or grilling.

See also:
Baked Courgettes with Mint and Chilli (page 140)
Mexican One-pot Courgettes (page 141)
Dev-Mex Pumpkin Soup (page 344)
Chicken, Leek and Corn Soup (page 369)

Courgettes and Marrows

All growers love planting courgettes. They are a doddle to grow, but a nightmare to sell in mid summer because, regardless of when you plant, they tend to glut in late July and August. To make matters worse, every gardener and allotment holder proudly distributes their surplus free of charge. This inevitably results in courgette mountains around the country as stocks build. We used to top and tail ten tonnes of them and send them off to be frozen for baby food but our high labour costs meant this was never profitable, so now we are brutal and abandon half the crop some time in late July. By then everyone is getting pretty sick of picking them anyway.

Marrows already suffer a bad name without the help of unscrupulous growers and overenthusiastic gardeners passing off outsized courgettes as marrow. A marrow grows in the same way as a courgette but the striped 'tiger cross' types seem to offer slightly more culinary potential, so stay clear of the telltale all-green fruit of courgette varieties and avoid anything more than a foot long.

All the *Cucurbita* are native to the Americas, where their ancestors grew wild as climbers. As well as courgettes and marrows, the family includes squash and pumpkin (see page 339). Courgettes are really just a highly selected form of summer squash, whose fruit is picked continuously and eaten immature. They have been bred and selected for their bush habit rather than the trailing habit more typical of pumpkins and squash.

We have tried many different varieties, including a number of yellow courgettes and several summer squashes in different shapes and colours. Though exotic in appearance, from a culinary point of view most were watery and tasteless and none of them had anything to offer over a conventional green courgette.

Courgettes are a great crop for the garden, producing an endless supply from just two or three plants. We work on two sowings: one under glass in early April for planting out under fleece later in the month. A second sowing directly into the soil in June for cropping through the autumn until the first frost can help to avoid the summer glut. Given water and sun, courgettes can be incredibly prolific, making it necessary to pick every day to prevent them getting oversized.

During the winter, most courgettes sold in the UK come from the south of Spain, Italy and Morocco. We don't often buy them because they are normally fairly travel weary and this is a crop where freshness really counts in terms of flavour. In the spring, when we are struggling to find enough local produce for the boxes, we may use a few, especially from the South of France when its season begins.

Storage and preparation

Eat courgettes quickly. They will maintain their appearance in the bottom of the fridge for a week or more but their flavour deteriorates rapidly, so that after a few days they are virtually tasteless. This is a good reason for not eating them out of season, as imported courgettes will generally be at least a week old before they reach the shelves. Marrows also need to be eaten reasonably fresh.

We don't often salt courgettes, but if they have got a bit big it can help reduce the wateriness. Sprinkle sliced or grated courgettes with salt and leave them in a sieve or colander for half an hour, then squeeze out the liquid, by hand or in a tea towel, before using.

Contrary to the opinion of some irritating chefs who have probably never been in a vegetable field, tiny courgettes are pretty tasteless. Like many vegetables they need a degree of maturity to develop their flavour. They are normally at their best when 12–17cm in length. The only virtue of a baby courgette is for frying in batter, tempura-style, with the flower still attached. Deep-fried courgette flowers – perhaps stuffed with ricotta and spinach – eaten in batches as they come out of the pan, are one of the best things on earth, but you will have to grow them yourself. There are two reasons why I have given up trying to put them in the boxes: firstly they are just too delicate and perishable to last the journey from the farm, and secondly slugs love to curl up and take a snooze in them. If you do grow courgettes, you can harvest most of the smaller, more pointed male flowers without affecting the yield. If the female flowers are used, you can pick and fry them with a courgette up to 7cm long attached.

Grilled Courgette, Tomato and Bean Salad with Basil Dressing

We served this salad the day we opened the Field Kitchen and use various versions of it throughout the summer. It is one of the recipes we are often asked for, so here it is …

Serves 4

200g dried cannellini or haricot beans, soaked in cold water overnight
    and then drained
3 tablespoons extra virgin olive oil
4 courgettes, cut into ribbons 5mm thick
a small punnet of cherry tomatoes, cut in half
sea salt and freshly ground black pepper

For the dressing:
a bunch of basil
½ garlic clove, crushed
100ml olive oil
a pinch of salt

Put the drained beans in a large pan, cover with fresh water and bring to the boil. Reduce the heat and simmer for an hour or so, until tender. Drain, season to taste and dress with 2 tablespoons of the olive oil.

Toss the courgettes with the remaining olive oil and grill on a ridged griddle pan (or under a hot grill) until tender and lightly charred.

For the dressing, put all the ingredients in a food processor or blender and whiz until smooth.

Gently mix the beans, tomatoes and courgettes together in a large bowl and add enough basil dressing to coat. Taste and adjust the seasoning.

Baked Courgettes with Mint and Chilli

Jane used to cook something similar to this at the River Café in London, where it was served on bruschetta. It would be equally good as an accompaniment to grilled fish.

Serves 4

4–5 courgettes
2 red chillies, finely sliced
2 garlic cloves, finely sliced
olive oil for drizzling
2 sprigs of mint, chopped
a dash of good-quality red wine vinegar
sea salt and freshly ground black pepper

Top and tail the courgettes, cut them in half, then quarter them lengthways. Remove the seeds. Place the courgettes on a baking tray, skin-side down. Sprinkle with the chillies and garlic, season with the salt and pepper and drizzle with olive oil, then bake in an oven preheated to 180°C/Gas Mark 4 for about 15 minutes, until the courgettes are tender and beginning to brown. Remove from the oven, sprinkle over the mint and vinegar and serve.

Mexican One-pot Courgettes

Jane likes this dish because everything is just chucked in together but the result is mouthwatering. The flavourings are unusual for courgettes, which are generally treated in a Mediterranean way.

Serves 6

750g courgettes, cut into small dice
350g tomatoes, skinned, deseeded and chopped (or use canned tomatoes)
6 peppercorns
4 sprigs of coriander
2 sprigs of mint
3 cloves
2cm piece of cinnamon stick
2 small chillies, left whole
120ml single cream
sea salt

Put everything in a large, heavy-based pan, cover and bring to a simmer. Cook slowly for about 30 minutes, stirring occasionally to prevent sticking, until the courgettes are tender and all the liquid has been absorbed. This sometimes tastes even better reheated the next day.

Slow-cooked Courgettes with Lemon, Dill and Capers

Usually we are told not to overcook vegetables but it's essential here. Don't be afraid to cook it for a long time, as the skin of the courgettes holds them together. The reward is a fantastic flavour.

Serves 4

6 courgettes
3 tablespoons olive oil
3 garlic cloves, thinly sliced
grated zest of 2 lemons
1 tablespoon chopped dill, plus extra to serve
10 capers, soaked in cold water for 20 minutes, then squeezed dry and chopped
1 tablespoon good wine vinegar
sea salt and freshly ground black pepper

Slice the courgettes on a slight diagonal into ovals about 8mm thick. Heat the oil in a large frying pan and fry the courgettes in batches until lightly coloured on both sides, removing each batch as it is done (don't put too many courgettes in the pan at once or they won't brown). When all are done, add the garlic to the pan. Before it browns, return all the courgettes to the pan and mix well. Add the lemon zest, dill and capers and cook for about 30 minutes over a low heat, stirring occasionally. When they are done, the courgettes will be a bit mushy, but delicious. Season well and sprinkle with the vinegar and more chopped dill.

Stuffed Marrow

Jane tried this on the Riverford staff a few years ago and it went down pretty well, nearly as well as the all-day breakfast does. You have to add loads of flavour to marrow, as it needs all the help it can get.

Serves 4

1 marrow
2 tablespoons olive oil, plus extra for drizzling
1 onion, thinly sliced
1 red pepper, thinly sliced
2 garlic cloves, crushed
4 anchovies (optional)
400g can of chopped tomatoes
3 tablespoons cooked Puy lentils
a small bunch of spinach or chard, cooked (optional)
100g feta cheese, crumbled
1 tablespoon shredded basil
1 tablespoon freshly grated Parmesan cheese (optional)
sea salt and freshly ground black pepper

Cut the marrow in half lengthways, drizzle it with olive oil and bake in an oven preheated to 180°C/Gas Mark 4 for about 20 minutes, until it is cooked through and starting to brown. Scoop out the seeds and season the marrow with salt and pepper.

Heat the 2 tablespoons of oil in a pan, add the onion and cook gently for about 10 minutes, until softened. Add the red pepper and garlic and cook for 15 minutes. Add the anchovies, if using, plus the canned tomatoes, and cook for about 10 minutes, until the tomatoes have reduced and thickened. Stir in the cooked lentils and the spinach or chard, if using, and season to taste.

Spoon the mixture into the marrow and sprinkle with the feta cheese, basil and Parmesan. Return to the oven and bake for about 20 minutes, until golden brown.

Chocolate Courgette Cake

We like to use this recipe to persuade children of the virtues of vegetables. It is a regular feature on the lunch menu we prepare for Landscove Primary School and the children seem to love it.

120g softened unsalted butter
125ml sunflower oil
100g caster sugar
200g soft brown sugar
3 eggs, lightly beaten
130ml milk
350g plain flour
2 teaspoons baking powder
4 tablespoons cocoa powder
450g courgettes, peeled and finely grated
1 teaspoon vanilla extract

Put the butter, sunflower oil and both sugars in a bowl and beat them together until light and fluffy. Gradually beat in the eggs and then the milk.

Sift the dry ingredients together and fold them into the mixture. Stir in the courgettes and vanilla, then spoon the mixture into a 20 x 35cm baking tin lined with baking parchment. Place in an oven preheated to 190°C/Gas Mark 5 and bake for 35–45 minutes, until a skewer inserted in the centre comes out clean. Cut into squares whilst still warm.

Easy ideas for courgettes and marrows

✦ To deep-fry courgettes, make a light batter by mixing 150g plain flour with 2 tablespoons of olive oil and enough lukewarm water to give the consistency of double cream. Leave to rest for 20 minutes. Just before use, fold in 2 stiffly whipped egg whites and some seasoning. Cut courgettes into chips, dip them in the batter and deep-fry until light brown.

✦ Layer sliced tomatoes and courgettes in a gratin dish, sprinkling the layers with a little olive oil, a few oregano leaves and some salt and pepper. Drizzle with more oil and bake for 30 minutes at 200°C/Gas Mark 6, until tender and patched with brown.

✦ Curried Courgettes – in a bowl, mix 400g courgettes (cut in half lengthways and then cut on the diagonal into chunks about 5mm–1cm thick) with 75g flaked almonds, 1 teaspoon of curry powder and some salt and pepper. Heat 2 tablespoons of olive oil in a large frying pan, add the courgette mixture and cook over a high heat for about 10 minutes, until tender, stirring well. Sprinkle with chopped mint.

✦ Cook grated courgettes slowly in oil until soft, then season and add a little chopped tarragon and some capers. Serve as a side dish, or as a pasta sauce with Parmesan and grated lemon zest.

See also:
Broad Bean and Courgette Soup (page 45)

Posh nosh to choke on

RIVERFORD ORGANIC VEGETABLES
GROWER & SUPPLIERS OF ORGANIC PRODUCE

An organic estate is in danger of becoming the latest must-have for the very rich trying to give some meaning to their wealth. It is certainly a more laudable way of spending a fortune than gambling or collecting sports cars but the accompanying air of Victorian philanthropy can be irksome to practitioners who have acquired their acres the hard way. There is also a tendency to want to create an exclusive brand to go with it.

During a recent tour around a large organic Cotswold estate, the brand manager boasted of how expensive their organic fillet steak was (£50 per kilo). Not how good it was or how happy the cow had been or even the environmental richness of the estate where it had grazed. The pinnacle of his achievement was the divisive exclusivity of the brand. For him, organic was a niche, a market opportunity, a means of differentiation, a unique selling point, or any of the other ridiculous corruptions of the English language that smooth-tongued marketeers use to ply their oily trade.

I grew up in a large family where several of the farm workers would join us every day for the fantastic and plentiful lunches that my mother created. Eating is something we all do – a common denominator, an opportunity to bring people together and break down barriers. Organic farming should be an extension of this process because it is more respectful of food and the processes required to get it to the table. But the table must be accessible to everyone for it to be relevant.

Yes, organic should mean quality, provenance and animal welfare but the organic I aspire to is also affordable, enjoyable and accessible with as little fuss as possible, regardless of people's income and background. You don't have to be posh or rich to enjoy your food. I feel at best ambivalent and often resentful of the exclusivity and divisiveness that the organic tag has acquired from some of the brands that have sprung up around it. Britain is a class-ridden society where people increasingly define themselves by what they eat. The founders of the organic movement were an earthy, practical lot with mud on their boots and a passion for the health of the soil and their livestock, and consequently that of the nation. I imagine they would be horrified by the exclusivity of brands such as Daylesford and Whole Foods and suspect they would be more at home in a Spud-u-like. To use exclusivity as a marketing tool is a betrayal of the essential inclusiveness and sharing at the heart of true organic farming.

Cucumber

Cucumbers are fickle and difficult to grow in our climate but have the virtue, from a farmer's perspective, of being as close to pure water as vegetables get. As such, they grow incredibly fast and can be hugely productive over the short season granted by our climate. Most non-organic cucumbers are grown hydroponically, never making contact with the soil, being drip fed water and a computer-controlled solution of nutrients down a gutter full of Rockwool glass fibres (yes, the same stuff that insulates your loft) – a lifeless, consistent and hugely productive medium for their roots and about as far from organic farming as you can get. Our cucumbers are planted in the soil and I like to think you can taste the difference.

We tend to grow the mini cucumbers, which are at their best when about 20cm long. They taste better and seem to be slightly more hardy than the standard ones. They also have the virtue of being too short to grow bendy. Cucumbers keel over in the slightest cool draught so, since on principle we do not heat our tunnels, we delay planting until early May. Even so, by mid June they have climbed their strings, flowered and borne their first fruit. They must be picked every day and pruned and trained once a week, until they succumb to disease or the first cool draughts of autumn in late September or October. It is possible to extend the season to November with supplementary heating but the energy cost is huge and, from an environmental perspective, if you must have cucumbers in winter it is probably better to truck them up from Spain.

Storage and preparation

Cucumbers can be stored in the bottom of the fridge for a week or more but are best when eaten fresh. They may keep their appearance for quite a while, but the flavour definitely deteriorates. Should you wonder why cucumbers are almost invariably sold in an irritating plastic sheath, it is to help keep the water in and preserve the illusion of turgid freshness, hence extending their shelf life.

It is hard to beat cucumber eaten in its raw and naked state. For salads, we sometimes peel them and take out most of the seeds, which gets rid of some of the wateriness. If you are using them grated, you usually need to 'bleed' them to remove some of the water – simply sprinkle them with salt after grating, leaving to drain in a sieve for about 20 minutes, then squeeze them out by hand or in a tea towel.

Cucumber and Radish Salad

The cucumber balances the heat of the radishes in this salad. It makes a fine accompaniment to spicy Asian curries.

Serves 4–6

2 cucumbers
a bunch of small red radishes, trimmed and quartered
2 tablespoons sunflower oil
1 teaspoon brown mustard seeds
1 teaspoon cumin seeds
1 chilli, chopped
2 tablespoons lime juice (or lemon juice)
75g cashew nuts, roasted
1 tablespoon chopped coriander
sea salt

Peel the cucumbers, cut them lengthways in half and scoop out the seeds with a teaspoon. Cut the flesh into 1cm dice and combine with the radishes in a bowl.

Heat the sunflower oil in a small frying pan, add the mustard and cumin seeds and cook over a medium heat for about a minute, until the seeds begin to pop. Add the chilli and cook for 30 seconds. Remove from the heat and leave to cool.

Pour the mixture over the cucumber and radishes. Add the lime juice, cashews and coriander, season with salt to taste, then toss to combine.

Spiced Cucumber

One of Jane's favourites. You can make it well in advance and the flavour develops as it stands. Beware, though, that the longer you leave it the hotter the chilli flavour becomes.

Serves 6–8

3 small or 2 large cucumbers
4 teaspoons salt
4 tablespoons Chinese rice vinegar or 3 tablespoons white wine vinegar
6 tablespoons caster sugar
2 tablespoons sesame oil
1 tablespoon groundnut or vegetable oil
3–6 dried red chillies (according to taste), deseeded and cut into pieces

Cut the cucumbers lengthwise into quarters. Scoop out and discard the seeds, then slice the cucumber across into 2cm pieces. Put them into a clean, grease-free bowl, sprinkle with the salt and stir well. Leave to stand at room temperature for 2–3 hours. During this time, the moisture will be drawn out from the cucumbers.

Drain the cucumbers, then squeeze out excess moisture either by hand or in a tea towel or a salad spinner. Transfer to a clean bowl, add the vinegar and sugar and mix well.

Heat both the oils in a small saucepan until just starting to smoke. Remove the pan from the heat and wait for a few seconds until the smoke has disappeared before adding the chillies – otherwise they will burn. Let the chillies sizzle in the oil, then tip them into the bowl with the cucumber and mix well. Leave to stand for at least 6 hours or overnight in the fridge. Serve as an accompaniment, or as a canapé with cocktail sticks for spearing the pieces.

Cucumber Pickle

This recipe is from my mother, Gillian Watson. My brother, Ben, adapted it for sale in the Riverford Farm Shop, where it has been very popular for many years. We used to have it on family picnics in sandwiches or pittas with cream cheese. It is good with a strong, hard cheese or with terrines and cold meats, especially ham. When it comes to pâtés and terrines, a bit of acidity to cut through the richness is always a plus.

Compared with other chutneys and pickles, it is easy, if slightly longwinded, to make. The only down side is that because it is so lightly cooked, it won't keep for ever and does need to be stored in the fridge once opened.

Make sure the cucumbers are good and fresh, so the pickle is slightly crunchy.

Makes 2–2.5kg

5 cucumbers
1kg onions, peeled and halved
about 80g sea salt (or cooking salt)
500ml distilled malt vinegar
350g granulated sugar (or soft brown)
4 teaspoons mustard seeds
generous ½ teaspoon ground cloves (or use a few whole cloves instead)
generous ½ teaspoon ground turmeric

Slice the cucumbers and onions very thinly (a mandolin is ideal for this). Layer them in a bowl, sprinkling with the sea salt as you go, then weight them down with a plate and leave for a few hours or overnight. Drain off the liquid, rinse the vegetables well and drain in a colander.

Combine the vinegar, sugar, mustard seeds, cloves and turmeric in a pan and bring slowly to the boil, stirring to dissolve the sugar. Add the well-drained cucumber and onion mixture and bring back to the boil for 1 minute. Transfer the mixture to sterilised jars, using a slotted spoon. Bring the liquid back to the boil and simmer until slightly reduced for about 15 minutes, then divide it between the jars, filling to the brim. Put on the lids and label. The pickle will keep for several months.

Easy ideas for cucumber

✦ Try replacing the lemon in a gin and tonic with a slice of fresh cucumber. It is amazing how much flavour comes from a single slice. I was introduced to this when the lemons ran out on a boozy camping trip to North Devon. A revelation.

✦ To make tsatsiki, peel and finely dice a cucumber, sprinkle with salt and leave in a colander for 30 minutes. Drain and squeeze out excess moisture. Mix with 300ml Greek yoghurt, 2 crushed garlic cloves, 2 tablespoons of finely chopped mint and some salt and pepper. Serve as part of a mezze, with olives, hummus and flatbreads.

✦ Raita – the Indian version of the above recipe. Fry 1 tablespoon of mustard seeds in a little oil until they pop. Add to 300ml thick yoghurt with ½ peeled and chopped cucumber, 1 grated carrot, ½ finely chopped red onion, 1 tablespoon of chopped mint and some salt and pepper. Serve with curries.

✦ Peel a cucumber, quarter it lengthways and remove the seeds. Chop the flesh into 2cm chunks. Melt 1 tablespoon of butter in a pan and toss the cucumber in it, stirring well. Cook gently for 5 minutes, then add lemon juice, salt and pepper to taste. Stir in chopped herbs, such as dill and parsley. Serve with fish.

See also:
Fattoush with Broad Beans (page 48)
Ceviche (page 130)
Gazpacho (page 378)

Fennel

When it comes to fennel, people seldom waver – like liquorice and Pernod, they either love it or hate it, making it a contentious item in our boxes. Jane and I are both enthusiasts, and eagerly await the first crop harvested from our fields in July. The strong, clear, light-aniseed flavour is quite unlike that of any other vegetable, offering a welcome additional dimension in the kitchen in both its raw and cooked forms. Jane's Braised Fennel, which goes particularly well with pork (see page 162), has converted many visitors to the Field Kitchen who had previously fallen into the anti camp. The slow cooking rounds off the anise flavour, bringing sweetness and a satisfying soul-food texture that most people find irresistible. When Gordon Ramsay wrote a generous and glowing review of the Field Kitchen after his visit, it was this fennel dish that temporarily interrupted the invective and led him to suggest I should be paying Jane more.

The local rabbit population shares our enthusiasm for fennel; once they have had a taste of the succulent leaves, they are hooked. Our standard high-voltage fence is a futile barrier in the face of their addiction, making lead shot the only lasting solution.

Herb fennel is cultivated for its seeds and leaves and is a highly decorative self-seeding plant to grow in a garden. It is easy to collect and thresh your own seeds from the flower umbels for use as a flavouring during winter. Florence fennel, the type we eat as a vegetable, is a cultivar of wild or herb fennel selected over many generations for the fleshy and succulent leaf bases, which form a bulb. Under any sort of stress, the cultivated form will revert to its wild ancestry and prematurely run to seed, before producing the fat bulb for which it is prized.

Fennel is usually sown under glass in plugs or blocks of compost and planted out after the last danger of frost has passed, for harvest from July onwards. Since it is damaged by all but the lightest frost, the UK season normally comes to an end in October. It can be grown in a greenhouse out of season but takes up a lot of space, so during the winter it is generally imported from southern Europe, most particularly Sicily. The secret to getting a good, plump bulb is fast and even growth, requiring a deep, fertile soil, regular watering in dry spells and, on our farm, a gun to shoot the rabbits.

Storage and preparation

Fennel has a reasonable shelf life (at least a week) but is best kept in the bottom of your fridge. If it comes with the leaves on and you are not planning on using them, it will keep better if you cut off and discard them. The outer layer of the bulb has a tendency to brown, particularly at the end of the season when it may have been caught by a frost. This is not necessarily an indication of lack of freshness.

It is often worth cutting the fennel in half lengthwise and removing most of the core and base before slicing, particularly if the bulb is starting to lengthen and push upwards prior to running to seed. The Sicilians we buy from in the winter tell me that they normally eat their fennel raw, sliced thinly, with black pepper and a squeeze of lemon.

Although fennel is grown primarily for the bulb, the feathery leaves can be used to flavour dishes in the same way as fresh herb fennel, but in more generous quantities due to their milder flavour. They also make a good garnish and, in small quantities, can be added to a green salad or used to garnish pasta dishes. They are particularly good for stuffing fish. Don't hold back; fill the whole fish with the feathery tops, perhaps adding a knob of butter and a squeeze of lemon, too.

Fennel Gratin

A good accompaniment to lamb or pork, or a light supper dish on its own with a green salad.

Serves 6

4 fennel bulbs, trimmed
150ml double cream
1 teaspoon finely chopped rosemary
2 garlic cloves, crushed
1 tablespoon freshly grated Parmesan cheese
sea salt and freshly ground black pepper

Cut each fennel bulb into 6 wedges and cook in boiling salted water for about 5 minutes, until just tender. Drain very thoroughly and place in a bowl.

Put the cream in a small pan with the rosemary and garlic and heat just until it comes to the boil. Remove from the heat and add to the fennel, along with half the Parmesan. Mix well and season to taste. Place in a gratin dish, cover with foil and place in an oven preheated to 180°C/Gas Mark 4. Bake for 30 minutes, then remove the foil and sprinkle with the remaining Parmesan. Turn the oven up to 200°C/Gas Mark 6, return the fennel to the oven and cook for a further 10 minutes, until the top is browned.

Fennel, Black Olive and Orange Salad

A classic Sicilian dish. Even though cooked fennel is delicious, sometimes it's best just raw, finely shaved, with a simple dressing. If you have only a couple of fennel bulbs, this is the way to serve them.

Serves 6

3 oranges
3 tablespoons extra virgin olive oil
1 tablespoon lemon juice
1 garlic clove, crushed
2 fennel bulbs, trimmed
12 black olives, stoned
1 tablespoon chopped flat-leaf parsley, plus a few leaves to garnish
sea salt and freshly ground black pepper

Cut off all the skin and white pith from the oranges, then cut out the segments from between the membrane, working over a bowl to catch the juice. Squeeze out the membranes into the bowl when you have finished, to extract the remaining juice. Pour off the juice into a separate bowl and whisk in the olive oil, lemon juice, garlic and some salt and pepper to make a dressing.

Finely shred the fennel with a sharp knife or on a mandolin. Mix with the orange segments, olives, parsley and dressing. Adjust the seasoning and serve.

Atafu Pork with Braised Fennel

When she was working in the Pacific, Jane was lucky enough to visit the atoll group Tokelau (three islands 500km north of Samoa), cooking for a group representing the New Zealand government, which was looking at independence for Tokelau. On one of the atolls, Atafu, the villagers brought pigs as gifts, both cooked and raw, as is their custom. Most of the cooked pigs were distributed to the villagers but Jane experimented with the smaller raw ones to make a version of the Italian dish, porchetta. It worked well and here it is adapted to a pork joint. The spare rib roll is most suitable because of its fat content but you could also use a good-sized loin.

Fennel makes an ideal marriage with roast pork, and braising it in this way changes the flavour remarkably.

Serves 4–6

1 spare rib roll (pork shoulder), weighing about 2kg
1 tablespoon chopped sage
1 tablespoon chopped rosemary
3 garlic cloves, crushed
2 teaspoons ground fennel seeds
3 rashers of pancetta or smoked streaky bacon
sea salt and freshly ground black pepper

For the fennel:
4 fennel bulbs, trimmed
2 tablespoons olive oil
2 garlic cloves, chopped
juice of 1 lemon

Unroll the pork and spread the joint out flat. Using a sharp knife, slash the meat at 5cm intervals to increase the surface area, being careful not to cut right through it. Rub the sage, rosemary, garlic, half the fennel seeds and some black pepper into the flesh. Lay the bacon rashers over the joint and re-roll it, tying with string. Rub some salt and the remaining ground fennel seeds into the pork fat and then put the joint on a baking tray. Place in an oven preheated to 160°C/Gas Mark 3 and roast for about 2 hours.

Meanwhile, prepare the fennel. Cut each fennel bulb into 8 wedges. Heat the olive oil in a pan that is large enough to hold the fennel in a single layer. When the oil is hot, add the fennel and brown over a high heat, stirring occasionally. Remove the fennel from the pan and set aside. Add the garlic to the pan and cook gently for a few minutes, until softened but not browned. Return the fennel to the pan, season and mix well. Stir in 2 tablespoons of water and cook over a high heat for 5 minutes. Reduce the heat to low, cover and cook for 30 minutes. Remove the lid and cook for a further 30 minutes, being careful not to let the fennel 'catch' in the pan. When it is done, the fennel should have a darker, mushy appearance. Season to taste with lemon juice, salt and pepper, then serve with the pork.

Easy ideas for fennel

✦ Slice fennel bulbs lengthways, brush with a little olive oil and cook on a ridged grill pan until charred and tender. Dress with finely chopped chilli and mint, plus some oil and lemon.

✦ Grill fennel as described above, then mix with the Basic Tomato Sauce (see page 380) and black olives.

✦ Substitute fennel for some of the potatoes in the Basic Potato Gratin on page 284.

✦ Use fennel wedges as well as or instead of leeks in the lemony marinade on page 250.

See also:
Warm Runner Bean Salad with Fennel, Apple and Walnut Dressing (page 169)

French and Runner Beans

Some years ago, while visiting friends in Kenya, in the middle of a ramshackle town where most food was bought amongst the colourful chaos of local street markets and people lived on a dollar or two a day, I found myself in a large, white-panelled room where a hundred women in white coats and hair nets stood at long tables sorting runner beans. The beans all looked perfect to me but they were being divided up with great skill and lightning speed according to their length and straightness. The perfectly straight ones went to Marks & Spencer and Waitrose, with an increasing tolerance of bend down the hierarchy through Sainbury, Tesco, Asda etc. The beans were then trucked to Nairobi and flown in a dedicated fleet of DC10s to Heathrow to be on the supermarket shelves the next day.

I can only guess what those women thought of a society that worried about the nth degree of bend on a bean while they could not afford the most basic medical care. Despite the kilo of aviation fuel used to ship each kilo of beans and the questionable use of scarce water resources to grow crops for export in a country that can barely feed itself, some argue that this is an opportunity for development, and that to thwart it on grounds of sustainability is just the latest form of imperialism. There may be occasions when this argument holds good but more frequently the companies are owned and managed by expats, who buy most of their seed, plastic, chemicals and machinery abroad. The living conditions of those working on the farms and in pack-houses might be slightly higher than the local norm but most of the benefit is leaving the country.

At Riverford we have always had a no-airfreight policy, so we have to struggle with a marginal climate and high picking costs. Beans like it hot and humid and, for a legume, are surprisingly hungry for nitrogen. They hate the wind and are easily stunted by a spell of cool weather. If the soil is warm, we might make a speculative sowing in April but the first French beans (slimmer than runner beans but still a long way from the very fine beans that come from the low-wage economies, where picking costs can be kept down) are usually sown in May for picking in late July. Later sowings will take picking through to the first frosts in early October. We have a picking machine that will do a reasonable job but can lead to bruising, so most of the crop is harvested by our more nimble-fingered pickers. I once constructed a machine where pickers lay prone over the rows on beds so that they could pick with both hands and did not have to bend down. I alone thought it was great, so it now lies at the back of the yard, being quietly overrun by brambles and nettles.

The runner beans are sown in early May and, as climbers, need a framework of strings or bamboo canes to grow up. In a good year their scarlet flowers and rampant foliage are a wonderful sight, making them a satisfying crop for a gardener. In cool years they may struggle to make it up the canes but have a better chance if you start them indoors. Runner beans are in season in August and September though, like French beans, they are airfreighted into the UK all year, even throughout our home-grown season.

Runner beans are an iconic part of the English summer for gardeners. They have a tendency to be tough in cooler years and towards the end of the season; a good French bean, picked young, is normally better.

Storage and preparation

Temperatures below 7°C can, in theory, cause chill damage but most domestic fridges don't get cold enough for this. In practice, the best place for beans is in a bag in the bottom of your fridge, where they should keep for a week. When fresh, the beans should snap in half cleanly. French and runner beans have a tendency to grow tough if not watered enough or picked when over mature. There should be none of the telltale bulges caused by developing beans inside most varieties, though this is not true of some of the flat-podded French beans. I cannot see the point of the very fine beans from Kenya. They are a nightmare to pick, taste no better than the larger ones, cost more, take longer to prepare and normally go off faster.

All beans should be topped and tailed before cooking, and runner beans can benefit from de-stringing by running a potato peeler down each side – though this should not be necessary if they have been picked young enough. The easiest way of cooking beans is in lots of boiling water – no lid if you want to maintain the colour – then drained and refreshed in cold water as soon as they are tender. You can reheat them in a little butter before serving. Jane insists they should squeak in your mouth when they are perfectly cooked; I like them just beyond squeaking.

French Beans with Tomato Sauce and Fried Breadcrumbs

This is particularly good with French beans but you could also serve runner beans, blanched fennel or courgettes in the same way.

Serves 6

150g stale bread, crusts removed
200ml olive oil
4 sprigs of thyme
3 garlic cloves, peeled
400g French beans, trimmed
sea salt and freshly ground black pepper

For the tomato sauce:
1 tablespoon olive oil
1 chilli, chopped
4 garlic cloves, thinly sliced
400g can of chopped tomatoes
1 teaspoon sugar

First make the tomato sauce. Heat the olive oil in a pan, add the chilli and garlic and cook over a medium heat for 2–3 minutes. Just before the garlic turns brown, empty the canned tomatoes into the pan and stir. Add the sugar, then lower the heat and simmer for about 40 minutes until the sauce has reduced and thickened. Season to taste.

While the sauce is cooking, prepare the breadcrumbs. Whiz the bread in a food processor to make crumbs. Put the oil in a small, deep pan and place over a medium heat for 5 minutes. Add the thyme and garlic. When the garlic is turning brown, add the breadcrumbs and fry until they are golden and crisp. Remove from the oil with a slotted spoon, place on kitchen paper to drain and discard the garlic cloves.

Cook the French beans in boiling salted water for about 4 minutes; keep testing them for the desired amount of crunch. Drain well, then combine with the tomato sauce and sprinkle with the crunchy breadcrumbs.

Warm Runner Bean Salad with Fennel, Apple and Walnut Dressing

We made lots of salads, including this one, for the Plymouth Flavour Fest. Big mistake – we should have been serving pork in a bun. Certain members of the public appreciated this salad and we now serve it regularly in the Field Kitchen.

Serves 4

100g walnuts
1 teaspoon walnut oil
a pinch of cayenne pepper
300g runner beans, sliced on the diagonal into 1–2cm lengths
2 apples, cored and cut into 1cm dice
1 fennel bulb, very finely shaved (a mandolin is good for this)
sea salt and freshly ground black pepper

For the walnut dressing:
1 garlic clove, crushed
2 teaspoons Dijon mustard
2 teaspoons honey
3 tablespoons good-quality red wine vinegar
100ml sunflower oil
1 tablespoon walnut oil

Mix the walnuts with the walnut oil, cayenne pepper and a pinch of salt and spread them out on a baking sheet. Place in an oven preheated to 180°C/Gas Mark 4 and roast for 5 minutes, until lightly toasted. Remove and leave to cool.

Whisk together all the ingredients for the dressing and season to taste. Lightly crush half the walnuts and add them to the dressing.

Cook the runner beans in a pan of boiling salted water for about 5 minutes, until just tender. Drain and toss with the apples, fennel, walnut dressing and the remaining walnuts. Taste and adjust the seasoning. Leave to sit for a white before serving, so the runner beans can absorb the flavours.

Salad of French Beans and Grilled Leeks with Tapenade Dressing

A wonderful high-summer salad, to be served with chicken or a meaty fish such as tuna. You could add a little shaved fennel before serving, if you like.

Serves 6

300g French beans, trimmed
500g leeks, trimmed
a little olive oil

For the tapenade dressing:
75g stoned black olives
1 garlic clove, peeled
2 anchovy fillets
1 teaspoon capers, soaked in cold water for 20 minutes, then drained and squeezed dry
1 fresh chilli (optional)
125ml olive oil
1 tablespoon chopped parsley/basil/tarragon (optional)
freshly ground black pepper

First make the dressing. Put the olives, garlic, anchovies, capers and chilli, if using, in a food processor and whiz to a rough paste. Gradually add the olive oil and mix to make a dressing with a coating consistency. At this point the chopped herbs can be added. Season with freshly ground black pepper.

Cook the French beans in boiling salted water for 3–4 minutes; they should still have some 'bite'. Drain and set aside.

Cook the leeks in boiling salted water for 5 minutes, then drain thoroughly. Cut them in half lengthways, toss in a little olive oil and then grill on a ridged grill pan until they are just tender and lightly charred. Cut into 6cm lengths.

Mix the beans and leeks together and then stir in enough dressing to taste.

Runner Bean Chutney

This recipe was sent in by a box customer, name unknown. Jane had never heard of runner bean chutney before she came to Devon but it's very popular down here, and a great way of using up a glut.

Makes about 4kg

1.6kg runner beans, trimmed
1.2kg onions, finely chopped
1 litre malt vinegar
6 tablespoons cornflour
2 tablespoons mustard powder
2 tablespoons ground turmeric
2 tablespoons mustard seeds
2 tablespoons sesame seeds, lightly toasted in a dry frying pan
400g light soft brown sugar
800g Demerara sugar

Blanch the runner beans in plenty of boiling salted water for 2 minutes, then drain well. Refresh in cold water and drain again. Chop them finely and set aside.

Put the onions in a large, heavy-based pan with half the vinegar and simmer for 20 minutes, then add the beans. Mix the cornflour, mustard powder, turmeric, mustard seeds and sesame seeds with a little of the remaining vinegar and then stir them into the onion and bean mix. Add the rest of the vinegar and cook gently for 10 minutes. Add both the sugars and stir until dissolved. Bring back to the boil, stirring constantly, then reduce the heat and simmer gently for about 1 hour until slightly thickened, stirring frequently to prevent sticking. Transfer to warm sterilised jars, seal and allow to mature for 6–8 weeks.

Easy ideas for French and runner beans

✦ Cook 300–400g French beans in boiling water until just tender but still squeaky. Melt 2 tablespoons of butter in another pan. Add the drained beans to the butter, raise the heat and stir in 2 tablespoons of grated Parmesan and some pepper.

✦ Toss warm cooked French or runner beans with crisp pancetta and sliced spring onions, plus a drizzle of good balsamic vinegar.

✦ Toss cooked beans with a little Salsa Verde (see page 216), some leftover roast lamb or freshly cooked sliced steak, and some rocket.

✦ Serve pesto in the traditional way – cook tagliatelle in boiling salted water, adding French beans and thinly sliced waxy potatoes at the same time as the pasta. Drain, return to the pan and toss with pesto (see page 209). You could add grated Parmesan and a little cream, if you like.

See also:
Summer Salad with Beetroot, Goat's Cheese and Green Beans (page 313)

Garlic

In our damp climate, it is difficult to produce good-quality garlic that will store, though there is one grower in the Isle of Wight who does a pretty good job. I always make a few strings for personal consumption but, inspired by a trip to Andalusia one spring, we sell most of our crop as fresh or 'wet' garlic in May and June.

Garlic can be planted successfully any time between October and early April, though earlier plantings will generally produce the biggest bulbs. Late October is perfect but in wet years we have been forced to plant in the spring and have still had worthwhile crops. Individual cloves should be planted (ideally point up but it is not essential) 15–20cm apart in a soft, fine seedbed. It is important that the seed garlic is sourced no further south than the Pyrenees. We have tried Spanish and Egyptian seed with disastrous results; not surprisingly they do not fare well in our winter. The cloves should be large and firm with no moulds or rots. By May the stems are somewhere between a child's and a farmer's fingers in fatness and the bulb is normally starting to swell. At this stage you can use the whole plant chopped into salads, dressings, marinades, salsas or stir-fries. This wet garlic has a milder flavour than mature, dry garlic and should generally be added later in the cooking process and in larger quantities. A whole bulb/stalk will not overwhelm a large dish.

As the season progresses, the bulb swells and differentiates into cloves, while the leaves senesce and inevitably succumb to the fungal disease, rust. At some stage in late June the skin of each clove becomes too tough to use without peeling and the wet garlic season is over. When all but the youngest central leaves have yellowed, it is time to lift and dry the crop. In a good year they can be dried in the field but more reliably they can be laid in shallow layers in crates and finished in the porch or polytunnel. Plaiting is the ideal way of storing them and is best done when the leaves are semi-dry.

Storage and preparation

Garlic should be kept in a dry, airy place to delay sprouting and the development of rot. If well dried, it should keep for several months even at room temperature, though it shows an increasing tendency to sprout as spring approaches. Fresh or wet garlic is best kept in the fridge, provided you are not too averse to the smell, and should be eaten within 10 days.

The timing of our garlic harvest changes every year, keeping Jane on her toes in the Field Kitchen, where she has to combine what is coming off the fields. She has found the milder flavour of wet garlic goes particularly well with roast new potatoes and braised artichokes, and also in risottos and gratins. Our wet garlic tends to be ready when wild garlic is out (known as ransoms in neighbouring Cornwall). If you live anywhere rural, you may well find a shady lane with the telltale smell and white flowers. Pick and wash the leaves and use in the same way as wet garlic. The flowers are also edible and look pretty sprinkled on salads.

Bagna Cauda

Originating from Northern Italy, this is an anchovy and garlic sauce traditionally served with crudités and good bread for dipping. It is delicious drizzled over steamed purple sprouting broccoli or cape broccoli too. In the days when she worked at the River Café, in London, Jane used to love bagna cauda on toast with a poached egg, as a sustaining breakfast before a long shift.

Serves 8–10

8 garlic cloves, peeled
200ml milk
10 anchovy fillets (preferably salted)
100g softened butter
olive oil, for drizzling

Put the garlic cloves in a small pan, cover with the milk and simmer for about 40 minutes, until the garlic is soft. Pour the entire contents of the pan into a food processor, add the anchovy fillets and process until smooth. Slowly add the softened butter and then drizzle in olive oil to taste. You should have a sloppy, emulsified sauce. Sometimes it has a tendency to separate; you can bring it back together by warming it gently while whisking.

Wet and Wild Garlic Risotto

I think it was the idea of 'wet and wild' that led Jane to try this risotto. Generally the two are around at the same time but if you can't get wet garlic, just use leeks. Wild garlic leaves are generally found in woods and country lanes in the spring and you can smell them before you see them.

Serves 4

1 litre vegetable or chicken stock
1 tablespoon olive oil
45g butter
3 heads of wet garlic, thinly sliced
2 garlic cloves, finely chopped
1 small onion, finely chopped
250g risotto rice, preferably Arborio
a splash of white wine or vermouth
a large handful of wild garlic leaves, roughly chopped
50g Parmesan cheese, freshly grated, plus extra to serve
sea salt and freshly ground black pepper
wild garlic flowers, to garnish

Heat the stock in a pan and keep at simmering point. Heat the oil and 15g of the butter in a heavy-based pan, add the wet garlic, ordinary garlic and onion and cook without colouring for about 10 minutes, until soft.

Add the rice, turn up the heat a little and stir until the rice is coated with the garlic mixture. Add a little salt and pepper and then pour in the wine or vermouth. Cook, stirring, until the liquid has been absorbed. Add enough hot stock just to cover the rice and turn down the heat. Maintain the rice at a gentle simmer and keep adding more stock as soon as each addition has been absorbed, stirring constantly. About 10 minutes into this process, add the wild garlic leaves. Continue to add the remaining stock in the same way. After another 8–10 minutes, when the rice is just cooked but still has a little bite, mix in the remaining butter and the grated Parmesan. Season to taste and serve with a sprinkling of cheese – and some wild garlic flowers if the fancy takes you.

Easy ideas for garlic

◆ If you have a glut of garlic, cut the bulbs in half across the middle, toss them in olive oil, then place in a baking dish with a few sprigs of thyme. Cover and roast at 180°C/Gas Mark 4 for about an hour, until the garlic is soft. Use to make garlic pizza bread (see below), or add to salsas and salads for a mellow garlic flavour.

◆ To make garlic pizza bread, make some pizza dough, following the method in Leek and Roquefort Pizza Bread (page 247), but bake it without a topping. When you take it out of the oven, rub with half a head of roast garlic (see above) and drizzle with olive oil.

◆ Add sliced wet garlic to roast new potatoes about 10 minutes before the end of cooking.

See also:
Tarragon and Garlic Stuffing for Chicken (page 215)

Globe Artichokes

Many farmers have a passion for one crop or animal that surpasses any rational consideration. For my father and grandfather it was pigs. For two generations they lost money and no amount of pleading from the accountant deterred them from having a few rooting around. For me it is globe artichokes: they have yet to make a penny but I live with an optimism that truly represents the triumph of hope over experience. It could be their handsome appearance in the field – the magnificent sculptural form, with the green-scaled globes towering above luxuriant foliage – or it could be that they are one of the few crops you don't have to bend over to pick. A Russian herbalist told me that it was because they cleanse the liver, the seat of anger. She attributed my obsession to my need, as an angry person, for self-medication.

The Ancient Greeks and Romans imported globe artichokes from North Africa and they spread throughout the aristocratic gardens of Europe. They are hungry plants, requiring a lot of space and nitrogen to produce a small amount of food. I can't imagine them catching on with the land-hungry poor but Henry VIII reckoned they made him horny, and his head gardener was charged with maintaining a supply throughout the summer. There is barely a vegetable to which someone somewhere has not ascribed this virtue, and despite copious consumption I can't vouch for artichokes.

In France, Italy and Spain, each area tends to have its own preferred artichoke varieties, suited to local weather and more particularly local culinary traditions. Most of the artichokes grown in the UK are similar to the Roscoff type grown along the coast in northwest Brittany. These tend to be green, fleshy, large and squat in shape. They seem to do well in our climate and need a fair amount of water in the period running up to harvest to produce good-quality heads.

It is possible to grow artichokes from seed but they are open pollinated and, whatever the seed catalogue tells you, there will be huge variation between the worst, which will be disturbingly similar to thistles, and the best. In subsequent years it is possible to select the best strains from your patch and multiply by division, but this is a lifetime's labour and the French and Italians have a head start of several generations. After following this approach for a few years, there were still too many thistles and I started casting my eyes across the Channel for some top-quality plants from Brittany. After hours on the phone trying to get all the right permits from both sides of bureaucracy, I gave up on the official route. My father and I crossed the channel in his 26-foot

sailing boat, sneaked up the Roscoff river, met some farmers in a cloud of Gauloise smoke in a shady bar and the deal was done. We sailed back with the small cabin stuffed with hessian sacks full of plants. We met my wife at a secluded cove rendezvous under Start Point, rowing our booty ashore and lugging it up the beach to a waiting Land Rover.

That was 15 years ago. Despite loving care, it took the artichokes two or three years to adjust to their new home this side of the Channel. Since then, however, they have gone from strength to strength. Each spring we take suckers from the mature plants and plant them out in a new field, so that the original 400 have now become 30,000. Despite the volume, they still don't make us any money because the labour costs of weeding them are so high. This year I plan to import a special weeding machine from Brittany to cut down on the hand work.

Each mature, over-wintering plant grows away strongly in the spring, throwing up a main stalk bearing the *grosse mère* (big mother), ready for harvest in late May or early June. The French thin the crowns and prune their plants to produce the biggest big mother they can get. Further south in Italy and, to a lesser extent, Spain, the smaller heads, or *figli* (children), and even smaller *nipoti* (nephews) that come later are more prized. It all depends on what you plan to do with them.

The main season is over by late July but the new plants, grown from the suckers taken in April, produce their heads in September and October. After harvest is completed, we cut down the senescing remains of the plants and sow a green manure of either rye or, if it is early enough, the vetch that is so good at fixing nitrogen, between the rows. This green manure is chopped in in February and, together with a liberal application of muck, will feed the next year's crop.

Artichokes have few pests and have the virtue of being one plant that I have never known a rabbit to eat. We tend to grow them on odd fields where we cannot control the rabbits. Aphids can be a problem but the plants provide such a good habitat for ladybirds and other predators that they are normally self-regulating. We keep a crop for three or four years, by which time they are usually starting to be overrun by perennial weeds such as the highly invasive and choking couch and creeping buttercup. Fortunately this is about the time to split up the crowns and move on to another field.

Storage and preparation

Globe artichokes will keep for a week or more in the bottom of your fridge. Discrete areas of discoloration are sometimes the result of a late frost and will not affect the flavour if trimmed out. But a lot of browning and dehydration is a sure sign that they have been too long out of the field and will be past their best. They should be picked while tight, and before a hole starts appearing in the centre. As they mature, the artichokes slowly open and, if given a chance, will reveal the beautiful purple, thistle-like flower sold dried in flower shops.

The more mature the artichoke, the tougher the leaves and the meatier and more substantial the base, or heart, will be. As a guide, if you cannot cut through the leaves reasonably easily with a sharp knife, they will be tough even when cooked (though the flesh attached to them may be quite edible). To trim artichokes, pull off the dark outer leaves, working round the artichoke until you are down to the pale green leaves. Then cut off the tops of the remaining leaves and trim the artichokes so no dark green bits are evident. The stem can be trimmed too – just lightly if the artichokes are young, but cut right back if they are old and tough. At this point, you can remove the hairy choke with a teaspoon.

Once cut, the exposed surfaces will soon brown. This can be avoided by acidulating some water with the juice of a lemon and dunking your prepared artichokes in it prior to cooking. If preparing a lot, you may find a tidemark on your bowl to challenge even the most powerful detergent.

The simplest way of cooking artichokes is to boil them in salted water acidulated with lemon juice for 20–30 minutes, according to size (until the lower leaves will pull off fairly easily, but with a bit of experience you can also tell by the smell). It helps to use a small lid as a weight to keep them under the surface. Drain them well upside down for 5 minutes and eat them either hot or cold with vinaigrette or melted butter (possibly with a little lemon juice in it). Good picnic food.

If you want to do more than boil and eat them with vinaigrette or melted butter, there are more ideas from Jane on the following pages.

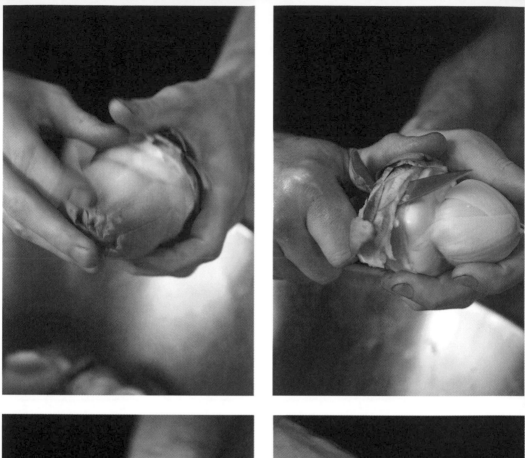

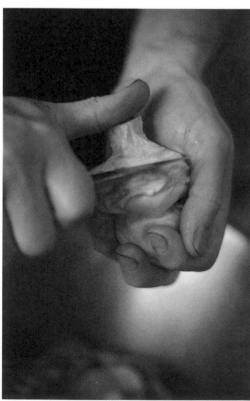

A friend of my wife married an Italian a few years ago. At one of the many meals spread over several days of celebrations, I happened to mention my enthusiasm for artichokes. It was like lighting a forest fire, as the argument raged around the table about the best way of preparing them. Everyone from a different region had the definitive recipe, which in true Italian style surpassed all others.

Another tip: don't waste any good wine with artichokes – there is something about them that ruins your palate. And one more thing; don't lick your fingers after cutting them; they will have that extreme bitter flavour reminiscent of dandelion juice.

Provided you have the time and the inclination, they are also lots of fun in the kitchen. I was delighted to find, when Jane joined us as our chef in the Field Kitchen, that she shared this passion, and thinks that ours are the best she has ever cooked – better than anything they got at the River Café (where she was nearly broken in her first week by being given two crates of old, tough artichokes to prepare). Every year Jane progresses from excitement when someone from the fields puts the first artichoke on her desk, through to despair a few weeks later when there is another crateful to prepare for lunch in the Field Kitchen, with everyone's fingers already blackened and rough. My advice is to stick to the Breton approach of boiling them whole, which requires minimal preparation, but Jane's preference is preparing them in ways that enable you to eat the whole lot. Even with the youngest and freshest artichokes, this can be hard work.

Artichoke, Salmon and New Potato Salad with Anchovy Sauce

This is a really stunning dish, using ingredients that are in season in early summer. Sea trout would make a good substitute for the salmon, as would a meaty white fish such as brill or turbot.

Serves 4

4 globe artichokes
300g new potatoes
olive oil for drizzling
150g salmon fillet
75g rocket
3 tablespoons Bagna Cauda (see page 176)
sea salt and freshly ground black pepper

Cook the artichokes in boiling salted water for 20–30 minutes, until tender (i.e. when the leaves can be pulled away easily), then drain. In the meantime, boil the new potatoes in a separate pan. Drain well, season with salt and pepper, then drizzle with olive oil and keep warm.

When the artichokes are cool enough to handle, peel off the leaves, trim the stalks and remove the hairy choke. Cut each artichoke into quarters or sixths. This should not be a problem, as the artichokes are cooked and easier to handle.

Grill the salmon until just cooked but slightly pink in the middle. Pull it apart into chunks, discarding the skin and any bones.

Place the artichokes, potatoes, salmon and rocket in a large bowl. Drizzle with the bagna cauda and toss everything together. Serve immediately.

Braised Artichokes with Broad Beans and Mint

Preparing the artichokes like this can seem like a daunting task but it is worth it. Stripping off the leaves is quite therapeutic when you have only a few to prepare. The novelty soon wears off, however, when you are faced with 40 or so every day, as we sometimes are in the Field Kitchen. If you like, you can add parsley and dried chilli to the braised artichokes with the mint.

Serves 4

4 globe artichokes
juice of 1 lemon
3 tablespoons olive oil
1 garlic clove, crushed (wet garlic can also be used)
a handful of shelled broad beans
1 tablespoon chopped mint
sea salt and freshly ground black pepper

Prepare the artichokes as described on page 183 and cut each one into sixths or eighths. Place in a bowl of cold water with the lemon juice added to prevent them going black.

Heat the oil in a frying pan over a high heat, add the artichoke wedges and stir constantly until they start to brown. Lower the heat, add the garlic and a few tablespoons of water and season with salt and pepper. Stir well, then reduce the heat, cover and cook for about 10 minutes, until the artichokes are tender.

Blanch the broad beans in a pan of boiling salted water for 4–5 minutes, then drain and add to the artichokes. Stir in the mint and adjust the seasoning.

Roast Artichokes and New Potatoes

How to make a couple of artichokes go a long way. If you can't get hold of wet garlic, just add some whole unpeeled cloves instead for a rustic look.

Serves 8

800g new potatoes, halved
80ml extra virgin olive oil
a sprig of rosemary, chopped
2 globe artichokes
1 wet garlic bulb, chopped
sea salt and freshly ground black pepper

In an ovenproof dish, mix the potatoes with the olive oil, rosemary and some seasoning. Place in an oven preheated to 200°C/Gas Mark 6 and roast for about 30 minutes, until the potatoes are starting to brown.

Meanwhile, prepare the artichokes as described on page 185 and cut each one into eighths. Add the artichoke segments and the wet garlic to the potatoes, mix together and return to the oven for another 30 minutes, until the artichokes and potatoes are cooked through.

Stuffed Artichokes

This recipe is based on one of Antonio Carluccio's. Normally we use baby artichokes and serve them as a canapé but it works just as well with larger ones, as long as they are well trimmed.

Serves 4

4 globe artichokes
juice of 1 lemon
4 tablespoons fresh breadcrumbs
4 tablespoons extra virgin olive oil
1 tablespoon chopped parsley
15 salted capers (or 25 capers in vinegar), soaked in cold water for 20
    minutes, then squeezed dry
50g Parmesan cheese, freshly grated
2 egg yolks
olive oil
sea salt and freshly ground black pepper

Prepare the artichokes by discarding the outer leaves and the tough stem. Trim the artichokes down, removing the leaves with a sharp knife so that no dark green ones remain, but leaving the pale inner leaves attached. Remove the chokes with a melon baller or teaspoon. If the artichokes are young, just trim the stalks, but if they are old and tough, remove them. Place the artichokes in a bowl of cold water with the lemon juice added to prevent browning.

For the stuffing, mix together the breadcrumbs, oil, parsley, capers, Parmesan and egg yolks to obtain a soft mixture. Season with salt and pepper. Stuff the cavities of the artichokes with the mixture.

Put the artichokes in a shallow saucepan in which they fit tightly. Pour in 1cm of olive oil and 1cm of water, then cover and cook on the hob for 30 minutes over a low heat. The artichokes are ready when a knife slides through them easily. Serve warm or cold.

Easy ideas for artichokes

✦ Boil artichokes whole, as in the Artichoke, Salmon and New Potato Salad on page 186, then leave upside down in a colander to drain. Open the leaves out slightly, turn the artichokes the right way up and drizzle with a little vinaigrette made by whisking together 150ml olive oil, the juice of 1 lemon, 30ml white wine vinegar, 1 crushed garlic clove, ½ teaspoon of Dijon mustard and some salt and pepper. Serve some of the vinaigrette on the side for dipping the leaves in. You could add skinned, deseeded and diced tomatoes to the vinaigrette, and/or some chopped parsley.

✦ Boil artichokes whole, as above, and serve with melted butter and lemon juice instead of vinaigrette.

✦ Braise artichokes as described on page 187, omitting the broad beans and mint. Serve with a Pine Nut Salsa made by mixing together 1 tablespoon of lightly toasted pine nuts, ½ finely chopped red onion, 1 crushed garlic clove, 1 finely chopped hardboiled egg, ½ tablespoon each of chopped tarragon and parsley, 2 tablespoons of olive oil, 1 tablespoon of good wine vinegar and some salt and pepper.

Supermarkets: a lifetime of loathing

My loathing for supermarkets was born almost 20 years ago, when I was making my first tentative approaches as a would-be supplier to Safeway (now consumed by Morrisons). The buyer asked me to come to London the following Thursday to meet his technologist colleague. When I asked if we could make it Friday, because I would be in London for the weekend, the phone went dead. I called back – 'I'm sorry, I think we were cut off' – and was met with the buyer's immortal words: 'No, sonny, when we whistle, you jump.'

I was new to the game and had not yet been beaten into the subservience that views this as normal behaviour. I tore down the beginnings of my modest pack-house and went back to selling wholesale.

Supermarkets regard it as normal practice to demand promotional prices well below the cost of production and retrospective payments at the end of the year if your product sells well. Suppliers are often expected to pay to get their products on the shelves and may be required to contribute to sometimes spurious marketing campaigns and promotions outside their control. I was once asked to pay £1,000 to talk to a consultant who would advise me how to talk to Sainsbury. Does it sound like dealing with the Mafia? It is; everyone knows it is wrong but they are powerless to change it. One could always say no but, since one of the conditions of business is often that you supply only one or perhaps two of the major supermarkets, such outrageous reasonableness would spell the end.

A few years later I met that Safeway buyer, who was now working for an organic packing company supplying the supermarkets, and found that he was not a demon; he was surprisingly reasonable and pretty decent. He had simply been doing what was expected within the environment he found himself in. The institution had manipulated and debased his humanity, normalising disgraceful behaviour to service its shareholders' insatiable appetite for profit. In my experience, supermarkets – with the exception of Waitrose and the Co-op, who are not stockmarket-listed and therefore don't constantly worry about their share price – demean human behaviour and are almost universally loathed by their suppliers, while being begrudgingly tolerated by customers on account of their convenience. Supermarket buyers make secondhand-car salesmen seem like priests but even they cannot maintain such unscrupulous unpleasantness with people they actually get to know – they are moved frequently before they form relationships with suppliers that might tempt them to decency.

The food industry, and vegetable growing and packing in particular, is a battlefield ravaged by the ruthless buying policy of the big four: Tesco, Asda, Sainsbury and Morrisons. The collateral damage of abandoned pack-houses, redundant staff and bankrupt growers is strewn across the country. The supermarkets have spent the last 30 years lecturing us on supply chain rationalisation (chopping out all but the largest suppliers), category management (pushing their costs on to their suppliers) and the need for continuity of supply (global supply chains), but now the wind has temporarily changed. Local is in, and their advertisements are all about local, seasonal sourcing (even though genuinely locally sourced products in Tesco currently amount to less than 1 per cent of sales). The reality is that ever larger, more concentrated suppliers are merging, buying and taking each other over in a miserable ongoing battle to curry favour and avoid being struck out by a buyer's pen at the next 'supplier review'.

I don't know whether to rant, laugh or throw up when the invitation arrives to a local suppliers' seminar organised by Tesco to reinvent the industry they have spent three decades systematically destroying. Let no one forget that the publicly quoted Big Four exist to deliver dividends and shareholder value, pure and simple. As amoral institutions priding themselves on their response to ever-shifting public opinion, they have no opinions of their own. Morality and decency are alien concepts because they cannot be measured in the financial terms reflected in share price and dividends. For corporate social responsibility, read 'brand management and risk reduction'. Their positions on local sourcing, GM food, organic farming, biodegradable packaging, climate change or any of the other issues used to grab tokenistic headlines are like autumn leaves, blown around by public opinion before being left to rot when the fickle wind of PR management moves on. The hypocrisy inherent in their proclamations of green credentials and concern for public health leaves me, for one, reaching for a bucket.

Gooseberries

I was driven to planting an acre of gooseberries by memories of my mother's gooseberry fool and by frustration at the lack of organic fruit grown in this country. In the closing years of the millennium, gooseberries fell into virtual obscurity and, without a market, most growers grubbed theirs out in favour of sweeter, more profitable crops.

A few people warned me of sawfly (a pest that attacks only gooseberries, in three waves of voracious larvae) and predicted disaster without an arsenal of chemicals. There are always prophets of doom – they keep the chemical companies in business – so I carried on regardless. For the first three years the bushes were indeed stripped bare by sawfly larvae, which emerged each April from their over-wintering pupae in the soil in a truly biblical-style plague. The plants are incredibly vigorous and soon put out new leaves, only to be stripped again at six-weekly intervals by successive generations. The skeletal plants, bare of leaves, made a depressing sight and a few did die, but five years on, the larvae have gone and the surviving plants are doing pretty well. Nature has established a balance and we have a mystery predator keeping the larvae in check. We can't find anything above ground so I suspect that one or more of the myriad organisms living in our soil has developed an appetite for the pupae.

Gooseberries are normally in season from mid to late June for jam making and cooking. There is a brief period, normally at the end of June, when they soften and sweeten to the extent that they can be eaten without sugar, but blink and you will miss it and they split or go mushy. Overripe gooseberries start fermenting on the bush and can be pretty nasty. There are red varieties that are sweeter, less thorny and hence more pleasant to pick. Unfortunately they are also less resistant to mildew and less vigorous than the traditional trusty and prickly variety, Invicta, that we continue to rely on at Riverford.

The British public is finally appreciating the joys and culinary possibilities of some of our more traditional home-grown fruit and vegetables, and getting an appetite for their stronger, sharper flavours. Gooseberries and rhubarb are back in fashion. Who would have believed it but now we never have enough of these tart berries and have planted another acre. Berries don't have to be flown around the world to be interesting.

Storage and preparation

If the gooseberries are hard, they will keep in the fridge for a couple of weeks. If you want them to ripen further, leave them out of the fridge.

Generally they need topping and tailing (just pinch off the stalk and the little 'tail' with your fingers) before cooking, unless they are going to be sieved.

Ripe gooseberries are ready more or less as the first mackerel of the season come down the Channel and arrive off our coast. Perfect timing by nature, as gooseberries make a great sauce (see page 200) to go with mackerel, or even salmon, Jane says. They are also good with pork.

Gooseberries combine particularly well with elderflower. It feels like the ultimate seasonal thing to put a few heads of elderflower in to cook with them.

Gooseberry and Elderflower Fool

If there is no fresh elderflower around when the gooseberries are ready, add a little elderflower cordial (about 2 teaspoons) instead. A few tablespoons of homemade custard (see facing page) can be folded in with the cream.

Serves 4

300g gooseberries, topped and tailed
2 heads of elderflower, as fresh as possible
a knob of butter
2 tablespoons caster sugar (or to taste)
250ml double cream

Put the gooseberries, elderflower, butter and sugar in a pan and cook over a low heat until the gooseberries start to soften and 'pop'. Leave to cool. Then remove the elderflower heads, mash the gooseberries with a fork and check the sweetness, adding more sugar if necessary. Whip the cream and fold it into the gooseberries. Chill before serving.

Gooseberries in Honey Saffron Custard

A recipe from *The Carved Angel Cookery Book* by Joyce Molyneux (William Collins, 1990). Jane worked at the Carved Angel in Dartmouth in its heyday and loved every minute of it. She has cooked Joyce's dishes everywhere, including the Solomon Islands in the middle of a military coup.

Serves 6

225g gooseberries, topped and tailed
50g caster sugar
6 egg yolks
600ml single cream
75g honey
scant ¼ teaspoon saffron strands

Put the gooseberries in a pan with the sugar and 2 tablespoons of water, then cover and stew gently for 5 minutes or until tender. Divide between 6 ramekin dishes.

Put the egg yolks, cream, honey and saffron in a bowl and whisk together just to combine. Sit the bowl over a pan of simmering water, making sure the water doesn't touch the base of the bowl. Cook the custard over a low heat for about 10 minutes, stirring constantly, until it thickens.

Strain the custard through a fine sieve over the gooseberries. Put the ramekins in a roasting tin containing about 3cm of hot water. Place in an oven preheated to 140°C/Gas Mark 1 and bake for 45 minutes–1 hour, until just set. Serve at room temperature.

Gooseberry Sauce for Oily Fish or Pork

If you are serving this with fish, you could let it down with a little fish stock for a lighter sauce.

Serves 6–8

400g gooseberries, topped and tailed
25g butter
1 tablespoon caster sugar

Place all the ingredients in a pan and cook slowly until the skins of the gooseberries start to burst. You can serve them rustically like this, or sieve them if you prefer.

Easy ideas for gooseberries

✦ Substitute gooseberries for blackberries and apples in the pie on page 362, or for the oranges, apples and dried fruit in the crumble on page 9, increasing the sugar to taste.

✦ Mix cooked sweetened gooseberries with crème fraîche and then layer in a serving bowl with crushed gingernut biscuits mixed with a little melted butter.

Herbs

We all use herbs differently and in vastly different quantities according to our taste, culinary traditions and experience. For some, a bountiful supply of coriander is essential. For others, a basil bush will be stripped bare every week. One thing is for sure: if you have access to your own supply near your kitchen, you will enjoy cooking and eating more.

On the whole, both annual (grows each year from seed and produces seed within a year) and perennial (either herbaceous or re-growing each year from a persistent root stock) herbs are easy to grow. The problem is that ensuring you have the right herb to hand for a particular dish requires a fair amount of space, time and organisation. Things are complicated by the vast number of varieties and strains of each herb, which really do differ quite markedly in their flavour and growth habit. Having said that, if you are a keen cook and interested gardener, but are frustrated by lack of growing space for bulkier vegetables, I would recommend that you try to establish some of the herbs listed below, all of which can be grown in pots. Start by growing at least parsley outside and some basil on a sunny windowsill inside. Putting down roots and planting some perennials might come next. If you have more space and more time, you might want to try tarragon, chervil and coriander.

The difference between fresh and dried herbs is generally most marked in the leafy annuals, where the dried version is heresy and the supermarket packets of fresh are overpackaged and breathtakingly expensive to those of us who know what the growers are paid. The pots of living herbs are an option but again they are expensive and soon die (don't condemn your gardening abilities on the basis of these plants: they are programmed to die so that you buy another one).

The important thing with all herbs is to develop a sense of their culinary properties: what they combine well with and when to add them in the cooking process. Unless you are the next Heston Blumenthal, a sense of cultural integrity and style of cooking is a useful starting point for your experimentation and will guide you when necessity forces you to improvise. Here are a few ideas that might help you along the way.

Basil

Basil can grow as a perennial in tropical climates but I challenge anyone to get it through a British winter without a sunlamp. It loves dry heat and, in my experience, needs high light intensity to thrive. Having said that, it is very easy to grow from May to September in a polytunnel or on a sunny windowsill and, as it tends to be used mainly in summer dishes, this is not such a problem for a seasonally oriented eater. Drying destroys the flavour – you might as well use hay – but freezing the leaves in plastic bags and then crumbling them into dishes is a reasonable option.

We grow vast quantities of basil in our polytunnels for use in the veg boxes and to supply local pesto fanatics. We plant out in early May (you could probably push it to April on a warm, sunny windowsill) and pick through to the end of September by pinching out the leading shoots (bud plus two full leaves) between thumb and forefinger once a week, just before they flower. Basil will develop a harsh flavour if you let it flower, and the plant will not fully recover even after removing the flower. It is sometimes worth making a second planting in mid summer to provide some younger, more vigorous plants for cropping into the autumn. As light levels and night temperatures drop at the end of September, the quality declines, and the crop is normally wiped out by disease associated with loss of vigour some time in October.

There are many different types of basil, and a degree of rivalry exists amongst some foodies and gardeners around how rare and esoteric their particular variety is. We have tried quite a few, including several of the red and purple ones. Most of them are nasty and we have reached the conclusion that bog-standard sweet Genovese basil is best for most purposes, the only exception being if you use it a lot cooked, in which case there may be virtue in a more bitter/robust variety for some dishes.

The flavour of basil is rapidly destroyed by cooking, so it is commonly used raw in salads (most famously with tomatoes and mozzarella) and sauces (such as pesto or pistou), or added to dishes right at the end of cooking. Pistou (see page 396) is wonderful for lifting dull dishes and invigorating a jaded palate. A dollop transforms a bowl of minestrone and can be as good on pasta as its cousin, pesto.

Bay

Bay leaves are an essential ingredient in a good stock and many stews, and are used frequently in vegetable and fish dishes. They give a depth of flavour, with a bitter edge, and are usually added whole and then discarded before eating. Dried bay leaves are fine, and may even be stronger in flavour, but I still prefer to use fresh.

Bay is part of the laurel family, and as such is evergreen and can grow to be a sizeable tree. If you have a friend or neighbour with a bay tree, or even notice one growing in the park, a smallish branch (twig, even) secreted in your pocket can be hung in the kitchen and will keep you going for months. Alternatively, bay grows happily in a large pot and responds well to the savage topiary favoured by more formal gardeners.

Chervil

Chervil is an annual but is otherwise similar to parsley in its cultivation and use (see page 206). It has a greater propensity to run to seed but generally contains itself for longer than coriander. The flavour is milder than that of parsley, with a gentle liquorice note. Try it with fish or eggs – it is also great in a simple *fines herbes* omelette (ideally mixed with tarragon, chives and parsley).

Chives

Chives reappear each year from bulbs and consequently grow in clumps like daffodils or wild garlic. They can be treated as perennials but are tolerant of shade and like a bit more fertility than bushy perennials such as rosemary and sage (see page 208). Once established, they will often compete well with grass; if you can establish them in a corner of rough grass, they will probably look after themselves and be there if and when you want them. Alternatively, they can be grown in a pot. Like most of the alliums, they are said to deter insects, though I have yet to notice this. Different varieties have varying tendencies to run to seed. The wilder cultivars appear in early spring and seldom flower. The cultivated ones seem to grow later but more vigorously, and will normally run to seed in mid or late summer.

In culinary terms, chives come somewhere between spring onions and fresh or wild garlic. They are great for garnishing and bringing slightly tired dishes to life: sprinkle them on soups or add to stir-fries and salads. Like most herbs, when you have them to hand you will discover new ways of using them. Chives can be added to scrambled eggs or omelettes (on their own or in a mixture of fines herbes – i.e. chervil, parsley and tarragon), or mixed with crème fraîche or soured cream to dress a potato salad.

Coriander

Coriander is a semi-hardy annual with a strong tendency to run to seed, so you will find that, unlike parsley, you need to make several (at least five) sowings to maintain a supply throughout the year. It is much quicker to germinate and establish than parsley so it is not worth buying plants to grow on. It is happy outside in summer and autumn but needs the protection of a windowsill or greenhouse in winter. The emerging leaves become more feathery as the plant runs to seed, and the flavour changes (I think many would say it deteriorates, but it is still acceptable for most purposes). From a commercial viewpoint, this makes it a cut-once rather than a cut-and-come-again crop. For personal use, the feathery leaves are fine, so if you are not so fussy you can keep cutting out the seed heads and extend your crop, thus reducing the number of sowings.

Of the green herbs, coriander is probably the most work to grow, so whether you bother will probably depend on your enthusiasm for Asian food and a few Mexican dishes. The roots, leaves and seeds can all be used in various ways but they have quite different flavours and are not interchangeable. As with herb fennel (see page 157), it is relatively easy to leave a sowing and collect your own seeds. You can use the seeds fresh or dry them by spreading them out in the sun, for sowing or later use.

Coriander roots and stalks can be included in curry pastes but most recipes call for the leaves only. Jane likes to use large quantities (think spinach rather than herb) and has secured an alliance with John, who manages the polytunnels and loves growing the stuff, to guarantee a supply for the Field Kitchen.

Dill

Like chervil, dill is similar to parsley to grow and has a liquorice flavour (slightly stronger than chervil's) and a propensity to run to seed. The fine, feathery leaves are used to flavour fish (essential in gravad lax), pickles and soups. Dill is a key ingredient of Russian and Scandinavian cooking, making a good addition to potato and beetroot salads, horseradish sauce and smoked fish. The seeds can be collected and dried for use in cooking (similar to caraway) or replanting.

Dill requires a lot of work or cash to ensure a continuous supply. As a grower, I would argue that, unless it is a personal favourite for cooking, most kitchens could live without it.

Mint

If you can't grow mint, you should give up gardening altogether. It will flourish just about anywhere, even between the cracks in your paving stones. The main problem is that, without a restraining influence, its creeping roots are invasive and will quickly take over a bed. Choosing from the hundreds of different varieties is also difficult. The best policy is to dig up some root from a plant whose flavour you like (most owners will be happy to part with it) and either start it in a pot of compost or plant it straight into the ground. Planting in a container such as an old bucket with the bottom knocked out, dug into the ground, will help to contain it. Mint likes a moisture-retaining soil and is tolerant of shade but will grow just about anywhere. You can start it from seed from a catalogue but then you will have little idea of what you are growing. Some of the seed we have bought in the past has produced rather nasty mint. Avoid peppermint, unless that is specifically what you are after – say, for tea. Spearmint is plain nasty for most things other than chewing gum.

Mint is vital to a good Pimm's, as well as being an essential accompaniment to roast lamb. My Northumbrian-born mother-in-law, scorning insipid shop-bought mint jelly, taught me to make proper mint sauce to go with lamb. Chop two or three sprigs of mint into a bowl and add about a tablespoon of boiling water to break down the cellulose (she later became a chemist) and release the flavour. Add a little sugar while it is still hot. Stir and leave for a few minutes to cool, then add a teaspoon of vinegar and more sugar if necessary.

Mint is a vital ingredient in many North African dishes, the best known of which is probably the bulgar wheat salad, tabouleh. Jane uses mint with cucumber and yoghurt in tsatsiki and raita (see page 156) and in many Asian-inspired salads. Its palate-cleansing properties make it a natural accompaniment to spicy dishes and Jane also recommends trying it in a gin and tonic.

Parsley

Probably the UK's most widely used fresh herb, and one that crops up frequently in almost all styles of cooking, from African to Asian. It is not as trendy as basil or coriander but much more versatile, and something that most cooks would not be without. It can be chopped and added at the end of cooking to give freshness and colour, or used in larger quantities earlier in the cooking to add base flavour to stocks, stews and with fish.

You can choose between the traditional curly parsley (Champion Moss Curled being the old favourite) or go for the more upmarket flat-leaved Italian – or snob's parsley, as we call it. The flat-leaved version, which is similar to coriander in appearance, is said to have a stronger flavour, but this is not my experience. Personally, I find it sweeter but less robust in flavour, and would favour it where used raw but prefer the traditional variety for cooking. Jane will only have the snob's stuff in her kitchen. Curly parsley is generally more vigorous and easier to grow and is definitely higher yielding, perhaps explaining my enthusiasm.

Both types are hardy biennials and will run to seed after their first winter and need to be replaced. A spring sowing outside may last through to the following spring but we tend to make a second sowing in late summer in our tunnels to see us through the winter. Parsley is notoriously fickle in germination and can take many weeks to emerge, so you may find it easier to buy a small plant to grow on. Although the plants are slow to establish, they are vigorous and high yielding once they get going. One or two plants (perhaps one of each type) in deep 15–20cm pots on a sunny windowsill will keep most households supplied throughout the year.

Parsley is traditionally used with butter to dress carrots and new potatoes but can also freshen up a wide range of cooked vegetable dishes and warm salads. It is also essential, along with mint, in the North African bulgar wheat salad, tabouleh, and in rice salads. Any stalks and trimmings will make a valuable addition to stocks. The flat-leaved variety can be finely chopped and mixed with grated lemon zest and finely chopped garlic to make the Italian gremolata. This is traditionally sprinkled on ossobuco (braised veal shin) but is also good with chicken casseroles, poached meats, braised leeks and fennel.

Sorrel

Sorrel is a close relative of our number-one perennial weed enemy, docks. It is almost as easy to grow and, once established, will look after itself in the same way as chives, coming back year after year from its deep roots to provide a trouble-free supply of the tart, intensely lemony leaves, so useful in soups, sauces and salads. It can sometimes be found growing wild in meadows and on the lawns of less controlling gardeners who tolerate the diversity. You can choose between French or garden sorrel, with the larger-leaved French variety normally being favoured except for wet ground.

Sorrel can be cut most of the year but is best in spring and autumn and will tend to run to seed in mid summer unless cut regularly. Cutting will stimulate the plant to produce new, tender growth. Older leaves, particularly when the plant is flowering, can be bitter and very nasty, so it is always worth tasting a few leaves before picking.

Jane is a big fan of sorrel and uses copious quantities to make her wonderful Sorrel and Onion Tart (see page 212). She also cooks it in a sauce to accompany fish (see page 216).

Tarragon

This perennial herb has an aroma similar to anise or fennel but is less sweet. It is widely used in French cooking and throughout central Europe to accompany chicken, fish and eggs and is also used to flavour soft drinks in Eastern Europe. It is much better fresh than dried.

French tarragon is less hardy but has a stronger flavour (and is generally considered superior), while the hardy and vigorous Russian tarragon is more succulent and easier to grow. It has, however, been rejected by our kitchen on account of its lack of flavour. We keep a patch of French tarragon going in the tunnels because Jane uses so much for stuffing her chickens (see page 215).

Some people get it to thrive outside, but we have had little success. Should you settle for the easier Russian variety, it should do well in a bed with the other perennials listed below.

It is traditional to cook chicken with tarragon, either by pushing sprigs under the skin before roasting or by adding it to marinades, sauces and stuffings. Jane also uses tarragon in dressings for warm salads and when braising vegetables.

Rosemary, Thyme, Marjoram, Oregano and Sage

These hardy, bushy perennials are fairly slow growing and can take a year or more to establish but are then pretty low maintenance. The dried version can be acceptable but fresh is better and it always feels so good just to step out and pick a sprig of something you have grown yourself, wherever the rest of the ingredients in your dish come from. Four foot of a two-foot deep bed in a reasonably sunny spot will accommodate enough for any domestic kitchen. The soil should be well drained, so a raised bed is good, but these herbs don't need much fertility. They are, in fact, indigenous to poor, semi-arid Mediterranean soils, where the most they can hope for is a goat dropping once in a while.

Rosemary: Good in marinades for lamb, or simply with roast lamb – also in anchovy sauces (a favourite with Jane) and tomato sauces. Add a small bunch when boiling beans such as haricot, borlotti or cannellini or when roasting squash.

Thyme: The strong flavour of thyme means that it is normally added early in the cooking, though the flowers can be used raw. Try roasting it with vegetables and using in gratins, tomato sauces, casseroles and stews.

Marjoram: For flavour, the best variety is sweet marjoram. It has many of the same uses as rosemary and thyme but is also good in sauces with blue cheese (gorgonzola is best) and walnuts to serve with polenta and pasta.

Oregano: As with so many herbs, the flavour can vary widely according to variety and growing conditions. The flowers can be used fresh but oregano is otherwise one of the few herbs that is better when dried. Jane's preference is for Sicilian wild oregano, which she claims has a distinctive flavour. At the

River Café she added it to ribollita, an Italian cabbage and bean soup, but for most of us oregano is associated with pizza.

Sage: Though sage is traditionally used in stuffings for poultry, I didn't develop a taste for it or appreciate its potential until Jane served it on top of a rotolo, a pasta roll filled with spinach, ricotta and squash. Her Sage Butter (page 217), served with roast squash, ravioli, veal or pork, is a revelation to the uninitiated. She also has a thing for Sage and Anchovy Fritters (see page 217).

Storage and preparation

All herbs, once picked, will keep best in the fridge in a plastic bag. If picked with a good stem, parsley, coriander and, to a lesser extent, chervil and dill can be stood in water as you would cut flowers, but it is dubious whether this is a better way of storing them. The perennials, such as rosemary, thyme and marjoram, can be kept for longer in the fridge than more delicate herbs. However, as they tend to retain their flavour through drying, if I have more than I can use fresh I tend to hang them in bunches in the kitchen and let them dry.

Pesto

There's pesto and there's pesto. This recipe is miles away from the bottled travesties that have never seen a pestle and mortar in their life.

Serves 6

leaves from a large bunch of basil
1 garlic clove, crushed
3 tablespoons pine nuts, lightly toasted in a dry frying pan
100–150ml olive oil
80g Parmesan cheese, freshly grated
sea salt and freshly ground black pepper

Put the basil, garlic, pine nuts and a pinch of salt in a pestle and mortar and grind to a paste (or process them in a food processor). Transfer to a bowl and stir in enough olive oil to give the consistency you like. Add the Parmesan cheese and adjust the seasoning.

Chunky Avocado and Tomato Salad with Coriander and Sweet Chilli Dressing

Serves this salad as an accompaniment to chilli con carne or marinated fish, or just on its own.

Serves 6–8 as a side dish

2–3 ripe avocados
500g tomatoes
¼ cucumber
½ red onion or 1 bunch of spring onions, chopped
sea salt and freshly ground black pepper

For the coriander and sweet chilli dressing:
1 garlic clove, crushed
1 tablespoon sweet chilli sauce
1 tablespoon balsamic vinegar
2 tablespoons sunflower oil
2 tablespoons chopped coriander
juice of ½ lemon or lime

Cut the avocados, tomatoes and cucumber into chunky 2cm dice. Mix together in a bowl with the onion and season well.

Mix all the dressing ingredients together and season well. Toss with the vegetables and serve.

Basil Dressing

A vibrant dressing to serve over grilled courgettes, fish or tomatoes.

Serves 4

a handful of basil leaves
olive oil
lemon juice
sea salt and freshly ground black pepper

Crush the basil leaves with a pinch of salt in a pestle and mortar or food processor, gradually adding enough olive oil to give a dressing consistency. Add a little lemon juice and pepper to taste.

Mint Tea

A few winters back, I took a long trip to visit some of our suppliers in Morocco and sample some of their famed surfing spots. There always seemed to be lots of waiting – waiting for tagines, waiting for surf, waiting for children, waiting for buses – and the waiting was invariably accompanied by mint tea. After a while I ceased craving beer or coffee, which tended to be unavailable, warm or nasty. When I got home I was the healthiest I have been for a long time but, even though I bought the inevitable teapot and tray, the mint tea habit has not stuck, probably down to the way I make it. Here is a basic recipe from Norddine, a Moroccan who has worked on the farm for many years.

Serves 4

1 litre water
4 teaspoons green tea
12 teaspoons sugar
a couple of handfuls of mint

Bring the water to the boil, add the green tea and most of the sugar and leave over a very low heat for 5 minutes. A slight froth will probably form on the surface. Remove from the heat, add the mint and leave to stand for up to 5 minutes. Add more sugar to taste and serve. The tea will become bitter with excessive brewing. This can be avoided by removing the mint.

Sorrel and Onion Tart

We serve this as a vegetarian option in the Field Kitchen – so much so that we've had to plant another massive patch of sorrel.

Serves 6–8

1 quantity of Shortcrust Pastry (see page 275)
50g butter
1 large red onion, thinly sliced
150–200g sorrel
3 eggs
250ml crème fraîche
50ml milk
1 tablespoon grated pecorino, Parmesan or Gruyère cheese
sea salt and freshly ground black pepper

Roll out the pastry, use to line a 24cm loose-bottomed tart tin and bake blind as described on page 275.

Melt the butter in a pan, add the onion and cook gently for 15 minutes, until soft. Cut off the stems from the sorrel and slice the leaves roughly. Add them to the onion and cook for about 2 minutes, until they change to a khaki colour and the volume decreases.

Whisk the eggs, crème fraîche and milk together with half the cheese and season well. Stir in the onion and sorrel. Pour the mixture into the prepared pastry case and sprinkle the remaining cheese on top. Place in an oven preheated to 150°C/Gas Mark 2 and bake for 35–40 minutes, until the filling is set and slightly brown on top. Serve warm.

Tarragon and Garlic Stuffing for Chicken

This stuffing is based on Chicken Spago, from the famous Los Angeles restaurant, which used parsley instead of tarragon.

1 head of garlic
1 tablespoon finely chopped tarragon
sea salt and freshly ground black pepper

Separate the garlic cloves, peel them and place in a small pan. Cover with water and simmer for about 40 minutes, topping up with more water if necessary, until the garlic is very soft. Drain the garlic and crush to a paste with the flat of a knife. Mix with the tarragon and season well.

The stuffing should be smeared between the skin and flesh of the breast and leg. A natural pocket can be found by easing the skin away from the flesh. With one hand and a tablespoon of the stuffing, venture under the skin, pushing the stuffing in and being sure not to break the skin. Spread the stuffing over as much of the flesh as possible, then roast the chicken in the usual way.

Parsley Salad

Packed full of wonderful Mediterranean flavours, this is almost a salsa rather than a salad. Perfect with grilled fish or lamb.

Serves 6

leaves from a large bunch of flat-leaf parsley
1 garlic clove, crushed with a pinch of salt
8 anchovies, chopped
1 tablespoon capers, soaked in water for 20 minutes, then drained and
   squeezed dry
8 sun-dried tomatoes, chopped
1 red onion, chopped
1 tablespoon balsamic vinegar
3 tablespoons good olive oil
sea salt and freshly ground black pepper

Put all the ingredients in a bowl and toss together well.

Salsa Verde

This versatile sauce crops up a lot throughout the book. You can customise it to your own taste, adjusting the quantities of anchovies, mustard etc.

Serves 4

1 garlic clove, crushed
1 tablespoon capers, soaked in water for 20 minutes, then drained and
   squeezed dry
2 anchovy fillets
a small bunch of flat-leaf parsley
10 mint leaves
1 teaspoon Dijon mustard
1 tablespoon red wine vinegar
olive oil
sea salt and freshly ground black pepper

Place the garlic, capers, anchovies, parsley and mint in a food processor and blend well (or chop finely by hand). Place the mixture in a bowl and add the mustard and vinegar. Drizzle in enough olive oil to give the correct consistency and season well. The consistency depends on how you intend to use the salsa. It should be quite thick if you are serving it as a sauce for lamb or fish, thinner if it is being used for coating vegetables or as a dressing.

Sorrel Sauce

A quick, simple sauce that can be served with fish or used to fill an omelette.

Serves 4

20g butter
200g sorrel, shredded
1 heaped tablespoon crème fraîche (or double cream)
sea salt and freshly ground black pepper

Melt the butter in a small pan, stir in the sorrel and cook gently until it has just wilted. Stir in the cream, cook for 1 minute, then season to taste. Serve hot.

Rosemary Garlic Butter

This is best used as a topping for hot smoked fish, but will go with any grilled fish or meat. For a subtler effect, use 2 or 3 cloves of roasted or boiled garlic (see pages 179 and 215).

100g softened butter
2 teaspoons very finely chopped rosemary
1 garlic clove, crushed to a paste with a pinch of salt
sea salt and freshly ground black pepper

Mix all the ingredients together, then shape into a log. Wrap in cling film or foil and chill until firm. Cut into slices to serve.

Sage Butter

Melt 2 tablespoons of butter in a shallow pan, add a handful of sage leaves and cook over a medium heat until the sage and butter brown slightly. The sage should be crisp but not burned. Remove from the heat and serve with ravioli or other pasta, or risotto.

Sage and Anchovy Fritters

To make each fritter, sandwich an anchovy fillet between 2 large sage leaves, dip in a light batter (the one for deep-fried courgettes – see Easy ideas on page 145 – works well) and deep-fry until golden brown. Drain on kitchen paper and serve straight away.

See also:
Stir-fried Chicken with Chillies and Basil (page 131)
Grilled Courgette, Tomato and Bean Salad with Basil Dressing (page 139)
Minted Braised Little Gems (page 316)
Toasted Bread Salad with Basil and Tomatoes (page 379)
Soupe au Pistou (page 396)

Jerusalem Artichokes

Jerusalem artichokes are in no way related to globe artichokes. The name Jerusalem is said to be a corruption of *girasole*, Italian for the closely related sunflower. This seems more plausible when they briefly burst into their yellow blooms in late September. The plant originates from North America, where artichokes were cultivated and gathered from the wild by the Native Americans. They arrived in the UK via Holland in 1617. After a period of popularity in the 1980s, they seem to have fallen from favour and are now grown mainly as pheasant cover. We have recently reduced the acreage we grow, but personally I think they are a taste well worth acquiring.

Farmers love to grow Jerusalem artichokes. They suffer no serious diseases or pests and are vigorous enough to out-compete even the most aggressive weeds, growing to a height of 3 metres in five months. Indeed, a more serious issue is getting rid of them when it is time for the field to be returned to grass or another crop. If we could fill our vegetable boxes with Jerusalem artichokes all winter, our lives would be simple. Unfortunately their agronomic simplicity is not reflected in their popularity; this is a vegetable that threatens marriages.

Given the litigious age in which we live, I always issue a warning in the newsletter the first time artichokes go in the boxes in autumn, about their legendary flatulence-inducing properties. Think baked beans and multiply by ten and you might be getting close. My wife will not have them in the house, although my sons always rather enjoy their effects. Some consolation for those with more delicate sensibilities can be drawn from the fact that, unlike the cabbage family, the effect is more thunderous than malodorous. I am advised by a herbalist friend that the disturbance can be reduced by cooking the artichokes with bay leaves, or possibly by eating fennel.

The tubers are planted in March or April in ridges, just like potatoes. They emerge with tremendous vigour and spend all summer growing a huge frame, before bursting into bright-yellow flower and concurrently filling their tubers as they senesce, just before the first frosts in October. Flowering normally coincides with the harvest festival and we often use the blooms to help decorate our parish church. The roots are frost hardy and are best stored in the ground, so we lift them as and when we need them for the boxes through the winter.

Storage and preparation

In early winter, artichokes will keep for several weeks in a vegetable rack in a cool, damp place (the main loss of quality is through dehydration, which is why a damp place is good). As spring approaches, they show a tendency to sprout; this can be delayed by keeping them in the fridge, ideally in a perforated plastic bag. Unlike potatoes, they do not turn green in the light, though they sometimes develop a harmless reddish tinge.

Artichokes are a very minor crop, so no one has done much breeding, but a few years ago we discarded the stock I had multiplied up from my mother's garden and replaced it with the larger, smoother, more regular and, crucially, easier to peel Fuseau variety. Even so, they are painstakingly slow to peel. If you grow them yourself (which I would not really recommend unless you have a large garden, because they tend to dwarf everything and are hell to get rid of), make sure you select large, round seed tubers. Not everyone feels you have to peel them – you can just give them a bit of a soak to loosen the mud and a good scrub.

The easiest way to use artichokes is in soups or roasted, though Jane has developed several more sophisticated uses in the Field Kitchen. They can be good in a gratin, as long as you don't add too much liquid or they can end up watery. The same applies to soup. They benefit from Jane's beloved truffle oil, especially in salad, and also go well with hazelnuts – Jane sometimes toasts these and uses them in the Jerusalem Artichoke Soup on the facing page.

Jerusalem Artichoke Soup

A classic soup with lots of possible variations (see below for a couple of ideas).

Serves 4

1 tablespoon olive oil
1 onion, chopped
500g Jerusalem artichokes, scrubbed and thinly sliced
800ml chicken or vegetable stock
100ml single cream
sea salt and freshly ground black pepper

Heat the oil in a large pan, add the onion and fry gently for 5 minutes. Add the artichokes and stock, bring to the boil and simmer for 20 minutes, until the artichokes are tender. Blend the mixture until smooth, then season to taste and reheat gently. Stir in the cream and serve.

✦ Try this soup with hazelnuts. Add 50g ground toasted hazelnuts when blending the soup.

✦ Or adding polenta croûtons, Parmesan and white truffle oil makes a tasty alternative. Deep-fry cubes of cooked polenta to make croûtons. Replace the cream with 2 tablespoons of freshly grated Parmesan cheese. Serve the soup with the croûtons, an extra sprinkling of Parmesan and a drizzle of white truffle oil.

Jerusalem Artichokes and Mushrooms in a Bag with Goat's Cheese

When in doubt, put it in a bag. These earthy flavours work so well together and look quite rustic when served in their parchment bags. As always with Jerusalem artichokes – and mushrooms – a drizzle of truffle oil would make a fabulous addition.

Serves 4

4 large Jerusalem artichokes, scrubbed and cut into rounds 1cm thick
juice of 1 lemon
4 tablespoons olive oil
1 teaspoon thyme leaves
200g mushrooms, sliced
10g dried porcini mushrooms, soaked in 400ml boiling water for 30 minutes
2 garlic cloves, chopped
75g goat's cheese, crumbled
1 tablespoon chopped chives
sea salt and freshly ground black pepper

Mix the artichokes with half the lemon juice, a tablespoon of olive oil and the thyme leaves, then set aside.

Sauté the fresh mushrooms quickly in 2 tablespoons of the remaining olive oil until they are just tender. Season well and remove from the pan.

Drain the porcini, reserving the soaking water. Chop roughly and cook in the remaining tablespoon of olive oil with the garlic for 2 minutes. Add the reserved soaking liquor and simmer until reduced and quite syrupy. Add the fresh mushrooms and the remaining lemon juice and season to taste.

Spread out a large square of baking parchment. Tip the artichokes over one half of it, sprinkle the mushrooms on top and then fold over the parchment. Seal the 3 open sides by folding them over tightly, or simply use a stapler.

Place the parcel on a baking tray and bake in an oven preheated to 200°C/Gas Mark 6 for about 45 minutes, until the artichokes are tender. Open the bag and sprinkle the contents with the crumbled goat's cheese and the chives.

Jerusalem Artichokes with Leeks, Bacon and Sizzled Sage

This recipe came about at the end of the Jerusalem artichoke season, when we decided to try them with leeks. The bacon and sage came later and the whole combination was a success.

Serves 4

500g Jerusalem artichokes, peeled and thickly sliced
2 leeks, sliced at an angle into 2.5cm lengths
3 streaky bacon rashers, chopped
1 tablespoon lemon juice
4 tablespoons olive oil
a handful of sage leaves, coarsely chopped
sea salt and freshly ground black pepper

Put the artichokes in a pan of boiling salted water and simmer briskly for 15 minutes. Meanwhile, steam the leeks for 3 minutes, until they are just tender and still bright green. Fry the bacon over a moderate to high heat until brown and crisp.

Drain the artichokes, put them in a warmed serving bowl and sprinkle with the lemon juice. Scatter the leeks and bacon over the top and season with salt and plenty of pepper.

Heat the olive oil in a small frying pan until very hot. Add the sage and sizzle for 30 seconds – it will crisp up as it cools. Pour the oil and sage over the vegetables and serve straight away.

Easy ideas for Jerusalem artichokes

✦ Jerusalem artichokes are delicious eaten raw (and you won't explode!). Slice them thinly and toss with a little lemon juice and olive oil. Lovely in a winter salad with chicory or radicchio, Parmesan slivers and white truffle oil.

✦ They are also great roasted: toss the artichokes with a few tablespoons of olive oil, spread them out on a baking tray with a few branches of thyme, some garlic cloves, and some salt and pepper and roast at 200°C/Gas Mark 6 for about half an hour, until tender.

✦ Dip 5mm-thick slices of Jerusalem artichoke in a light batter (try the one for courgettes on page 145), deep-fry them in oil and serve with Salsa Rossa (see page 132).

✦ Substitute Jerusalem artichokes for half the potatoes in the Basic Potato Gratin on page 284.

Kale

Is it cattle food? It all depends on the variety and when and how you pick it. But who cares anyway? The fact that cows like it should not put you off; they can be discerning too. Having said that, if you don't eat it, the cows normally get their chance to munch their way through the last plants in March or April. Of the varieties we grow, curly, red and cavolo nero are all bred for the table but the thousand-head kale, which is normally grown for cattle, can actually be the best, provided we pick only the young, tender shoots that come up in early spring and leave the rest for the cows. We have a few farmers, mainly in Cornwall, who grow this variety for their cows but in a hard winter, when greens are short, will make a tidy sum by picking it over for the broccoli-like spears that appear in spring.

We always get a few complaints from customers outraged that they might be sharing with the bovines but I make no apology for the kales, and much prefer them to the late winter cabbages, which follow the last of the Savoys and are often stalky, tough and tasteless by comparison. Most of the kales are either field sown in late June or planted out in early August. With the exception of cavolo nero, which is good in the autumn, kales are at their best in the late winter as other greens become scarce. The season ends in April, to be replaced by purple sprouting broccoli and spring greens.

Recommendation of any food on the grounds of health is normally enough to convince me that it must be nasty so, as a big fan of kale from a culinary perspective, it is with trepidation that I labour their nutritional benefits here. Don't let this stop you enjoying it, but if kale was not so cheap and mundane in image it would undoubtedly have been heralded as a superfood. It is amongst the richest sources of vitamins A and C and calcium, as well as being high in manganese, iron, copper and the B vitamins. In addition, it is at least as high as broccoli in antioxidants and other phytochemicals that endow the brassica (cabbage) family with its cancer-fighting qualities. It is these same protective compounds that give brassicas their bitterness.

Red Russian kale (October–April, mainly March)

Small, tender, deeply indented (frilly) leaves with a purple tinge. Russian kale is very sweet and succulent, including the leaf ribs and stem, which are seldom tough even as the plant runs to seed. It needs very little cooking and is best steamed as whole leaves. We normally sow this kale late and close together to produce small plants, which are harvested whole for the boxes in February, March and early April. The seeds are sold as an ornamental plant. I have never met anyone else growing it commercially.

Cavolo nero or black kale (October–January)

Very dark green, even blue-black, long, crinkled leaves with a heavy mid rib. Sold as a whole head or as a bundle of leaves, normally in early winter. It is the slowest-growing, least hardy, and hungriest of the kales and needs to be planted early in a good field to produce a reasonable-sized plant. Jane gets really cross if we harvest it before the frost has been on it because this makes it sweeter and more tender.

I cannot help begrudging, in the way that I do most food fashions, cavolo nero's rise in popularity during the 1980s and 1990s. If it had continued under the name of black kale, as I originally bought it from our local seed merchant, I suspect it would have languished in the 'cattle-food' category that has tarred other kales. There is no doubt that much of its popularity can be attributed to Rose Gray and Ruth Rogers at London's wonderful River Café, where Jamie Oliver (and Jane Baxter) honed their skills in the 1990s. It does have a fantastically robust texture and flavour, making it suitable for hearty soups such as the Italian ribollita. It is very similar in flavour and texture to the humbler Savoy cabbage and the two are interchangeable in many recipes. The ribs are tough and best discarded except in the smallest leaves.

Curly kale (September–March)

This has curly leaves on a tough rib. Curly kale is the one that is normally sold in supermarkets, often ready chopped. We grow a small amount but it is the least interesting of the kales and tends to be tough and excessively bitter. It is best boiled briefly, as overcooking turns it to soggy leather.

Red kale (September–March)

A red version of curly kale that is often even more bitter. I am fighting to ban it from the fields of our growers' co-op but somehow some always seems to turn up. It does look nice in the bag mixed with the green but that is about all you can say in its favour.

Thousand-head or hungry-gap kale (March–April)

We pick this over a short season, just before the plant goes to seed. The leaves cluster around a tender shoot, making it surprisingly good to eat and not unlike purple sprouting broccoli. Test the stem (does it snap cleanly?) and, if succulent, prepare and serve as you would broccoli. It is a pain to pick, so it normally gets included in the boxes only in hard winters when we are short of other greens.

Storage and preparation

Life expectancy in the fridge varies according to the variety: 3–4 days for red Russian, a bit longer for curly kale, and nearer a week for thousand-head or cavolo nero, especially if it is on the stalk.

If a stem or leaf rib snaps cleanly, it will not be tough and can be included in your cooking with the leaf, particularly if you slice it thinly. If not, you will need to strip the leaf from its rib. Red Russian and thousand-head (provided only the young shoots have been picked) are normally fine to eat whole; the others usually require separation for all but the smallest leaves. Jane tends to be rather more pedantic than I am when it comes to preparation, and perhaps this is only right, as her guests are paying.

In terms of robustness of flavour and texture, the ranking of kale goes: cavolo nero, curly, red, thousand-head and red Russian, with the latter needing least cooking (and suffering most from over-cooking). For a quick vegetable accompaniment, steam red Russian for just a few minutes. For soups, stews and sauces needing something more robust, go for cavolo nero. Jane's time at the River Café established her as a cavolo nero fan, but I am glad to say that she has been won over by red Russian, though it does need to be eaten fresh.

Black Rice with Black Kale and Truffle Oil

Jane found Italian black rice in the Riverford Farm Shop, run by Ben Watson. Its nutty, earthy flavour and baked-bread aroma are amazing. We've only tried it with cavolo nero so far but it's a wonderful combination. If you can't get black rice, you could use wild rice instead.

Serves 6

1 tablespoon butter
3 tablespoons olive oil
1 onion, chopped
300g venere nero (black rice)
400g can of chopped tomatoes
2 garlic cloves, crushed
1 litre vegetable or chicken stock
500g cavolo nero
3 garlic cloves, thinly sliced
2 tablespoons freshly grated Parmesan cheese
a drizzle of truffle oil
sea salt and freshly ground black pepper

Heat the butter in a large pan with 2 tablespoons of the olive oil. Add the onion and cook gently for about 10 minutes, until soft. Stir in the black rice, season well and cook for 3 minutes. Add the tomatoes and garlic and cook over a low heat for 5 minutes. Meanwhile, heat up the stock in a separate pan. Add it to the rice and simmer for 30 minutes, until the rice is just tender and the stock has been absorbed.

While the rice is cooking, strip the cavolo nero leaves from their central ribs and blanch them in a large pan of boiling salted water for 3 minutes. Drain, refresh in cold water, then drain again. Squeeze out excess water and chop the leaves roughly.

Heat the rest of the olive oil in a pan, add the garlic and cook for about 3 minutes. Add the chopped cavolo, cover and braise slowly for 5 minutes. Season to taste.

When the rice is just cooked, mix in the cavolo nero and Parmesan. Drizzle with truffle oil and serve.

Kale, Chorizo and Potato Hash

You can substitute any cabbage for kale here, or even sliced Brussels sprouts. To make a complete supper dish, top with a poached egg.

Serves 4

300g kale
1 tablespoon olive oil
300g chorizo sausage, chopped
1 onion, chopped
2 garlic cloves, crushed
500g cooked potatoes, cut into 2cm dice
sea salt and freshly ground black pepper

Strip the kale leaves from their central ribs and blanch them in a large pan of boiling salted water for 1 minute. Drain well, refresh in cold water and drain again. Squeeze out excess water and chop roughly.

Heat the oil in a large frying pan, add the chorizo and cook over a medium heat for 10 minutes, until just starting to brown. Remove the chorizo with a slotted spoon and set aside. Add the onion and garlic to the chorizo fat in the pan and cook gently for 5 minutes. Add the diced potatoes, turn up the heat to get some colour in them and cook for 5 minutes, turning the potatoes until browned all over. Return the chorizo to the pan with the kale and cook slowly for another 10 minutes, until well mixed and thoroughly heated through. Season and serve.

Cavolo Nero and Potato Soup with Red Chilli

We served this soup at the Exeter Food Festival. It took on a khaki colour, so we changed the name to 'swamp soup', but the public still came back for more.

Serves 6

about 400g cavolo nero or other kale
3 tablespoons virgin olive oil
1 onion, diced
6 garlic cloves, sliced
1 small dried red chilli, chopped
1 bay leaf
1 teaspoon salt
4 medium potatoes, peeled and diced
1 litre water or stock
freshly ground black pepper
soured cream, to serve

Strip the kale leaves from their central ribs. Cut the leaves into roughly 5cm pieces and wash well.

Heat the oil in a large pan, add the onion, garlic, chilli, bay leaf and salt and cook gently for 3–4 minutes. Add the diced potatoes and a cup of the water or stock and cook for 5 minutes. Add the kale, pour in the remaining water or stock and simmer for about 30 minutes, until the potatoes are soft.

Purée a cup or two of the soup in a blender and then return it to the pot. Season with black pepper and serve with a dollop of soured cream.

Easy ideas for kale

✦ To braise kale or cavolo nero, blanch it in a large pan of boiling salted water for 1 minute for kale, 3 minutes for cavolo nero, then drain, refresh in cold water and squeeze out excess liquid. Fry 1–3 very thinly sliced garlic cloves in olive oil. Just before the garlic is about to turn brown, add the kale, turn the heat down and mix together. Season well and serve.

✦ Braise some kale as described above, then blitz it with cream, Parmesan and dried chilli to make a quick sauce for farfalle or penne.

✦ Braise some kale as described above, then stir in cooked white beans or Puy lentils, heat through and drizzle with good olive oil.

✦ Finely chop braised kale, then stir it into wet polenta with butter and Parmesan. Good served with stews as an alternative to mash.

✦ Substitute kale for Brussels sprouts in Bubble and Squeak Soup (see page 66).

✦ Use kale to make the classic Irish dish, colcannon (see Perfect Mash variations, page 288).

Kohlrabi

The engorged stems of kohlrabi make it one of the weirder-looking vegetables that we grow. They tend to be thought of as root vegetables but in botanical or morphological terms they are the swollen stem base of a cabbage. In the field they resemble tennis-ball-sized characters from the Teletubbies or the Mr Men. In the kitchen they are somewhere between a large radish, a French-style summer turnip and a broccoli stem, with a mild flavour. For us their great virtue is speed from seed to harvest, making them one of the first crops to be harvested in the spring. We sow them under glass in February, plant them out in early April under crop covers to protect them from the worst of the weather, and expect to be harvesting by late May, when we are desperate for home-grown produce for the boxes. Like most sprinters, they are highly strung and need everything to be right; in particular they need lots of water in the field and to grow fast and unchecked if they are to retain their succulence. White Vienna (pale green) is the best and most reliable variety, being fast growing and succulent most years. Purple Vienna usually looks wonderful but is a week later to harvest and has a greater tendency to become tough.

Though they undoubtedly have their place in May and June, opinion is divided as to whether the culinary virtues of kohlrabi warrant cultivation later in the season. In the wet summer of 2007 they kept their succulence through to a good size, and customers who had previously shown some resistance were intrigued by their culinary possibilities and, for the most part, converted.

Storage and preparation

Kohlrabi keeps fairly well but, like most vegetables, will last longer when stored in the fridge. If it is supplied with the leaves attached, these should be removed to avoid drawing moisture from the root (like beetroot and carrots).

To prepare, cut off any remaining root and trim the base, which is normally the toughest part and will sometimes show signs of cabbage root fly damage. Very small, young kohlrabi should not need peeling but as they age, the skin can become tough and is best peeled away. Kohlrabi can be grated or very thinly sliced and eaten raw in a salad, perhaps with carrots – think mild turnip when planning the flavour. We once had a German working at the farm who ate them like apples. They can also be stir-fried, steamed or boiled. The leaves are fairly sparse but are often very tender and can be cooked separately as a green.

Kohlrabi, Apple and Walnut Salad

This recipe is based on one from the book *Cool Green Leaves and Red Hot Peppers* by Michel Michaud and Christine McFadden (Frances Lincoln, 1998).

Serves 6

3 kohlrabi, peeled and cut into small segments
2 crisp, red-skinned apples, cored and diced
2 Little Gem lettuces, shredded
a little lemon juice
a handful of watercress (optional)
75g walnuts, lightly toasted and then broken into pieces

For the walnut dressing:
1 tablespoon lemon juice
½ teaspoon sugar
½ teaspoon Dijon mustard
2 tablespoons light olive oil
2 tablespoons walnut oil
a pinch each of celery salt, salt and pepper

Combine the kohlrabi, apples and Little Gem lettuces in a serving bowl and sprinkle with lemon juice to prevent browning. Add the watercress, if using, and the toasted walnuts.

Whisk together all the ingredients for the dressing. Pour the dressing over the salad and toss well.

Kohlrabi and Peanut Stir-fry

Kohlrabi is a worthwhile vegetable but needs a lot of help. The Asian seasonings give it a real boost.

Serves 4

250g thread egg noodles
2 tablespoons sunflower oil
2 garlic cloves, crushed
2cm piece of fresh ginger, grated
1 carrot, peeled and cut into thin sticks
1 kohlrabi, peeled and cut into thin sticks
1 fresh chilli, chopped (optional)
1 bunch of spring onions, sliced
150g sugarsnap peas or French beans
3 tablespoons hoisin sauce
2 tablespoons soy sauce
2 tablespoons water
1 teaspoon peanut butter
2 tablespoons peanuts, toasted and crushed

Cook the noodles according to the instructions on the packet.

Meanwhile, heat the oil in a wok, add the garlic, ginger, carrot, kohlrabi and chilli, if using, and stir-fry for 4 minutes. Add the noodles with the spring onions and the sugarsnaps or French beans and cook for a further 2 minutes. Stir in the rest of the ingredients, heat through and serve.

Easy ideas for kohlrabi

✦ Peel some kohlrabi, cut it into batons and cook in a little butter until soft. Stir in chopped parsley or dill, then season with lemon juice, salt and pepper.

✦ Substitute kohlrabi for cabbage in Asian Coleslaw (see page 79).

✦ Substitute kohlrabi for turnips in Braised Carrots and Turnips (see page 92).

✦ Use kohlrabi like celeriac in a rémoulade (see page 118).

Where did all the growers go?

A trip around the formerly thriving traditional horticultural areas of the UK reveals a depressing picture of dilapidated glass houses, machinery gently rusting under brambles and horticulture disappearing under wheat, as the skills and associated culture of a once-proud industry, built up over generations, are lost for ever. Be it the Vale of Evesham, the Isle of Thanet, the mosses of Lancashire, the Tamar Valley or the orchards of Kent, the story is one of an industry on its knees, drawing its last gasps before quietly slipping beneath the sod.

Until 30 years ago, these areas supplied the neighbouring conurbations with most of their seasonal fruit and vegetables, initially through thriving wholesale markets and then increasingly through supermarkets, which were at that time happy to buy locally. The last generation of growers has seen supermarkets become increasingly dominant and progressively impose trading terms that can be met only by the largest companies. The smaller regional growers have quietly gone to the wall, to be replaced by agribusinesses employing gang labour in vast factories, often under highly questionable working conditions. Continuity and consistency are achieved with the help of aircraft streaming into Heathrow and fleets of trucks from southern Europe, so that shoppers are never troubled by the seasons or the vagaries of the weather.

Change happens and, one might argue, why should horticulture be any different from the coal, steel or shipbuilding industries? The difference is that this change is unnecessary, wasteful and, in a world threatened by climate change and oil depletion, unsustainable. It is not the result of market forces but of oligopoly. Supermarket supply chains, with their technology, protocols and audits, are fantastically efficient at the centralised distribution of uniform, continuously available products from large suppliers who obediently follow their rules. They struggle badly with the human interactions typical of smaller-scale, local businesses. Many supermarket customers want local food and would like to feel some connection with where it is produced, but somehow the sterile aisles have swept us along with the ridiculous pretence that vegetables can be produced with the uniform, hygienic perfection to match the plastic trays and shelves they sit on. Supermarkets, with their over-packaged, anonymously own-brand, travel-weary offerings, are only now, reluctantly and very belatedly, responding to public pressure. As the family businesses that constitute local horticulture quietly disappear, the supermarkets that have presided over their demise are announcing their desire to buy locally. Well, they are too late. The farms, skills and infrastructure that go with local production have gone, leaving only pony paddocks and wheat fields. After three decades of being kicked, screwed and twisted, it will take more than the Tesco policy initiative to get growers to pick up their hoes again.

Leeks

Leeks were the first crop I grew on a substantial scale and to this day they remain an important staple for us, keeping the boxes full and our staff busy throughout the winter. They tested my back and my organic resolve during my early days as a grower and, what with the escapee that always seemed to be decaying under the car seat, plus the pervasive odour on my clothes, they kept me celibate through my first winter. Only pig farmers smell worse. Jane Grigson credits this sulphurous stench with leeks' fall from popularity, which, according to her, lasted three centuries. After I had been planting and weeding all summer, the early winter of 1987–8 was horrendously wet; the field descended into a quagmire and the crop succumbed to the fungal disease rust. As I watched the previously vigorous foliage melt into a slime of decay, the advisers and chemical salesmen were whispering, serpent-like, in my uncertain ears that all my woes could be solved with a few potent kilos of fungicide.

Somehow I maintained my resolve and a sudden drop in temperature proved more powerful than any fungicide, halting the disease while the leeks carried on growing. By February the plants had replaced the infected leaves with new ones and I had learnt that rust is a disease of warm, damp Devon autumns and that I should not listen to chemical salesmen. By April, with an aching back and incipient rheumatism in my fingers, there was £6,000 in the bank and Riverford Organic Vegetables was on its way.

It is possible to be pulling leeks by late July but the erect, quick-growing early varieties tend to be soft and pale and can be disappointing at a time when there are plenty of other vegetables around. The slower-growing, stouter, shorter, firmer, more frost-hardy varieties are typical of December onwards. We normally start picking in September and harvest increasing volumes through the winter as the supply of other vegetables declines. By March, with the first hint of spring, the leeks are getting lusty; if you dissect one lengthways you may find, thrusting up through the leaves, the start of the 'bolt' that would eventually carry the starburst flower characteristic of the allium family (onions, garlic, chives). Initially this bolt is tender and perfectly edible but as it lengthens and pushes up through the leaves it rapidly becomes tough and unpleasant to eat. By early May the UK season is over and you should be wary of buying leeks without closely examining the centres for hard yellow stalks (bolts), until the new crop is ready.

Harvesting leeks by hand through the winter is a cold and back-breaking job. There are some very clever machines that will lift and rough trim the leeks but they soon get bogged down when the weather turns wet. If you buy leeks in mid winter, the chances are that some hardy soul or far-flung desperado has pulled them up by hand in a windswept field.

Storage and preparation

Leeks should last for at least a week in the bottom of your fridge without significant deterioration. The leaves are perfectly designed to trap soil particles resulting from rain splash or careless hoeing. Unless you specifically want rings, or want to cook the leeks whole, the best way of washing a leek is to split it lengthwise in half, pushing a knife in just above the base and working up so the two halves remain attached at the base but are then easy to wash under a running tap. If you want rings, wash the outside of the leek, slice and then leave the rings to soak in water, giving them an occasional slosh before scooping out with a colander.

We are often asked about the virtues of the green and white parts of leeks. The green parts are less tender but more nutritive and are especially good in stocks and stews. It is a bit extravagant to trim off all the green top, as the white part goes up further inside, and by a judiciously layered attack you can use a lot more.

Leek and Potato Soup with Chicken, Bacon and Sage

This is a different take on leek and potato soup – according to Jane, a sort of 'soupy roast dinner'. It's a good way of using up leftover cooked chicken. Alternatively, you could poach 4–6 chicken thighs in vegetable stock and then use the liquid to make the soup. Take the cooked chicken meat off the bone and stir it in at the end.

Serves 6

50g butter
1 onion, chopped
75g smoked streaky bacon, chopped
1 tablespoon chopped sage or 1 teaspoon dried sage
450g leeks, finely sliced
450g potatoes, peeled and sliced
about 1 litre chicken stock
200–300g shredded cooked chicken
a little cream (optional)
sea salt and freshly ground black pepper

Melt the butter in a large pan, add the onion, bacon and sage, then cover and sweat for about 10 minutes. Add the leeks and potatoes and stir well. Add enough chicken stock to cover the vegetables, bring to the boil and simmer for about 30 minutes, until the vegetables are tender.

Take a few cups of the soup and purée them in a food processor, then stir back into the rest of the soup and mix well. This should bring the soup together.

Stir in the cooked chicken, reheat thoroughly and season to taste. Add a dash of cream, if you like, and serve.

Leek and Roquefort Pizza Bread

Jane was absolutely blown away by this when she came across it at Harvest, a restaurant in Coolum, Queensland. A pizza stone gives the best result. It's important to roll the dough as thinly as possible to get a good, crisp base.

Serves 4

40ml olive oil
1 garlic clove, peeled
1 bird's eye chilli, halved
25g butter
2 small leeks, halved lengthwise and then thinly sliced across
30g Parmesan cheese, freshly grated
100g mozzarella cheese, grated
1½ tablespoons finely chopped oregano
1½ tablespoons finely chopped flat-leaf parsley
60g Roquefort or other blue cheese, crumbled
sea salt and freshly ground black pepper

For the dough:
300g strong white flour
7g sachet of dried yeast
1 teaspoon salt
180ml lukewarm water
1½ tablespoons olive oil

Put the olive oil, garlic and chilli in a small bowl and set aside to infuse the oil. To make the dough, combine the flour, yeast and salt in a bowl, then stir in the water and oil. Turn out on to a lightly floured surface and knead for 5–8 minutes, until smooth and elastic. Place in a lightly oiled bowl, cover with cling film and set aside in a warm place for 1 hour or until doubled in size.

Meanwhile, heat the butter in a small frying pan, add the leeks and cook over a low to medium heat for about 10 minutes, until soft but not coloured. Season with salt and pepper. Remove from the heat and leave to cool.

Place 2 heavy-based baking sheets or terracotta tiles in the oven and preheat the oven to 250°C/Gas Mark 10. Combine the Parmesan, mozzarella and herbs in a small bowl.

Cut 4 sheets of baking parchment, each large enough to hold a 22cm pizza. Divide the risen dough into 4. Dust the pieces of baking parchment with a little flour and roll out each piece of dough on the parchment, making a round about 22cm in diameter. Brush with the flavoured oil and scatter with the cheese mixture, followed by the leeks, then the Roquefort. Slide one pizza, still on the paper, onto each hot baking sheet or tile and bake for 8–10 minutes, until golden. Serve immediately. Cook the remaining pizzas in the same way.

Braised Leeks with Shallot and Caper Vinaigrette

A simple, light alternative to the usual buttery leek dishes. Serve as a starter, sprinkling grated hardboiled eggs over the leeks, if you like, to finish them off.

Serves 2

4 small–medium leeks
1½ teaspoons sherry vinegar or white wine vinegar
1 tablespoon chopped shallot
½ teaspoon Dijon mustard
2 tablespoons extra virgin olive oil
1 teaspoon capers, soaked in cold water for 20 minutes, then squeezed dry and finely chopped
1 tablespoon chopped parsley
sea salt and freshly ground black pepper

Top and tail the leeks, then cut them in half lengthways and rinse well. Place the leek halves, cut-side down, in a large frying pan and add enough water to come halfway up the sides of the leeks. Bring to the boil and simmer for 5 minutes, until just cooked.

To make the vinaigrette, whisk together the vinegar, shallot, mustard, olive oil and some salt and pepper. Whisk in the capers and parsley.

Move the leeks from the pan on to paper towels and gently squeeze them dry. Place in a serving dish and spoon the vinaigrette on top.

Mussels, Leeks and Bacon on Toast

The inspiration for this came from a dish at the Hardwick Arms, just outside Abergavenny. The owner, Stephen Terry, has created the ultimate gastropub and this dish typifies his approach – full-on flavours and a complete lack of pretension.

Serves 4

500g mussels
1 tablespoon olive oil
25g butter
4 leeks, thinly sliced
100g bacon lardons, or chopped smoked streaky bacon or pancetta
100ml white wine
4 pieces of sourdough or ciabatta bread
2 garlic cloves, peeled
1 tablespoon chopped parsley

Scrub the mussels under cold running water, pulling off the 'beards' and discarding any open mussels that don't close when tapped lightly on the work surface.

Heat the oil and butter in a pan, add the leeks and bacon and cook for about 15 minutes, until the leeks are soft and flavoured with the bacon. Meanwhile, heat the white wine in a separate pan, add the mussels, then cover and cook over a medium-high heat for 3–4 minutes, until the mussels open (discard any that remain closed). Remove from the heat and strain the liquid through a fine sieve into a small pan. Simmer until reduced by half its volume.

Remove the mussels from their shells and stir them into the leek and bacon mixture. Toast the bread, rub with the garlic and divide the mussel mixture between each piece. Drizzle with the reduced mussel cooking liquor, sprinkle with the parsley and serve.

Easy ideas for leeks

✦ Sweat finely sliced leeks in butter for 5 minutes, until softened. Pour in a glass of red wine and simmer until reduced. Season and serve as an accompaniment to grilled fish or roast meat.

✦ Blanch 4 whole trimmed leeks (cut in half lengthways if large) in boiling salted water for 2 minutes, then drain and refresh in cold water. Drain well, brush lightly with oil and sear on a hot griddle pan. In a wide pan, gently heat the juice of 2 lemons, 1 tablespoon of sugar and 100ml water. As the leeks come off the grill, place in the warm marinade. Leave for 5 minutes, then sprinkle with chopped coriander or parsley and serve.

✦ Blanch and grill leeks as described above, then serve with Pine Nut Salsa (see page 191) instead of the marinade.

✦ Cook sliced leeks in butter or oil for 10 minutes, then add to Braised Artichokes (see page 187) instead of broad beans, substituting parsley for the mint.

✦ Make the shortcrust pastry on page 275, roll out into a rough circle and cover with leeks that have been sweated in butter with a few sprigs of thyme. Roughly crumble some goat's cheese over the top and bake at 200°C/Gas Mark 6 for 15–20 minutes, until the cheese and pastry are lightly browned.

✦ Make a leek, pancetta and potato gratin (see Basic Potato Gratin variations, page 284–285).

See also:
Warm Salad of Romanesco, Grilled Leeks and Haricots (page 55)
Salad of French Beans and Grilled Leeks with Tapenade Dressing (page 170)
Jerusalem Artichokes with Leeks, Bacon and Sizzled Sage (page 224)

Onions and Shallots

There can be few smells less appetising than the rank, sulphurous odour of a rotten onion. If you are one of our veg box customers, you will surely have encountered one at the sink and probably cursed us for supplying it. Imagine, then, the farmer, after a summer of planting, weeding, harvesting and drying, who is faced with a barn full of unsaleable, festering bulbs as they develop the telltale rings of neck rot.

Growing onions in the damp southwest without the benefit of fungicides is difficult in the best of years, but in a wet season has cost us more customers and led to more bad blood within our co-op than any other crop. The challenge is keeping mildew at bay and the leaves alive until the crop has matured and formed the natural seal around the neck of the onion that will prevent the entry of disease and allow the bulb to store through the winter. For every five years, we would expect, say, three good crops, one disaster and a year when we will risk annoying our customers with dodgy onions while trying to sell enough to save the farm from economic disaster. After 12 years, not surprisingly, the co-op has rebelled, and we are the only ones left growing the crop. On economic grounds, we should have given up long ago but it seems a travesty not to be producing such a major crop ourselves.

We grow an over-wintered crop, sown in August, which produces an early crop for harvesting as bunched green onions with their tops on from May or as dry onions in July. In August we start harvesting the main-crop, spring-planted onions, most of which would have traditionally been dried and stored for use throughout the autumn and winter. Given the frustrations of our customers and growers, we now plan to finish our own onions in November before moving to Donald Morton, a grower in Norfolk who, with a drier climate, is usually able to take us through to January. We are then reliant on Dutch onions until April, sometimes bridging the gap with a few other imports before our own crop starts in May. The global trade in alliums may sound like an abomination to proponents of local food but experience has taught us that, faced with the alternative of peeling and trimming a smelly onion at the sink, even the most hardcore advocates tend to lose their commitment to reducing food miles. We have not done the calculation but I have a strong suspicion that the high energy costs associated with growing, drying and storing onions in marginal climates may well be even greater than those associated with transport anyway.

Shallots

I made a brief foray into growing shallots 15 years ago but rapidly gave up when, after all my efforts, some customers suggested that we were just palming them off with undersized onions. Perhaps our customers are more sophisticated now and it is time for another attempt. However, we have a close relationship with a group of growers a short ferry trip away in Brittany, who do such a good job that I am in no hurry. Though related to onions, shallots are a different species and require considerably more effort to grow and dry. The reward – and the justification for the much higher price tag – is a milder, sweeter flavour, making them suitable for use raw in salads or as a flavouring for vinegars and dressings, as well as in dishes where a less astringent flavour is required. Slow-cooked whole in stews or roasted in their skins, they lend a wonderful sweetness to dishes.

There are two main types of shallot. The Dutch grow both but are better know for the round, onion-shaped shallots that are grown from seed and can indeed taste quite similar to onions. The elongated French-style shallots, which normally have copper-brown skins but can be pink or yellow underneath, are milder, sweeter and generally held to be superior. Until recently they were grown exclusively by planting multiplier sets, which by the end of the season have divided, typically into six or eight shallots, for harvesting and drying. This time-consuming process is being banished to history by the, as ever, fiendishly clever Dutch, who have developed varieties of lookalike shallots that can be grown from seed. I have yet to form an opinion as to whether they taste as good but needless to say the shallot growers of Brittany are unanimous in condemning them as inferior.

Spring onions

Spring onions, salad onions, scallions or green onions are simply immature onions harvested while the leaves are still green and vigorous. They have a milder flavour than mature bulb onions and the whole plant can be eaten, leaves and all. There are specialist salad onion varieties, such as the traditional favourite, White Lisbon, which have been selected specifically to grow at high density to produce slender shanks rather than bulbs. Some would argue that these varieties are sweeter than immature plants from varieties normally grown for seed but I am sceptical. The problem with the pencil-thin onions from a farmer's perspective is that if the outer leaves have any blemish, as they normally do when not pumped up with nitrogen and protected by a barrage of pesticides, the grower is faced with a phenomenal amount of work peeling away these leaves to make them presentable. No surprise, then, that we tend to grow larger, bulbed salad onions. I take support for my belligerent rejection of the Marks & Spencer-style neat and tidy, trimmed and packed little salad onion from the prevalence of bunches of fat, golf-ball-sized green onions in markets throughout France, Spain and Italy. The green tops of these onions can be chopped finely as a substitute for chives or, if they are starting to look tatty, make a good allium basis for stocks, replacing leeks or bulb onions.

Storage and preparation

Onions should be firm and free from any sign of sprouting. To store well, the neck of the onion, where the leaves were attached, should be tight, firm and well sealed. Onions like to be cool and dry, preferably with a bit of air movement. The only exception is the fresh onions that we harvest direct from the field, complete with their tops, and put in the boxes during May and June. These will not store and should be kept in the fridge, as you would a spring onion. The tops are edible while green. Use chopped, like spring onions, in stir-fries.

If well dried and disease free, shallots should keep for up to six months in a dry, airy spot. Like onions, they keep best hung up in traditional strings.

Red Onion Salad with Beetroot, Lentils, Feta and Mint

This is delicious served in a mezze with Crushed Roast Carrots with Cumin and Goat's Cheese (see page 95) and some hummus. The flavour of the raw onions is tempered by soaking them in sugar and vinegar.

Serves 6

500g beetroot
2 red onions, thinly sliced
2 tablespoons light soft brown sugar
2 tablespoons good-quality red wine vinegar
3 tablespoons cooked Puy lentils
50g feta cheese, crumbled
1 tablespoon chopped mint
sea salt and freshly ground black pepper

Roast the beetroot according to the method in Warm Beetroot Salad with Orange, Bacon and Caraway (see page 26). When they are cool enough to handle, peel them and cut into wedges.

Mix the sliced red onions with the sugar and vinegar and set aside for 1 hour, stirring occasionally. Season with salt and pepper and mix with all the other ingredients, including the beetroot. If the beetroot has just been cooked and the lentils are still slightly warm, the resulting salad will be superior.

Pissaladière

The Provençal equivalent of pizza, made with onion and anchovies. Sliced tomatoes, brushed with a little oil, could be added with the anchovies, if you like. Serve as a starter or a light lunch.

Serves 6

2 tablespoons olive oil
4 large onions, finely sliced
1 quantity of Shortcrust Pastry (see page 275)
6 anchovy fillets, cut in half lengthways
10 black olives, stoned
sea salt and freshly ground black pepper

Heat the olive oil in a large pan, add the onions, then cover and cook gently for about 45 minutes, until soft. Season to taste.

Roll out the pastry on a lightly floured work surface into a rough 25cm square. Place on a baking sheet, prick with a fork and chill for 10 minutes.

Spread the onions thickly over the pastry base. Crisscross with the anchovies (or you can write your name in them, if you like) and dot with the olives. Place in an oven preheated to 200°C/Gas Mark 6 and bake for 20 minutes.

Sausages with Onion Gravy

We all love gravy and we never get enough. This recipe includes generous amounts to satisfy even the most diehard gravy fanatic. Add the mustard, Worcestershire sauce and soy sauce to suit your taste – Jane likes hers pretty strong.

Serves 4

25g butter
1 tablespoon olive oil
8 good-quality pork sausages
4 large onions (use half red onions, if possible), thinly sliced
1 dessertspoon sugar
1 dessertspoon plain flour
400ml chicken or beef stock (if you are cooking swede as well, the cooking liquid makes good gravy)
100ml red wine (or beer)
about 1 tablespoon each of mustard, Worcestershire sauce and soy sauce
sea salt and freshly ground black pepper

Heat the butter and oil in a large, heavy-based pan, add the sausages and cook until browned all over. Remove from the pan and set aside.

Add the onions to the pan, then cover and cook over a low heat for about 45 minutes, until they are completely soft, stirring occasionally to prevent sticking. Stir in the sugar and turn up the heat to caramelise the onions slightly. Add the flour and mix well, then turn down the heat and gradually stir in the stock and wine. Bring to a slow simmer and return the sausages to the pan. Cook for about 20 minutes, to reduce and concentrate the flavour. Stir in the mustard, Worcestershire sauce and soy sauce to taste and season well. Serve with lots of mashed potato (see page 288).

Caramelised Shallots

The boxes tend to include just a small amount of shallots and this is an ideal way of cooking them. It makes a delicious accompaniment to steak and roast vegetables.

Serves 2

1 tablespoon butter
200g shallots, peeled
2 sprigs of rosemary
1 teaspoon sugar
175ml red wine
1 teaspoon balsamic vinegar

Heat the butter in a heavy-based pan, add the shallots and toss over a high heat until they are starting to brown. Add the rosemary and cook until the shallots start to caramelise. Add the sugar and stir until dissolved, then pour in the wine and vinegar. Cover and simmer for about 20 minutes, until the shallots are tender. Uncover the pan, raise the heat and cook until the liquid has reduced enough to coat the shallots in a shiny, syrupy glaze.

Twice-cooked Belly Pork with Spring Onions and Ginger

This is a wonderful way of cooking a cheap cut of meat, resulting in succulent, tender flesh packed with flavour. Lovely with boiled rice and steamed greens, such as French beans, pak choi, broccoli or chard.

Serves 4

1kg belly pork, cut into slices 2cm thick
1 bunch of spring onions, chopped (reserve the green tops)
2cm piece of fresh ginger, chopped (reserve the trimmings)
1 tablespoon sunflower oil
1 garlic clove, chopped
2 tablespoons oyster sauce
1 tablespoon soy sauce
1 tablespoon coriander (optional)

Put the pork belly in a pan and add enough water just to cover, plus the green ends from the spring onions and the trimmings from the ginger. Bring to the boil, then reduce the heat, cover and simmer very gently for 1 hour or until the pork is tender (this can be done well ahead of time). Remove the pork from the pan, reserving the cooking liquor, and allow to cool. Slice the pork thinly widthways.

When you are ready to serve, heat the oil in a large frying pan until very hot, add the pork pieces and cook for about 10 minutes over a high heat, stirring constantly, until browned all over. The pork will disintegrate slightly and start to stick, but keep stirring and scraping the pan with a wooden spoon. When the pork is slightly shredded, brown and crisp, add the chopped garlic and ginger and stir for 1 minute. Add the oyster sauce, soy sauce and spring onions and mix well, adding a little of the reserved cooking liquor for a moister result. Stir in the coriander, if using, and serve.

Easy ideas for onions and shallots

✦ If using red onion in a salad, slice it thinly and mix with a couple of teaspoons of brown sugar and a splash of vinegar. Leave for an hour or so, then drain (the sugar and vinegar can be included in the dressing). This takes away the astringency of the onion.

✦ To roast onions, peel back the outer layers of skin and then cut a cross right down to the root. Stuff with some sprigs of thyme and a peeled garlic clove, sprinkle with olive oil and balsamic vinegar, then place in a dish and cover with foil. Roast at 200°C/Gas Mark 6 for about 45 minutes, until tender.

✦ Joyce Molyneux's lemon onion sauce – in a tightly covered pan, cook 450g chopped onions in 25g butter and a dash of olive oil with the pared zest of 1 lemon for 30 minutes. Purée with the juice of the lemon and season. Joyce used to serve this with brains but it is lovely with grilled fish, too.

✦ Spring-onion mayonnaise is easily made by blending crushed garlic, finely chopped spring onions and a little green chilli with mayonnaise. It was originally served in the Deep South of the United States in oyster po' boys – a sandwich made with deep-fried oysters, crisp lettuce and the mayo, all stuffed into a baguette.

✦ Use spring onions to make the classic Irish dish, champ (see Perfect Mash variations, page 288–289).

See also:
Sorrel and Onion Tart (page 212)
Braised Leeks with Shallot and Caper Vinaigrette (page 248)
Duck with Little Gem, Spring Onions and Peas (page 317)

Has cooking become a spectator activity?

Two decades of celebrity chefs, countless hours of primetime TV cookery, endless pages of glossy food porn, combined with government campaigns for us to eat five-a-day, have done little to avert the decline in activity in the huge majority of kitchens. We may be conversant in the language of a multicultural twenty-first-century foodie but many of us are at a loss as what to do with a Savoy cabbage or a piece of brisket. How can it be that, as a nation so interested in food, over 50 years the percentage of household income devoted to it has slipped from 33 per cent to 15 per cent, and is still falling?

We have all the symptoms of a collective national eating disorder, with an astonishing ability to disconnect perception and professed beliefs about food from reality and actual behaviour. Despite the best efforts of Jamie, Hugh, Gordon, Nigella et al, there is less cooking than ever going on. Moreover, what unprocessed ingredients there are in our kitchens are even less seasonal in nature than they were ten years ago. When we started the box scheme in 1993, before the current media frenzy around local and seasonal, our typical customer ordered a weekly box of seasonal vegetables and cooked them with little fuss, probably much as their parents had, perhaps with the addition of the occasional curry or stir-fry. It was a matter of course, a part of normal life. Fifteen years later, when all the column inches would suggest that such behaviour was at the epicentre of a national movement, the number of people willing and able to cook with the seasons and accept the limitations that they bring, has, if anything, declined. Our longstanding core customers carry on cooking but, of the customers who have joined us over the last two years, particularly in wealthier areas, there is limited appetite for what we really like to grow and sell: seasonal, home-grown veg. They will buy the fruit and the tomatoes, the broccoli and the peppers but many reject the boxes that include even moderate amounts of core seasonal roots and greens, which demand more traditional cooking skills.

Why do we have this mismatch of aspiration and behaviour? Memories of appalling school dinners don't help when it comes to vegetables such as cabbages and swede, and a dogmatic adherence to 'local' can be hard work in April and May, but I am convinced that a lack of skills, time and confidence in the kitchen is the main issue. Indeed, I suspect that some of the media attention may have actually sapped confidence in this area, and made cooking seem unattainably distant. Food fashions, as portrayed in the media and on restaurant menus, are skin deep, they come and go like the cut of a pair of jeans, yet everywhere in the world people are very conservative about food. For generations, we learned from our parents how to make the best use of local ingredients; changes in real-life home cooking have been slow and incremental, which is why it is such an important part of our culture. Unfortunately all the change in the last 40 years or so has been in the wrong direction – helped along by the advertising budgets of food manufacturers and supermarkets, beamed out from the same televisions that have ensured we 'don't have time to cook'. We are now raising a generation whose parents will rarely be seen cooking and even more rarely with local ingredients. Cookery programmes are a poor substitute for assimilating skills over years of growing up in an active kitchen. It has taken two generations to decline to the shameful national culinary trough that we now wallow in. Though there is undeniably a counter–current emerging, it is a small eddy or turbulence in the general flow, which is still one of decline. Though our celebrity chefs and food writers must take some credit for this change, the battle is far from won and there is a real danger that, as the gap widens between what is on television and the reality in our kitchens, cooking will become a spectator activity. The nation will slump back with a takeaway and watch it on TV instead.

Parsnips

Parsnips are considered a peculiarly British crop nowadays, yet until the arrival of the potato from America they were a major source of starch across much of Europe during the winter. The cultivated crop has been developed from the wild parsnips that grow throughout central and southern Europe. The wild progenitor is similar to cow parsley, the hedgerow biennial so common in damper parts of Britain.

The UK is, as far as I'm aware, the only nation where parsnips are grown as a significant commercial crop. The French are particularly dismissive and use *le panais*, their word for parsnip, in various insults belittling anything from intelligence to genitals. All the French people I have spoken to dismiss parsnips as fit only for cows, but we know that they are blinded to one of the joys of winter. Parsnips are also richer in most vitamins and minerals than the more highly bred carrot, which has largely displaced it.

Most vegetable seeds are now bred and traded by international companies with little heed for provenance or local growing conditions. Parsnips, being a largely British crop, are mainly home bred by Tozers of Cobham, one of the few independent plant breeders who have not been swallowed up by the biotech companies in the course of their ambitions to control world food supplies and have us all eating designer GM crops. Long may Tozers and their like survive.

The flat, thin, disc-like seeds are notoriously difficult to handle, causing blockages in the seed drill and resisting the best engineer's search for the holy grail of singulation (the separation, and subsequent regular spacing, of individual seeds down the row). To compound these difficulties, parsnip seed is notoriously fickle in its germination and can take anything from ten days to a month to emerge, making it very difficult to establish an even crop and to achieve anything like a uniformly sized root. In the days when we grew for the supermarkets, we expected to throw away over half the crop because they were too large or misshapen. Box customers tend to be more accommodating. A large parsnip, whose neighbours have failed or been late to germinate, is no older or tougher than a smaller one grown in a crowd, and has the benefit of being quicker to prepare in the kitchen.

Parsnips are susceptible to carrot root fly, which attacks all the *Umbelliferae* (parsley, celeriac, carrots and parsnips, plus their wild relatives, cow parsley and beaked parsley). To avoid these small flies laying their eggs in the crop, we try to select our more windswept fields at least 400 metres from where an umbelliferous crop has previously been grown.

Early sowing greatly increases the risk of damage from canker and attack by carrot fly, so we normally wait until early May. The slow germination means that the weeds normally emerge first, allowing us to take a flame strike (a quick burst of heat over each row) to kill the weeds before the crop emerges. The foliage is fairly thick and vigorous and suppresses the weeds better than carrot foliage does. By late August there is normally a full canopy, and the plants start loading their tap roots with the starch that, given a chance, would be the energy source for throwing up a flower and seed head the following spring. There is normally a crop by September but we generally wait until the first frosts – usually November – to start harvesting it. Cold weather causes some of the starch in the root to convert to sugar and greatly improves the flavour. Parsnips are not worth eating in the mild southwest until at least November and are at their best from December to February. We sometimes lift a late crop in early March and cold store them for a few weeks to prevent them becoming woody, but the worthwhile season is certainly over by early April. Be wary of buying a parsnip outside this season: it will either be woody and tasteless or will have travelled from the other side of the world.

Storage and preparation

Parsnips lose moisture more quickly after harvest than carrots and most other roots and are not normally stored for more than a few days on the farm. We almost never wash them and you will find that, with some mud on and without the damage caused by washing, they will keep for two or three weeks in a cool vegetable rack or the bottom of your fridge. Even if they have gone a bit rubbery, this will not detract from the flavour.

From February onwards they are preparing for spring, which means throwing up a seed head from their central core. In preparation they start regrowing root hairs and sprouting leaf, and the core can start to go tough and woody. At this time it is worth slowing the clock down by keeping them in the fridge.

As with most of our roots, the easiest way to clean them is to soak them in water for a few minutes to soften the mud before scrubbing or peeling. The central core should be tender but, if pushing the boundaries of the season (March onwards) consider quartering the parsnips lengthways and trimming it out.

Spiced Parsnip Soup

Many parsnip soup recipes include curry flavours – understandably, as parsnips work well with Indian spicing. The addition of coconut milk here gives a subtler flavour, resulting in a delicious, warming soup.

Serves 6

2 tablespoons butter
1 tablespoon sunflower oil
1 onion, finely chopped
3 garlic cloves, finely chopped
2cm piece of fresh ginger, finely chopped
1 chilli, deseeded and finely chopped
1 teaspoon ground cumin
1 teaspoon ground coriander
½ teaspoon ground turmeric
2 cardamom pods
1 carrot, finely chopped
1 celery stalk, finely chopped
1 leek (white part only), finely chopped
4–5 parsnips, peeled and roughly chopped
2 tablespoons chopped coriander
400ml coconut milk
600ml hot vegetable stock
sea salt and freshly ground black pepper

Heat the butter and oil in a large pan, add the onion, garlic, ginger and chilli and cook over a medium heat for 5 minutes, until softened. Stir in the spices and cook for 1 minute. Add the carrot, celery and leek, reduce the heat and cook for 5 minutes. Finally add the parsnip chunks and half the chopped coriander. Mix thoroughly and cook for 2 minutes, then pour in the coconut milk and hot stock. Bring to the boil, then reduce the heat, cover and cook for 15–20 minutes, until the vegetables are soft. Cool slightly and blitz in a food processor or with a handheld blender. Reheat gently, season to taste and sprinkle with the rest of the chopped coriander.

Creamed Parsnips with Almonds

A fine alternative to conventional mash, or you can serve it as a dip – just increase the amount of oil and add a little more of the cooking milk until you get a consistency you like.

Serves 4–6

500g parsnips, peeled and cut into 1–2cm chunks
about 250ml milk
2 garlic cloves, crushed to a paste with a little salt
juice of ½ lemon
25g ground almonds
50ml olive oil
1 tablespoon flaked almonds, lightly toasted in a dry frying pan
sea salt and freshly ground black pepper
chopped parsley, to garnish

Put the parsnips in a pan, add enough milk just to cover and bring to the boil. Reduce the heat and cook until very soft. Lift out the parsnips and purée in a food processor with the garlic, lemon juice, ground almonds and a little of the cooking liquid. With the machine still running, slowly add the oil. Season to taste and turn the mixture into a serving dish. Sprinkle with the toasted almonds and chopped parsley before serving.

Parsnip Couscous

This recipe comes courtesy of Peter Gordon, who Jane was fortunate enough to work in the early days of the Sugar Club. He's now ensconced in the fabulous Providores restaurant on Marylebone High Street, where his food is as innovative as ever. You can find out more about Peter at www.peter-gordon.net. Serve this dish with a tagine or Moroccan-style stew.

Serves 6

500g couscous
115ml olive oil
250ml hot water
4 parsnips, peeled and cut into 1cm dice
juice and grated zest of 3 lemons
1 tablespoon each chopped coriander, mint and parsley, plus extra to
    garnish
1 tablespoon pine nuts, lightly toasted in a dry frying pan
sea salt and freshly ground black pepper

Mix the couscous with a tablespoon of the olive oil and ½ teaspoon of salt, working them through with your hands. Add the hot water, mix thoroughly, then cover and leave to one side.

Put the diced parsnips in a pan, add just enough water to cover, plus a little salt, and bring to the boil. Simmer for 10 minutes or until the parsnips are tender. Uncover the couscous and add the parsnips and their cooking water, plus the remaining olive oil, the lemon juice and zest and the herbs. Mix well, season to taste and then leave, covered, in a warm place for about 30 minutes. Serve sprinkled with the pine nuts and more herbs.

Parsnip Cake

This unusual recipe comes from Stella Berrisford, a box customer in Sussex. We tested it in the kitchen and everyone was very happy with it – it's a delicious nutty cake, very similar to carrot cake.

250g unsalted butter, softened
250g caster sugar
4 medium eggs
250g self-raising flour, sifted
1 teaspoon ground mixed spice
175g toasted hazelnuts, finely chopped
250g peeled and finely grated parsnips (weight after preparation)
4 tablespoons milk

For the topping:
125g cream cheese
60g unsalted butter, softened
about 250g icing sugar, sifted
60g toasted hazelnuts, roughly chopped

Cream together the butter and sugar until light and fluffy, then beat in the eggs one at a time, adding a spoonful of flour with each one. Fold in the remaining flour, plus the spice, nuts, parsnips and milk.

Use baking parchment to line a rectangular tin, roughly 28 x 18cm. Spoon in the mixture and place in the centre of an oven preheated to 180°C/Gas Mark 4. Bake for 40–50 minutes, until a skewer inserted in the centre comes out clean. Remove from the oven and leave in the tin for 10 minutes before turning out on to a wire rack to cool completely.

To make the topping, place the cream cheese and butter in a bowl and beat until soft. Beat in enough icing sugar to give a thick consistency. Spread the icing over the cake and scatter on the chopped hazelnuts. Cut into squares or triangles to serve.

Easy ideas for parsnips

✦ Peel parsnips, cut them into chunks and toss with a drizzle of maple syrup, a little wholegrain mustard, some orange juice and salt and pepper. Put in a roasting tin, dot with a little butter and roast at 200°C/Gas Mark 6 until tender.

✦ Roast parsnips in olive oil until tender, then toss with a little harissa (rose harissa is best) and drizzle with seasoned yoghurt and chopped parsley.

✦ To make parsnip crisps, peel parsnips, then take thin slices off them along their length. Deep-fry in sunflower oil until crisp, drain on kitchen paper and sprinkle with salt.

Peppers

How did peppers come to be a staple of the British shopping basket? I am at a loss to understand our enthusiasm for this overpriced cousin of deadly nightshade, which hates our climate and can be coaxed into life locally only with so much heat that it must compete for the title of our most environmentally destructive vegetable. When thoroughly cooked, red peppers have some virtue, but green peppers are a complete waste of the glass and heat needed to produce them.

Okay, I'm in a minority of one in my tirade, and I am frequently outvoted in our weekly discussion of box contents, but for a nation supposedly so enthusiastic about local seasonal food, it seems absurd that we now spend twice as much on peppers as on cabbages, which are naturally in season 11 months of the year and are part of our heritage. Without using heat in cultivation, peppers are in season in the UK for a mere two months in September and October, and even then require plastic, or preferably glass, to crop reliably. To feed the national pepper habit, they are either grown under heated glass at huge environmental cost or, slightly less madly, trucked from Spain and Italy. Growers there are always bemused by the UK preference for bell peppers – the most monotonous and tasteless member of this genus – which account for 95 per cent of the UK market. It's another example of consistency overruling flavour. I prefer the longer, tapering varieties, such as Ramiro, as they invariably taste better. The contorted shapes they tend to grow in offend supermarket buyers but are luckily not a problem for the boxes.

Capsicums, of which sweet peppers are one group, come in a fantastic range of colours, shapes, sizes, sweetness and, most notoriously, the heat attributable to their capsaicin content (see Chillies, page 125). Bell peppers themselves, in all their many varieties, are mild, with little or no heat. Immature peppers are green and tend to be bitter, but as they ripen they sweeten and turn red, yellow or orange.

I invariably fry or roast peppers, and have never been able to comprehend why they are enthusiastically eaten raw as a salad vegetable. I am bemused by the space on supermarket shelves devoted to the traffic-light packs of green, yellow and red peppers. At least yellow and red ones add colour to a salad but raw green peppers are just nasty, giving me an uncomfortable reminder of just how closely they are related to the deadly nightshade.

Storage and preparation

Peppers have a remarkably long shelf life and will normally last for at least two weeks in the fridge. Even when they become a little withered, this does not seem to detract from their flavour. A handy tip, courtesy of Gordon Ramsay, is to break off the stalk and stand a bell pepper on its head. The flesh can then be sliced away in three or four pieces, leaving the seeds and pith attached to the base; much quicker and less messy than cutting them in half and scraping out the contents.

Recipes often call for peppers to be roasted, which gives them a smoky, concentrated flavour. Roast them either in the oven at 200°C/Gas Mark 6 or over the naked flame of a gas hob, turning them until the skin is blackened and blistered. Place them in a bowl immediately and cover with cling film – this allows the peppers to sweat and makes them easier to peel. Leave until cool enough to handle, then peel off the skin and remove the seeds.

Sweet and Sour Pepper Tart with Basil Custard

Jane has fond memories of working at a great little restaurant in Dartmouth in the 1980s, called Bistro 33. The chef/owner, Richard Cranfield, cooked amazing food. This is based on a simple tart that he often served as a starter but it would work just as well for any occasion.

Serves 8 as a starter

2 tablespoons olive oil
1 onion, thinly sliced
3 red peppers, thinly sliced
2 garlic cloves, crushed
1 tablespoon sugar
1 tablespoon balsamic vinegar
2 eggs
200ml crème fraîche
1 tablespoon freshly grated Parmesan cheese
a handful of shredded basil leaves
sea salt and freshly ground black pepper

For the shortcrust pastry:
175g plain flour
1 teaspoon caster sugar
a pinch of salt
125g cold unsalted butter, cut into small cubes
about 3 tablespoons cold water

First make the pastry. Put the flour, sugar and salt in a food processor and process briefly to mix. Add the butter and pulse until the mixture resembles fine breadcrumbs. Transfer to a bowl and stir in enough water to make a dough. Wrap in cling film and chill for at least 30 minutes.

Roll out the pastry on a lightly floured surface and use to line a 24cm loose-bottomed flan tin. Cover the base and sides with a piece of baking parchment and fill with baking beans (or ordinary beans or rice, which can be kept and used again for the same purpose). Place on a baking sheet in an oven preheated to 180°C/Gas Mark 4 and bake for 15–20 minutes, until golden brown, removing the paper and beans for the last 5 minutes or so. Remove from the oven and leave to cool.

To make the filling, heat the olive oil in a pan, add the onion and cook gently for 10 minutes. Add the red peppers and cook for 20 minutes, until soft. Stir in the garlic and cook for 5 minutes. Turn the heat up, add the sugar and cook until caramelised. Stir in the balsamic vinegar, reduce the heat and cook for 5 minutes. Remove from the heat and leave to cool.

Lightly beat the eggs with the crème fraîche, some seasoning and half the Parmesan. Mix the shredded basil leaves into this custard.

Place the pepper mixture in the pastry case, pour in the basil custard and sprinkle over the remaining Parmesan. Bake at 140°C/Gas Mark 1 for 30 minutes or until set. Serve warm.

Roasted Red Pepper Soup

This is another soup that was developed on 'soup day' in the staff canteen. Roasting the peppers gives it a greater intensity of flavour. Serve topped with a blob of crème fraîche or a chunky avocado salsa.

Serves 4

4 red peppers
2 tablespoons olive oil
4 garlic cloves, chopped
1 onion, sliced
1 leek, chopped
1 red chilli, chopped, or 1 teaspoon dried chilli flakes
1 bay leaf
400g can of chopped tomatoes
1 teaspoon sugar
1 tablespoon balsamic vinegar
1 tablespoon sweet chilli sauce
sea salt and freshly ground black pepper

Roast the peppers as described on page 274, then peel, deseed and roughly slice the flesh.

Heat the olive oil in a large pan, add the garlic, onion, leek, chilli and bay leaf and cook over a low heat for 5 minutes. Add the tomatoes and sugar, turn up the heat and cook for 10 minutes, stirring to make sure the vegetables don't stick. Add the red peppers, then reduce the heat and cook for 20 minutes. Stir in the vinegar, sweet chilli sauce and 300ml water, bring to the boil and simmer for 10 minutes. Purée until smooth and then pass through a food mill as well, if you want a particularly smooth texture. Season to taste, adding more vinegar or chilli sauce if required.

Shakshouka

There are many different versions of this North African recipe. It makes a great brunch dish – particularly good for a hangover.

Serves 4

2 tablespoons olive oil
2 onions, thinly sliced
1 red pepper, sliced
1 yellow pepper, sliced
1 red chilli, deseeded and finely chopped
4 garlic cloves, crushed
200g can of chopped tomatoes
1 teaspoon salt
¾ teaspoon ground black pepper
½ teaspoon ground cumin
½ teaspoon ground coriander
4 eggs
chopped parsley, to garnish

Heat the oil in a large, heavy-based frying pan, add the onions and cook gently for 5 minutes, until softened but not coloured. Add the peppers and chilli, then cover and cook for 8 minutes or until the peppers are just tender. Stir in the garlic, canned tomatoes, salt and spices, then cover again and cook for 8–10 minutes, until the sauce has thickened.

Using the back of a tablespoon, make 4 indentations in amongst the vegetables and carefully break an egg into each one. Cover and cook over a low heat for about 5 minutes, basting occasionally with the juices, until the eggs have set. (If you prefer the eggs scrambled, you can mix them with a fork before covering the pan.) Sprinkle with chopped parsley and serve. It's good with salad and warm pitta bread.

Easy ideas for peppers

✦ To make peperonata, cook 1 sliced onion in olive oil for about 10 minutes, until soft. Add 1 chopped clove of garlic and 2–3 thinly sliced red peppers and cook gently for about 10 minutes. Add 1 drained can of tomatoes and a pinch of cayenne pepper, then cook for another 10 minutes or so, until thick. Season, adding more cayenne if you like. Serve with grilled steak (lamb or beef) or sausages – or on its own on toast, with some cheese on top.

✦ Sauté 2 sliced peppers (preferably 1 red and 1 yellow) in olive oil until tender. Mix 1 teaspoon of honey with 2 tablespoons of red wine vinegar and 1 tablespoon of raisins. Add to the peppers and simmer until all the liquid has evaporated. Stir in 1 tablespoon of toasted flaked almonds and serve.

✦ Cut some red peppers in half, scoop out the seeds and put a cherry tomato, an anchovy fillet and a teaspoon of capers in each half. Drizzle with olive oil, season and then roast at 200°C/Gas Mark 6 for about 20 minutes, until the peppers are soft and slightly coloured. Serve warm.

See also:
Braised Shoulder of Lamb Stuffed with Salsa Rossa (page 132)
Corn on the Cob with Red Pepper and Chive Butter (page 373)
Gazpacho (page 378)

Potatoes

Are our taste buds too jaded to appreciate the subtle flavours of potatoes? Their reputation has sunk a long way since they left their home in the Andes, where they are still so revered. They have become, for many, a bland, low-cost bulking item on the side of the plate, requiring a smothering of ketchup, mayonnaise or gravy to make them palatable.

Does it have to be that way? Potatoes have suffered the fate of so much of our food: selected for yield, grown fast and sold cheap to a public most of whom no longer have the knowledge to differentiate on anything other than cost and cosmetic appearance. Compared with the potatoes sold in France, ours are staggeringly bland. Variety is certainly key to flavour but the soil type and growing conditions are equally important. Potatoes respond well to huge amounts of nitrogen and water but there is no escaping the general rule – the faster they grow, the less they will taste. When I planted my first potatoes 25 years ago, it was normal to grow them on mixed farms on a relatively small scale without the use of irrigation. Much of the crop was sold locally to customers who knew what they liked. Since then, the industry has become concentrated in the hands of fewer and fewer highly mechanised large players. It is hardly any wonder that the nation is turning to rice and pasta.

To satisfy the appetite of the potato for nitrogen, organic producers usually grow them early in a rotation after a legume crop (e.g. clover). Even then, they normally require a generous application of manure. The main challenge for organic growers is controlling potato blight (*Phytophthora infestans*), a virulent fungal pathogen that can reduce a healthy crop to a field of black stumps in a few days, and which was responsible for the starvation of one and a half million people in Ireland, and the emigration of a million more, in the Great Famine of the mid-nineteenth century.

Non-gardeners are often surprised to hear that potatoes are a tender and demanding crop. Neither leaves nor potatoes can withstand frost. We plant our earliest potatoes on coastal fields, where the maritime influence protects them from frosts, in February/March for digging in mid June. The main-crop potatoes are harvested in September and October and stored in huge wooden bins for use during the winter. Valor is our best keeping variety and can still be in good condition in June.

Varieties

Reluctantly I have to concede (I hate the branding of fresh produce) that Jersey Royals take a lot of beating, though I suspect even their flavour is suffering, as growers move away from the traditional use of seaweed as fertiliser in a bid to reduce costs. Most Cornish Early potatoes are an offence to the name. There has been a rush towards fast-growing varieties such as Rocket, which are all pretty tasteless and have destroyed the traditional seasonal trade for loose-skinned earlies from April to June. We find that even on our warmer coastal fields, the earliest variety that really passes the taste test is Charlotte, which typically arrives a full month after the watery sprinters.

The choice of main-crop varieties depends on intended use. Waxy potatoes with low dry matter (like the average Maris Peer and the nasty Nadine or very good Charlotte) hold their shape and are best for boiling, though most are fairly bland. At the other end of the spectrum are the floury varieties with high dry matter (such as the wonderful but very hard to grow King Edward and Santé), which are best for mash, chips, roasting and (in my view) baking. In between are Estima, Desiree and Maris Piper, which are okay for most things. Inexplicably, as a nation, we seem to prefer white-fleshed varieties, though in most cases the yellow-fleshed ones have more flavour and always look more appetising to me.

Our favourite varieties to follow Charlotte are Cosmos (excellent flavour but a tendency to crack when rain follows a dry spell), Desiree (though our co-op members find it hard to grow organically and prefer Raja) and, to finish the season, Valor, which is a very good keeper with good blight resistance. We spent years experimenting with wacky and specialist varieties, such as Pink Fir Apple, Kerrs Pink and La Ratte, but most are a nightmare to grow and harvest. On the whole we have decided that, at least for general use, they are not worth the effort and hype ascribed to them by some foodies and gardening enthusiasts.

Storage and preparation

New (loose-skinned) and main-crop or old (set-skinned) potatoes are quite separate beasts. They can sometimes be the same varieties but, due to their different state of maturity, cook and keep very differently. Traditional, loose-skinned new potatoes, normally harvested from May to early July before the skin is set, dehydrate rapidly and will not keep in good condition for more than a week, so store them in a paper bag in the fridge and eat them quickly.

Once the skin is set, the potato has equipped itself to be the plant's natural storage organ for starch and should keep for weeks or even months, provided it is stored in the dark and cool but free of frost. The best way to keep potatoes is in a paper bag, to allow breathing while excluding light.

From Christmas onwards the potatoes start to prepare for spring and might show signs of sprouting arms and legs at temperatures above 4°C (a tendency usually controlled in non-organic potatoes with chemical sprout suppressants). Don't be too alarmed if your potatoes have started sprouting; provided they have not turned green, it is okay to remove the sprouts and use the potatoes, and though you will find they have a tendency to go soft, this will not detract from the flavour. The tuber is actually a modified swollen stem and the eyes are dormant buds from which new roots and leaves would naturally emerge. Some varieties are much more sleepy and slow to wake up in the spring than others but the tendency increases progressively from January, as the tuber's internal clock tells it to prepare for another season. Any rise in temperature is taken as confirmation of spring, so sprouting can be stopped by putting the potatoes in the bottom of your fridge at this time. Temperatures below 4°C can cause the potatoes to accumulate sugar, which will result in blackening during cooking, especially when frying.

Like all members of the *Solanum* family (which includes tomatoes, aubergine and the nightshades), potatoes contain variable amounts of the alkaloid toxin solanin, the level rising when tubers are damaged or exposed to light. I recommend peeling away any small green areas and discarding tubers that show extensive greening. We also advise against leaving peeled or cut potatoes for more than a couple of hours before cooking, making the widespread practice in catering of preparing potatoes and sealing with preservative in a plastic bag for use days later a bit worrying.

Potato Salad

After being saturated by cookery shows on television, the one with Neneh Cherry and Andi Oliver was a breath of fresh air. We cooked this variation on their potato salad for a Caribbean barbecue and it did the job. You could try adding chopped parsley, spring onions, red onions or chives.

Serves 6

1kg new potatoes, scrubbed
100ml white wine vinegar
1 tablespoon olive oil
5 eggs, hardboiled, shelled and chopped
150ml Greek-style yoghurt
150ml mayonnaise
150ml crème fraîche
2–3 tablespoons chopped gherkins
1 tablespoon capers, soaked in cold water for 20 minutes, then squeezed dry and chopped
1 tablespoon English mustard
1 tablespoon wholegrain mustard
1 tablespoon chopped dill
sea salt and freshly ground black pepper

Cook the potatoes in boiling salted water until tender, then drain. While they are still hot, cut them into quarters and mix with the vinegar, oil and some salt and pepper.

Mix all the remaining ingredients together in a bowl. Add the potatoes, mix well and adjust the seasoning.

Basic Potato Gratin

There are various approaches to this dish and if you start looking for a definitive recipe you have a long journey ahead. This version works well but don't be afraid to add other vegetables and seasonings, as in the variations below. We tend to use all varieties of potato but find that a good all-rounder, such as Junior or Cosmos, works best.

Serves 6

300ml double cream
100ml milk
2 garlic cloves, crushed to a paste with a pinch of salt
800g potatoes, peeled and cut into slices 2–3mm thick
1–2 tablespoons freshly grated Parmesan cheese
sea salt and freshly ground black pepper

Put the cream, milk and crushed garlic into a pan and bring to the boil. Season and add the potatoes, mixing well.

Transfer the mixture to a gratin dish, spreading it out so that there is an even distribution of cream. Cover with foil and bake in an oven preheated to 180°C/Gas Mark 4 for about 50 minutes, until the potatoes are tender. Remove the foil, sprinkle with the Parmesan and return to the oven for 10 minutes, until browned on top.

✦ Try using chicken stock instead of cream for a different finish, or substitute thinly sliced fennel for some of the potato.

✦ Using half Jerusalem artichokes and half potatoes, or half celeriac, half potatoes and a little grated apple are also good variations.

✦ Or alternatively try using half sweet potato and half potato, adding 1 chopped red chilli and 2 teaspoons of chopped rosemary to the garlic and cream mixture.

✦ Soak some dried porcini mushrooms in hot water for 30 minutes, then simmer them in their soaking liquid with some crushed garlic until the liquid has reduced by half. Add a little cream and grated Parmesan and use to coat the sliced potatoes before baking as above.

♦ Sweat 2 sliced leeks in butter for 10 minutes, then add 100g cooked pancetta, plus the crushed garlic and a handful of roughly sliced wild garlic leaves. Add the cream and milk and bring to the boil, then add the potatoes and continue as above.

Panackelty

This dish from the northeast of England has been around for ever. There is no definitive recipe for it but it is a great way of using up leftover meat from a roast. Legend has it that it was the fuel the Jarrow marchers survived on.

Serves 2

2 onions, chopped
1 tablespoon lard or dripping
200g corned beef, leftover meat or sausages, sliced
1 carrot, sliced (plus any other root vegetables you have; swede is
    especially good)
2 large potatoes, peeled and sliced
500ml hot stock
sea salt and freshly ground black pepper

Fry the onions in the fat for 10 minutes, until soft, then place in an ovenproof dish. Add the meat, then the carrot and any leftover vegetables. Finish off with a layer of sliced potatoes, seasoning each layer as you go. Pour in your hot stock and bake in an oven preheated to 180°C/Gas Mark 4 for 1 hour, until everything is tender. Serve with buttered cabbage.

New Potatoes Baked in Parchment

This lovely way of cooking potatoes is usually associated with fish, and the little parchment bag seals in all the flavours. It is based on a recipe in *The Greens Cookbook* by Deborah Madison and Edward Espe Brown (Bantam Books, 1987), of Greens restaurant in San Francisco.

Per person:

6 or 7 small new potatoes, scrubbed but not peeled (if the potatoes are large, cut them in half)
3 garlic cloves, crushed (wet garlic can also be used)
leaves from a sprig of rosemary or a few sprigs of thyme or summer savory, chopped
1 tablespoon virgin olive oil
sea salt and freshly ground black pepper

Place the potatoes in a bowl with the garlic, herbs and olive oil. Season well and toss so they are coated in the oil and seasonings.

Cut a square of baking parchment large enough to hold the potatoes comfortably and fold it in half to make a crease. Unfold it and lay the potatoes on the lower half. Bring the rest of the paper over the potatoes and roll it up lightly along the edges to form a pouch (a bit like making a pasty). Make sure that the package is well sealed. You can staple it, if you like.

Bake in an oven preheated to 200°C/Gas Mark 6 for 40 minutes and then serve immediately. The packages will puff up. Put them on serving plates so everyone can open theirs at the table.

✦ Try adding a little saffron to the potatoes with the oil and seasonings.

Perfect Mash

…Well, sort of perfect. For the very best results, the potatoes should be boiled in their skins and peeled while still hot, but this is time consuming and messy. By all means try it, but you can still get excellent results by following the method below. In his fantastic saffron mash recipe, Simon Hopkinson instructs us to beat the mash with an electric mixer. If you can do this, the result is amazing with any type of mash. But don't be tempted to use a food processor, which can make the potatoes gluey.

Serves 4–6

1kg floury potatoes, such as Cosmos, Sante, Cara or Maris Piper, peeled
   and cut into chunks
100ml milk
100ml double cream
100g butter
sea salt and freshly ground black pepper

Put the potatoes in a pan of cold salted water, bring to the boil, then reduce the heat and simmer until tender. Drain well in a colander and leave for a few minutes for excess water to drain off.

Heat the milk, cream and butter in a large pan just until the butter has melted. Pass the potatoes through a mouli-légumes or a potato ricer into the hot cream and then beat well. Season to taste.

✦ Try infusing some saffron in the warm cream mixture and add up to 100ml good olive oil with the mash for a tasty alternative.

✦ Or beat loads of mustard into the mash; wasabi is good, if the fusion route is your thing, but add it more sparingly.

✦ Mix lots of fresh herbs into the finished mash or beat in 50g freshly grated Parmesan cheese with the potatoes.

✦ Alternatively to make colcannon, cook ½ shredded cabbage or some shredded kale in butter for about 10 minutes, until tender, and beat into the mash.

◆ Or to make champ, omit the butter from the cream mixture. Instead, add a bunch of chopped spring onions and heat through. Beat in the potatoes, as above, and then serve topped with lots of diced butter; it will melt into the potato.

Baked Fish and Potatoes with Salsa Verde

A fantastically quick and easy supper dish. Salsa verde works well with fish and potatoes, but you could use pesto instead (see page 209).

Serves 4

500g potatoes (any type), peeled but left whole
500g white fish fillets, preferably hake, skinned and pin-boned
2 tablespoons Salsa Verde (see page 216)
4 tomatoes, thinly sliced
olive oil for drizzling
2 tablespoons freshly grated Parmesan cheese
sea salt and freshly ground black pepper

Parboil the potatoes for 5 minutes, then drain and leave to cool. Slice them thinly.

Place the fish in an ovenproof dish just large enough to hold it in a single layer. Season with salt and pepper, drizzle with the salsa verde, then top with the sliced tomatoes and season again. Arrange the potatoes on top, drizzle with a little olive oil and sprinkle with some pepper and the grated Parmesan. Place in an oven preheated to 200°C/Gas Mark 6 and bake for 10–15 minutes, until the fish is cooked through and the potatoes are golden brown.

Our Chips

'Chip Day' at the staff canteen seems to be the most popular day of the week and there is quite a stampede at lunchtime. Generally we cut our chips quite fat, sometimes getting only 6–8 chips out of a large baking potato. They are less fattening than thinly cut chips, which have more surface area overall and therefore absorb more oil.

Ideally, the chips should be made in a thermostatically controlled deep-fat fryer, which makes it easier to maintain the temperature of the oil. You can use a large, deep pan, if necessary, but make sure you don't fill it more than a third full with oil – the level can rise alarmingly when you add the potatoes.

large potatoes (we tend to use Cosmos baking potatoes but any decent
   floury/baking variety will do), peeled and very thickly sliced
sunflower oil for deep-frying
sea salt

Rinse the chips under cold water for a few minutes, then drain them well, spread out on a tea towel and pat dry.

Heat some sunflower oil to 140°C in a deep-fat fryer or a deep saucepan. Cook the chips in batches, being careful not to overcrowd the pan, for about 5–6 minutes, until they are soft all the way through but not browned. Remove each batch and drain on kitchen paper when they are done. This first frying can be done well in advance and the chips finished off just before serving.

When ready to serve, heat the oil to 190°C and plunge in the chips to brown, again cooking them in batches. They will only take 2–3 minutes this time. Drain on kitchen paper, sprinkle with salt and serve immediately.

Easy ideas for potatoes

✦ Use leftover mash with grated beetroot to make pink bubble and squeak (see page 28).

✦ To make potato latkes, peel and grate 2 large potatoes and squeeze out as much liquid as possible. Mix together 1 finely chopped small onion, 1 egg and 1 tablespoon of self-raising flour, then stir in the potato and season with salt and pepper. Heat a thin film of oil in a frying pan, add tablespoonfuls of the mixture and flatten them with the back of the spoon. Fry for 2 minutes on each side, until golden brown and crisp.

✦ Use up leftover mash, or the insides of leftover baked potatoes, to make fishcakes: combine with canned tuna or salmon, seasoning and herbs, shape into cakes and fry until golden brown on both sides and thoroughly heated through.

✦ Use diced cooked potatoes to make a hash (see Kale, Chorizo and Potato Hash on page 230), substituting cooked chicken or corned beef for the chorizo, if you like.

See also:
Apple, Potato and Cheese Casserole (page 8)
Cauliflower and Potato Dal (page 102)
Artichoke, Salmon and New Potato Salad with Anchovy Sauce (page 186)
Roast Artichokes and New Potatoes (page 188)
Cavolo Nero and Potato Soup with Red Chilli (page 232)
Leek and Potato Soup with Chicken, Bacon and Sage (page 245)

Fresh: what does it mean and when does it matter?

Carrots harvested in October and held in store until April will normally taste better than ones that have been left in the ground and eaten 'fresh'. Some potatoes certainly improve in storage up to the point where they start sprouting. A Crown Prince squash can be every bit as good after six months on a dusty shelf as the day it was harvested. A Russet apple will taste better at Christmas than on the day it was picked. Onions harvested in September will keep quite naturally until March as long as they are healthy and, with refrigeration, can be stored till April or May. My point is that fresh is not always best. Sometimes it doesn't matter and it drives me nuts that so many food journalists don't understand this. The indiscriminating adulation of freshness encourages the trade to be less than honest about storage and deflects attention from areas where freshness really matters.

You can't have local food and always expect everything to be fresh. Sensible storage is an important part of reducing food miles and the associated environmental impact while maintaining an acceptable amount of choice. Tubers, bulbs, corms and some roots and stems are the plant's energy stores. Towards the end of the growing season, they are loaded with sugars, which are made by photosynthesis in the leaves. These sugars are converted to starch for storage between seasons, like a squirrel burying acorns. As spring approaches, a combination of an internal clock and rising temperatures causes the starch to be mobilised by converting it back to sugars, ready to fuel a quick getaway with next year's growth. There is nothing shameful or unnatural in using this capacity for storage to keep us fed throughout the winter without resorting to imports.

In modern storage, refrigeration is used to delay the spring awakening by tricking the root, bulb or tuber into thinking it is still in the depths of winter. It works up to a point, but as soon as the vegetables are brought out of store the quality declines rapidly, and there comes a time when (assuming you subscribe to the generally held view that year-round availability of everything is a prerequisite of an acceptable diet) it is justifiable to import on grounds of quality. Of course, it would be better for the planet if we just ate in season. Why anyone would want parsnips and swedes in summer is a mystery to me, but I would struggle without an uninterrupted supply of onions and potatoes.

When it comes to greens, however, there can be no doubt that fresh is best. As soon as the plant is cut, photosynthesis is shut down and with it goes the ability to maintain healthy cells and fight off infection. In some cases the leaves can continue to maintain themselves to a degree, especially if the plant is harvested whole: heads of lettuce, kale or cabbage will always keep longer than individual leaves; likewise Brussels sprouts keep better on the stalk. Generally, however, flavour and nutritional value start being lost from the minute the connection to the soil is severed.

Refrigeration can help to extend the shelf life of these plants. As a general rule, the rate of most biological processes doubles for every 10°C rise in temperature: thus a lettuce stored at 5°C should keep for twice as long as at 15°C and four times as long as at 25°C. Unfortunately refrigeration also consumes a lot of energy and contributes massively to greenhouse gas emissions (a quarter to a half of Tesco's declared carbon footprint and about 8 per cent of ours). It can be used intelligently, as described above, to reduce waste and improve quality but these potential benefits have frequently been abused by the trade, which has instead used refrigeration to extend supply chains and the length of time from field to shelf – viewing it as a means of making their own lives easier rather than offering improved quality to customers. Some fruit and vegetables, such as courgettes and tomatoes, can be kept in cold store for weeks and will still look fine but will have lost virtually all flavour and, I suspect, most of their nutritional value. By all means make use of your own refrigerator to prolong what life the produce has when you get it home – but wherever possible, try to make sure when buying green vegetables that what you're getting is genuinely fresh.

Quince

Rather than shelling out pocket money, my father encouraged the five of us, from a tender age, to hone our entrepreneurial skills on various enterprises on the farm. I was given a pig to raise for my eighth birthday and by the age of eleven I had inherited from my brother, Ben, a business bagging up manure for sale at the farm gate. The sacks were stacked up alongside the logs (another brother's enterprise) under a quince tree at the back of the house, planted by my mother when she first came to the farm in the 1950s.

One autumn a woman, as broad as she was tall, pulled up for some manure, but at the sight of the ripening quinces erupted into a stream of unintelligible (perhaps Armenian?) exclamations, accompanied by wild gesticulations. It turned out that quince was something of a national fruit in her country and this was the first one she had seen since leaving home during the war. She bought most of the quinces, leaving just enough to teach my mother how to make membrillo, and returned every year to strip the tree bare. The tree still limps on, way past its prime, producing less fruit each year, but with no one having the heart to cut it down. Meanwhile, membrillo has become fashionable and Jane is buying quinces from a wholesaler, so I have planted a few around the Field Kitchen. They seem incredibly vigorous and free from pests, so I am planning an orchard to supply my brother Ben's membrillo factory. Maybe we will offer them to select enthusiasts with the veg boxes. I'm not sure they will ever be a mainstream taste.

Quinces originate from southwest Asia, where their cultivation is said to pre-date that of the apple. They are highly fragrant and are steeped in history and ritual in the eastern Mediterranean. Among the Ancient Greeks, the quince was an offering at weddings. Plutarch reports that a Greek bride would nibble a quince to perfume her kiss before entering the bridal chamber, 'in order that the first greeting may not be disagreeable nor unpleasant'. It was a quince that Paris awarded Aphrodite, and it was for a golden quince that Atalanta paused in her race.

Quinces are closely related to the ornamental japonica and both can be used to make excellent jellies. The fruits rarely reach full maturity (when they can be eaten as a dessert fruit) in this country and are normally picked just before the first frost for cooking. The most common variety is Vranja.

Storage and preparation

The fragrance of quinces makes them lovely to have around just for their smell. They are deceptively hard – a lot harder than apples or pears – and hence their cooking time is longer. Jane generally peels, halves and cores them, then poaches or bakes them in a light sugar syrup. Once cooked, the quinces can be cut up and added to apple crumbles or pies. They are also great served with game and often used in tagines and casseroles with lamb or chicken. The cores and trimmings can also be cooked with sugar and water, strained and the resulting liquid simmered down to make a fragrant syrup. Add to custard or whipped cream, or use to glaze an apple tart.

If you are able to get quinces in reasonable numbers, I highly recommend trying Membrillo (see below). It is a wonderful way to round off a meal, eaten with a cheese such as Manchego or possibly pecorino or Parmesan. Or whisk a cube of membrillo (or a teaspoon of quince jelly) into gravy to serve with roast game birds.

Membrillo

2kg quince, or a mixture of cooking apples and quinces if you don't
   have enough, unpeeled and roughly chopped
granulated sugar

Put the quince in a pan with 300ml water. Cover and cook very gently until tender – you may have to mash it a bit towards the end.

Push the cooked fruit through a sieve or a mouli-légumes to make a purée. Measure the purée in a measuring jug and then put it in a deep, heavy-bottomed saucepan. For each litre of purée, add 550g granulated sugar. Heat very gently, stirring occasionally, until the sugar is thoroughly dissolved. Then raise the heat to bring the mixture to the boil and cook until thick. It will become a darker red and start popping as it leaves the sides of the pan. The trick is to stir continuously with a heavy wooden spoon so it never catches and burns. As it reduces you will need to protect your hand with a tea towel or oven glove. Once you can hardly move the spoon, take the pan off the heat and transfer the mixture to a baking tray lined with baking parchment, spreading it out in a layer about 1cm thick. Leave it, uncovered, for a few days in a warm room or airing cupboard, or even in an oven on the lowest possible setting. Then cut it into cubes with a hot knife. To store, pack them in an airtight container, sprinkled with sugar.

Rhubarb

Rhubarb was popular in Victorian times and throughout most of the twentieth century. However, along with many of our traditional home-grown fruit and vegetables, it suffered from the emergence of supermarkets and the associated globally traded, season-free produce that they have promoted over the last 30 years. Commercial production of rhubarb had largely retreated to the traditional stronghold of Yorkshire until a revival started at around the turn of the century, when crumble started to replace tiramisu on restaurant menus and chefs began to use the sharp flavours in sauces to accompany savoury dishes such as pork and mackerel.

Rhubarb is a perennial and is propagated by digging up and dividing the dormant root during December to February. The roots appear rotten and lifeless at this time of year and can easily be divided with a spade. It is common to plant them at one-metre spacing in both directions but we have developed a system of planting them more closely in widely spaced rows two metres apart. This allows us to sow a green manure between the rows in July or August, which is incorporated in February to feed the plants the following season; that, along with a liberal dressing of manure in late winter, satisfies their strong appetite for nitrogen, needed to produce firm stalks. The wider spacing also allows us to cultivate between the rows to control weeds throughout the season.

The new plants should not be picked in the first year and then only lightly in the second, to allow the roots to build up strength. In following years the stalks are pulled from late March to June, or even later if the roots are strong. Picking can be advanced by placing pots over the crowns or by lifting the roots in early winter, once they have been thoroughly chilled, and storing them in the sand in a warm, dark forcing house for picking from January to March. Forced rhubarb produces long, thin, etiolated stems, which are undoubtedly sweeter and more tender than the open-grown crop that follows.

Apart from slugs, often a problem in the first year, rhubarb has no serious pests, though, as with all perennial crops, perennial weeds such as couch grass, creeping nettle and dock can be troublesome; fortunately its vigorous, shading growth makes rhubarb a good competitor once established.

We have tried a number of varieties but have found nothing to beat Timperley Early, bred by H. Marshland in 1945. Sutton Seedless is a good later variety, which needs less feeding to produce good-quality stalks.

Despite its recent rise in popularity, rhubarb remains a contentious item in our veg boxes. The pedantic argue about whether it is a fruit or a vegetable, which all depends on whether your view is culinary or morphological. As it is now increasingly used in sauces to accompany savoury dishes I like to view it as a vegetable.

Storage and preparation

Rhubarb keeps for a week without much deterioration if stored in a plastic bag in the bottom of the fridge (cut off any leaves). If the sticks go rubbery quickly, this may be the result of moisture stress (rhubarb is a moisture lover and can suffer in dry years). Provided the floppiness is not due to hollow sticks, they will normally cook satisfactorily and are worth using up to the point where the cut ends are obviously drying and shrinking.

The leaves contain a significant amount of the toxin oxalic acid, and are said to have been the cause of a number of deaths during the Second World War, when people tried eating them as greens. They must have been very hungry because the LD50 (lethal dose for 50 per cent of people) of these very bitter leaves is about 5kg. The concentration in the sticks is much lower but still enough to give that rough feeling on the teeth.

Rhubarb Butter Sauce for Fish

Try serving this with salmon cooked by placing it on an elderflower head in a baking parchment parcel with a dash of white wine, then baking in a hot oven so the bag puffs up and the salmon steams inside. It's also good with other oily fish and with pork.

Serves 6–8

500g rhubarb, cut into batons
2 teaspoons sugar
juice and grated zest of 1 orange
150ml fish stock
40g chilled butter, cut into small pieces
sea salt and freshly ground black pepper

Put the rhubarb, sugar, orange juice and zest in a pan and cook gently for about 15 minutes, until the rhubarb has broken down into a purée. Meanwhile, in a separate pan, boil the fish stock until reduced by half its volume. Stir in the rhubarb, season and cook for 5 minutes, then push through a sieve into a clean pan. Just before serving, heat the sauce and whisk in the pieces of butter a few at a time to give a glossy finish. Season to taste.

Rhubarb and Strawberry Crumble

Jane used to think cooking strawberries was an abomination but this combination came as a very pleasant surprise. It is a favourite crumble in the Field Kitchen when the rhubarb and strawberry seasons coincide.

Serves 4

2–4 rhubarb stalks, cut into slices 2cm thick
1 punnet of strawberries, hulls removed, large ones cut in half
165g plain flour
50g soft light brown sugar
150g rolled oats
125g unsalted butter

Place the rhubarb in a deep pie dish. Toss the strawberries with a tablespoon of the flour and add to the rhubarb. Sprinkle half the sugar on top.

Put the oats, butter and remaining sugar and flour in a food processor and pulse until the mixture starts to come together. Spread the crumble over the fruit and bake in an oven preheated to 180°C/Gas Mark 4 for 35–40 minutes, until the rhubarb is tender and the crumble is browned. Serve with delicious clotted cream – preferably from the Riverford Dairy!

Rhubarb and Cardamom Fool

This is based on a recipe by the food writer Richard Cawley. Rhubarb and cardamom are a perfect match. You can omit the cream and use just yoghurt for a healthier option, if you prefer.

Serves 6

450g rhubarb, coarsely chopped
150g caster sugar
juice and grated zest of 1 orange
3 cardamom pods
100ml double cream
100ml yoghurt

Mix the rhubarb, sugar and orange juice and zest together and place in an ovenproof dish. Add the cardamom pods. Cover and bake in an oven preheated to 190°C/Gas Mark 5 for 30–45 minutes, until the rhubarb is completely soft. Remove from the oven and leave to cool completely. Take out the cardamom pods and purée the fruit.

Whip the cream with the yoghurt until it just holds its shape. Carefully fold the purée into the cream so you have a ripple effect, then transfer the mixture to serving glasses. Chill before serving.

Easy ideas for rhubarb

✦ To make a rhubarb and orange compote, chop some rhubarb into batons and cook gently in a little brown sugar and orange juice until tender but still holding its shape. Cut all the peel and pith off an orange and slice it into rounds. Add to the rhubarb, stir thoroughly and chill. Serve the cold compote with warm custard (see below).

✦ For traditional rhubarb and custard, bake some rhubarb as described in the fool recipe on the facing page, omitting the cardamom if liked. To make the custard, whisk 6 egg yolks in a large bowl with a teaspoon of cornflour and 1–2 tablespoons of caster sugar. Bring 400ml double cream and 200ml milk to boiling point in a pan with the seeds from a vanilla pod (or ½ teaspoon of vanilla extract), then whisk gradually into the egg mixture. Pour back into the pan and cook, stirring constantly, over a low heat for about 5 minutes, until thickened. Strain and serve with the rhubarb.

✦ Make a pavlova as described on page 356. Fill with whipped cream, drizzle with custard and cover with poached rhubarb (cooked as in the first Easy idea, above, or as in the fool recipe on the facing page). If you don't have time to make a pavlova, use broken bought meringues and mix them with the whipped cream, poached rhubarb and custard to make a rhubarb Eton Mess.

Salad Leaves

My early lettuce-growing career coincided with the rise of the iceberg and I spent the summers of the late 1980s and early 1990s struggling to grow these tasteless, nutrient-free aberrations of nature for Sainsbury and Waitrose. Thankfully, fashions have changed and the box scheme gives us the freedom to grow lettuces with flavour, which don't regularly melt into a slime (we used to call it snot rot in the field) if denied their supply of agrochemicals.

The first lettuces are sown under glass in January and planted out under crop covers in late March for harvest in early May. Weekly plantings up to early August provide a supply through to the first frosts in October. Lettuces need plenty of light to thrive and be at their best at harvest but actually don't do well in excessive heat, so in July and August even the less highly strung Cos can suffer from the dreaded snot rot. All lettuces become bitter when over mature, and stress (normally caused by heat or lack of water) can bring this on in younger plants.

There is considerable folklore surrounding the milky sap that exudes from the butt of a lettuce when cut. The Egyptians ate lettuce to promote virility, based on the supposed similarity of the sap to certain body fluids. This can hardly be consistent with the more commonly held, and pharmacologically sound, belief that lettuce is soporific. Mr MacGregor, the irate gardener in Beatrix Potter's stories, finally captured the greedy Benjamin and his Flopsy Bunnies after they feasted on his lettuces and 'by degrees, one after another, they were overcome with slumber, and lay down in the mown grass'. Some of my staff would also verify this effect; I once found a group of them spending their lunch hour cutting, gathering and drying the sap from the butts of a crop of bolted lettuces before they were mown off. Like Sherlock Holmes and so many before him, they enjoyed the opiate properties of the resulting goo.

A good number of salad leaves other than lettuces can be grown successfully in Britain and a surprising number of them are winter hardy, making it possible to prepare a seasonal salad from your garden throughout the year. Lots are relatively new to the British market and it is well worth experimenting with different mixes. We do our best on the farm but if you are a big salad eater and have even a tiny garden or a window box, my recommendation is that you choose your favourites from the list below and grow your own. Most of them can be cut several times from a late-summer or autumn sowing and some will go right through the winter. An August sowing will give at least three cuts

before Christmas, followed by sporadic picking throughout the winter. Spring and early-summer sowings are made trickier by attacks of flea beetle (which give the leaves a shotgun-blasted appearance but normally don't affect eating quality) and a tendency to run to seed if sown before June – making it hard to get more than one cut.

Another reason for honing your gardening skills on salad leaves is that it means you can avoid the air-freighted, nutrition-free leaves, pre-soaked in powerful chlorine solutions, that you will typically find in supermarkets.

American land cress

Dark-green, lobed leaves, very similar in appearance and taste to watercress but about four times stronger and half the size. It is best combined with milder leaves in a green salad to tone down the flavour. Land cress is very winter hardy but much slower growing than most salad leaves. A sowing in August will provide picking through the winter until it runs to seed in March. It can be substituted for watercress in soup but, due to its stronger flavour, you should only use about a third of the quantity.

Baby chard

Chard is part of the beetroot/mangold family but, if cut small enough, the leaves can be tender and add another flavour (sour and a bit earthy) to salads. Having said that, my children always pick this stuff out and leave it on the side of the plate. Just like the full-sized version (see page 324), chard can come with white, red or green stems with green leaves. Baby beetroot leaves, which are a deep ruby red, are also sometimes used to add colour.

Batavia

The most popular lettuce on the Continent. They can be red or green and are normally fairly crunchy. Less sweet and more earthy in flavour than Cos or Little Gem, they are the easiest lettuces to grow. Red Batavia are pretty bombproof and will stand in the field at maturity longer than most lettuces, so if you are going to grow just one lettuce in your garden, this is a good choice. Not winter hardy.

Butterhead, round or floppy lettuce

No crunch, not very sweet, and deeply unfashionable, but they have a pleasant, mild flavour, providing a base to which more interesting leaves can be added. Their main virtue is that, unlike most lettuces, they thrive at low light intensity and can be grown under glass or plastic, providing the basis for a winter salad. They are often sprayed with soap to control aphids, so if you buy them in winter give them a particularly good wash.

Cos

These are the upright, old-fashioned Mr MacGregor-style lettuces. They can form a loose heart, which is all that most supermarkets will sell, insisting that growers discard half the lettuce in the field. They are wonderfully sweet and crunchy but brown rapidly once the leaves are broken or washed. Fickle in the field during hot spells. Not winter hardy.

Lamb's lettuce, corn salad or mâche

This hardy, low-growing plant forms a rosette of small, dark-green leaves, which can be harvested with care virtually all year from protected sites or a polytunnel. Because you cut the whole plant, it is less suited to cut-and-come-again cultivation than many other salad leaves. Vast areas are grown in highly mechanised systems around Machecoul, in western France. The whole process has become incredibly sophisticated: massive quantities of sand are spread in a thin layer after sowing so the crop emerges cleanly and can be cut mechanically. One has to wonder at the scale and level of technical proficiency but production is dependent on soil sterilisation and agrochemicals and is in many ways the antithesis of organic production. I am told that the underlying aquifer is the most polluted in Europe.

Lamb's lettuce has a wonderfully subtle flavour. Our crops tend to be uneven, so we have to cut the tiny leaves by hand, which makes them very expensive. My recommendation, if you are a fan, is to grow it yourself.

Little Gem

Mini Cos with less crunch, but they can be very sweet. They become bitter if over mature. Little Gems look great in a salad and last well in the fridge. Not winter hardy.

Mizuna

Pretty, feathery leaves with a fairly mild, peppery flavour. It germinates quickly and evenly and is very fast growing but not as hardy as rocket and, in my opinion, not as good to eat. Most varieties are green but there is a good red variety called Ruby Streaks, which can add colour to your salad.

Oak leaf

Delicate, pretty, highly indented red or green leaves with a short shelf life and a mild, earthy flavour. Frost tender.

Pak choi, bok choy, tatsoi

This is a range of quick-growing, moderately hardy leaves of Oriental origin which can be used in salads while young (up to 10cm, say). They are easy to grow and can provide variations in texture and colour but they are all from the brassica family and share the same one-dimensional flavour, which can easily overwhelm a salad if you add too much. I think these leaves are best used in stir-fries and Oriental-style soups.

Rocket

Also known as arugula, roquette and rucola, rocket has a strong, peppery taste but not such an overwhelmingly mustard flavour as the other brassica salad leaves. It has been a popular salad in southern Europe since Roman times (when it was used as both salad and aphrodisiac) but, given the British resistance to the joys of bitter flavours (radicchio, escarole, etc), I am surprised by it's rise to popularity here during the 1990s. Of all the salad leaves, it is justifiably most people's favourite but is also probably the most difficult to grow.

Salad or 'sky' rocket is larger, milder flavoured and slightly less fickle to germinate than the 'wild roquette' favoured by the trade, making it the best choice for your garden or window box. It has a shorter shelf life and its leaves are more delicate but if you are going to eat it straight away, rather than fly it halfway around the world and then expect it to sit on a shelf for a week, this is not a problem. You can carry on picking individual leaves even as it runs to seed, and the pretty, cream-coloured flowers (which also taste good) look great scattered on a salad.

Most people find rocket too strong to eat on its own, so it is most frequently used to add an edge to a green salad composed of blander, sweeter leaves. Fifteen years after it came into fashion, and ten years after it went out, I still love a rocket and Parmesan salad, or – again if you can cope with being unfashionable – warm goat's cheese on toast on a bed of rocket. The cheese attenuates the bitterness of the leaves. One of my favourite sandwiches is a baguette filled with rocket and cheese – normally Parmesan shavings or a mature goat's cheese but a runny Brie, or Cheddar with a little mayonnaise, can also be good. During rocket's heyday, there was also a fashion for cooking with it. Given its price from a supermarket and the sometimes dubious results, it is not surprising that this seems to have slipped from the cookery pages of the weekend papers. One use that is worth trying, though, is with pasta; cook and drain the pasta and dress with a little olive oil or butter before mixing in a handful of rocket leaves, which should wilt in the heat of the pasta.

Rocket pesto can be made by replacing the basil with rather less rocket – see page 209. Again, the peppery bitterness of the rocket goes well with the Parmesan or pecorino. Don't overdo the rocket or it tends to taste too herbaceous.

Winter purslane

We used to call this by its other name, claytonia, until Jane commented that it sounded particularly unappetising, so we have gone back to winter purslane. Another name is miners' lettuce, acquired during the Californian Gold Rush when miners gathered it from the wild on account of its reputed ability to fend off scurvy. The heart-shaped leaves are borne on long stalks and have a very succulent texture and slightly lemony flavour reminiscent of sorrel.

Salad bags

Whole leaves attached to the butt of the lettuce will keep two to four times as long as a broken or chopped and washed leaf – which means the producers of convenient washed salads have a problem. Washing them in what effectively becomes a bacterial soup also promotes decay and has the potential for spreading pathogens such as Listeria and E. coli. The answer is to disinfect the leaves by rinsing them in a chlorine solution 20 times stronger than that used in most swimming pools. This is largely, though not completely, effective as a disinfectant but also has the effect of destroying most of the nutrient value and flavour and of leaving potentially toxic chlorine compounds on the leaves. Organic bags are better because chlorine washes are banned but pre-prepared salads are still a distant second best to making your own.

Storage and preparation

Lettuce should always be kept in the bottom of your fridge, where it will last for 4–10 days, depending on variety, age and health at purchase. Little Gems will last longer than the more delicate cultivars such as oak leaf. Be prepared to discard a few of the outer (older) leaves, which, particularly in organic lettuce, can be affected by mildew without condemning the whole head. A good indication of the age and health of the lettuce is given by the state of the butt, which, though browning rapidly after cutting, should never develop the softness resulting from rot or dehydration.

The leaves of a lettuce tend to get sweeter, milder and more blanched towards the centre but, as with most leafy vegetables, most of the vitamin and minerals are in the green, outer leaves. It always seems a shame that supermarkets insist on growers trimming and discarding these leaves – which also act as the plant's natural packaging – and then replacing them with plastic packaging in the never-ending quest for sweetness and neat presentation. The extreme is the virtually nutrient-free iceberg, but heavily trimmed 'sweet heart romaines' or even Little Gem are only marginally better.

Making a good green salad is all about balancing a variety of leaves, of differing flavours, textures, colours and shapes, with the right dressing. Most plain lettuces can be boring on their own, though the variation in colour and flavour from heart to outer leaves is a good start. Plain lettuces such as Cos and butterhead make a good base for a salad, to which you can add peppery leaves such as rocket, mizuna, land cress or the bitter radicchio/endive family (see page 30). If you share my dread of pre-prepared salad bags and eat loads of salad but don't have the space or inclination to grow your own, I would recommend buying the basic lettuces and sowing a window box with your favourite specialist salad leaves.

I eat salad virtually every day and tend to prepare about four days' worth at once. Tear or cut your leaves into a sink of cold water (I am not convinced that cutting is the sin that certain celebrity chefs would have us believe), mix well and leave to soak for 5 minutes with occasional agitation, then drain and dry. There are some truly appalling and very irritating salad spinners on the market; all the ones that involve pushing a button or winding a handle drive me mad. A tolerable and invigorating job can be done by loading the leaves into a plastic colander, wrapping it in a tea towel, then stepping outside and whirling it around your head. A better option is to buy a salad spinner with a drawstring action. Once washed and thoroughly dried, the leaves can be kept in a plastic bag in the fridge for 3–4 days.

Summer Salad with Beetroot, Goat's Cheese and Green Beans

A very simple salad that goes well with grilled lamb. For an autumnal version, substitute roasted squash (see page 342) for the beetroot.

Serves 4–6

300g mixed summer salad leaves
150g French beans
200g cooked beetroot (see page 21), cut into 2cm cubes
4 tablespoons olive oil
1 tablespoon good-quality red wine vinegar or sherry vinegar
100g soft goat's cheese, crumbled
sea salt and freshly ground black pepper

Wash the salad leaves and dry well. Cook the beans in boiling salted water for 3–4 minutes, until just tender, then drain, refresh in cold water and drain again. Put them in a large bowl with the salad leaves and beetroot.

Whisk the olive oil, vinegar and some seasoning together to make a dressing. Toss with the salad, then sprinkle with the goat's cheese.

Winter Salad with Spiced Pecans, Pears and Devon Blue

The spiced pecans are so delicious that you will have to guard them or they will disappear before you have a chance to serve the salad. You could always cut out the salad and serve the pecans on their own with drinks! If you can't get Devon Blue, gorgonzola or dolcelatte make good substitutes.

Serves 4–6

300g mixed winter salad leaves
75g pecan nuts
a pinch of cayenne pepper
1 teaspoon Worcestershire sauce
a dash of Tabasco sauce
½ teaspoon salt
3 ripe pears, peeled, cored and sliced
3 tablespoons Basic Vinaigrette (see page 319)
75g Devon Blue cheese, crumbled

Wash and dry the salad leaves and set aside. In a small bowl, mix the pecans with the cayenne pepper, Worcestershire sauce, Tabasco and salt. Scatter them over a baking tray and bake in an oven preheated to 200°C/Gas Mark 6 for 5–6 minutes, until lightly toasted. Remove from the oven and leave to cool.

Put the pears and salad leaves in a bowl and toss with the dressing. Divide between 4 plates, scatter over the blue cheese and pecan nuts and serve.

Minted Braised Little Gems

This is based on a recipe in a wonderful book by Sally Butcher with the unlikely title of *Persia in Peckham* (Prospect Books, 2007). It's very good served with roast lamb. Frozen peas can be added in the last 5 minutes of cooking.

Serves 4

2 tablespoons sugar
1 tablespoon good-quality white wine vinegar
4 Little Gem lettuces
5 sprigs of mint
100ml chicken or vegetable stock
sea salt and freshly ground black pepper

Put the sugar, vinegar and 2 tablespoons of water in a small pan and heat gently until the sugar has dissolved. Remove from the heat.

Remove and discard the outer leaves from the lettuces. Cut each lettuce into quarters, place in an ovenproof dish with the mint, stock and sugar/vinegar syrup and season well. Cover and cook in an oven preheated to 180°C/Gas Mark 4 for 20–25 minutes, until the lettuces are tender.

Duck with Little Gem, Spring Onions and Peas

A dish for a summer's day. The light spring vegetables offset the richness of the duck. Don't forget to save any excess duck fat for roasting potatoes – or for cooking Yorkshire pudding.

Serves 2

2 duck breasts
2cm piece of fresh ginger, finely grated
1 bunch of spring onions, sliced
2 Little Gem lettuces, shredded
200g fresh or frozen peas
a few mint leaves
1 tablespoon soy sauce
1 tablespoon balsamic vinegar
sea salt and freshly ground black pepper

Heat a medium heavy-based frying pan until very hot. Add the duck breasts, skin-side down, then reduce the heat and cook for about 6 minutes, until the skin is nicely browned. Turn over and cook for another 6 minutes, until the duck is cooked but still pink in the centre. Remove from the pan and leave to rest in a warm place.

Drain off all but 2 tablespoons of the fat from the pan. Add the ginger and spring onions and cook for a few minutes, until softened. Add the lettuce and peas and cook gently for 5 minutes or until the lettuce has wilted and the peas are cooked. Stir in the mint leaves, soy sauce and balsamic vinegar, then season to taste. Slice the duck breasts and serve on top of the vegetables.

Pak Choi with Chicken Broth

This recipe is ideal for chilly autumn evenings and, like so many chicken soups, makes an excellent and comforting antidote to colds and flu. If you want a more substantial broth, just add some noodles.

Serves 6–8

1 chicken
4 garlic cloves, sliced
2cm piece of fresh ginger, sliced
2 onions, sliced
1 star anise
2 corn cobs
2 carrots, cut into batons
1 celery stalk, cut into batons
600g pak choi, cut into chunks
soy sauce, to taste

Place the chicken in a pan in which it fits snugly and add enough water to cover. Add the garlic, ginger, onions and star anise and bring to the boil. Reduce the heat and simmer very gently for about an hour, until the chicken is cooked through. Remove the chicken from the pan and set aside.

Strain the stock into a clean pan. Stand the corn cobs upright on a board and slice off the kernels, then add them to the stock, together with the carrots and celery. Bring to the boil and simmer for 10 minutes.

Remove the meat from the chicken in strips. Add the chicken and pak choi to the pan and cook for 1 minute. Season with soy sauce to taste.

Simple Rocket Salad with Prosciutto and Parmesan

So simple it barely needs a recipe, but it's worth knowing how to do it properly.

Serves 4

2 tablespoons good olive oil
juice of ½ lemon
300g rocket
30g Parmesan cheese, cut into slivers
8 thin slices of prosciutto (or Serrano ham)
sea salt and freshly ground black pepper

Whisk the olive oil and lemon juice together with some salt and pepper to make a dressing. Put the rocket leaves in a bowl and toss with the dressing. Divide between 4 plates, sprinkle with the Parmesan slivers and drape each serving with 2 slices of prosciutto.

Basic Vinaigrette

A reliable vinaigrette for dressing any type of salad.

Makes about 300ml

240ml sunflower oil
4 tablespoons good-quality balsamic vinegar or red wine vinegar
½ garlic clove, crushed to a paste with a little salt
1 tablespoon Dijon mustard
sea salt and freshly ground black pepper

Put all the ingredients in a jar and shake furiously, or whisk them all together.

See also:
Fattoush with Broad Beans (page 48)
Waldorf Salad (page 121)
Artichoke, Salmon and New Potato Salad with Anchovy Sauce (page 186)

Growing vegetables organically makes you a better person

How can a Bachelor of Science make such an absurdly irrational claim? Clearly I have lost my way and should get off the farm more before I become a fully crazed theosophical Luddite. Yet for me, the foundations of organic farming are even broader than the environmental, nutritional, animal welfare and food safety benefits that have driven the market; organic farming is about our relationship with the planet we inhabit, including the six billion or so people we share it with. At its best, it is about humility, understanding and learning from nature, rather than arrogance, domination and destruction. It is about peace and respect rather than violence.

These might sound like wild claims. But if you go to war with nature without the back-up of an arsenal of fossil-fuel-based agrochemicals, you will lose. With that defeat comes humility, closely followed by re-evaluation, introspection and learning. With the arsenal, you also lose, but the illusion of power is maintained, and many farmers are too single-minded to realise what it is they are losing and what a high price the planet is paying.

Conversion to organic farming takes two years for the farmer's soil but normally much longer for his or her mind. It is not a step backwards into a world of nostalgia; it is part of a step forward into an age of wisdom where, just possibly, we use our knowledge and ingenuity as custodians rather than rulers of our planet.

Looking back over my early years as a grower, it is hard to believe how personally I used to take it when things went wrong. Perhaps my self-centred arrogance would have subsided with age anyway, but I am convinced that the vulnerability inherent in organic farming helped. For most converting farmers, there comes an epiphany when they realise they have got the relationship wrong; that organic farming is not about replacing ammonium nitrate with chicken shit, pyrethrum with soft soap, or herbicides with flame throwers; that the conflict is unnecessary and ultimately self-defeating, and that the key to organic farming is observation, empathy and understanding rather than power.

True organic farming requires a deep, long-term understanding of the ecology of our farms and crops. It is about a subtle management of our environment to get what we want (vegetables, in our case) with the minimum of interference and disturbance. Spraying a field with a nerve poison to kill aphids (and all other insects along the way) is a violent and ignorant act; planting phasealia to attract adult hoverflies and lacewings, whose larvae will eat the aphids, is a peaceful and truly knowing one. Similarly, sterilising soil with the fumigant methyl bromide to kill a few weed seeds and pathogens when 99.99 per cent of the soil's population is beneficial is as dumb and intellectually lazy as expecting carpet-bombing Vietnam to lead to peace and freedom.

Nature can provide what academics would call 'elegant' solutions – which include the kind of balance and subtle relationships between organisms that make conventional farming's clumsy, energy-consuming and often thoughtless abuses seem grotesque by comparison. It has so much to teach those who are receptive, and organic farmers normally become more receptive than most. If Bush and Blair had spent their bonding time on an organic allotment with their hands in the soil rather than driving around in a golf cart, they would have realised that they are not omnipotent, and I am pretty sure their countries would not be fighting their futile wars.

Spinach and Chard

Most box schemes grow more Swiss chard (white mid ribs, deep-green leaves), ruby chard (red mid ribs) and perpetual spinach (green mid ribs) than their customers know what to do with. The temptation of a simple and vigorous cut-and-come-again crop with few pests and diseases is more than most farmers can resist. After 20 years of chard abuse from customers (surpassed in volume only by cabbage abuse), I like to think youthful enthusiasm with the seed drill has been curbed by sensitivity to customer preferences.

Chards and their cousin, perpetual spinach, are actually more closely related to beetroot, sugar beet and mangolds (all *Beta vulgaris*) than to true spinach (*Spinacea oleracea*). True spinach is undoubtedly more succulent and, for most purposes, superior. Supermarkets normally sell only baby spinach with 5–8cm leaves but it is my experience that this has little culinary advantage over the larger-leaved types we grow. Unlike the more tolerant chards and perpetual spinach, true spinach is a highly strung sprinter, needing consistent and ideal growing conditions (irrigation, perfect soil, and, I hate to admit, fungicides). Since it is normally cut only once, a programme of frequent sowings is needed to provide true spinach throughout the season. It is difficult to grow organically (and consequently much more expensive), suffering from mildew and prone to bolt or go yellow in the presence of unrequited love, menstruating women, certain wind changes or just for the hell of it. We go on trying, but fail as often as we succeed.

In Devon we sow chard and spinach from April to August for harvest from June to November. Some growers seem to get away with sowing earlier, and you might be lucky in your garden, but without the advantage of fungicide-treated seed, the seed or seedlings too often rot in the ground. In a protected garden, chard and perpetual spinach will survive the winter and, with patient and selective picking, can provide a source of greens right through to the following May, when they will run to seed. We lack the patience, and our customers are fussier than some gardeners, so picking tends to stop with the first hard frost or big gale. Richard Rowan, one of our Cornish co-op growers, who has a protected farm on the banks of the River Tamar, runs some hungry sheep over his crop after picking in November. They graze the plants down to the ground and, in a good year, new, clean shoots appear after Christmas ready for a very welcome picking in April, when we are desperately short of home-grown produce.

Chard originated around the Mediterranean, possibly in Sicily, where it is prized more for the fleshy, white mid ribs than for the greens themselves. Perhaps not surprisingly, given its origins, it is more tolerant of heat and drought than the damp- and cool-loving spinach and has a better shelf life. There are various cultivars of Swiss chard, including the red-ribbed ruby, rainbow or rhubarb chard (probably three marketeers' versions of the same thing). Though a pretty novelty, these variations tend to be bitter and tough when we have grown them and, like so many novelty vegetables, ultimately disappointing. Southern European cultivars are usually more compact in their growth, with thicker ribs reflecting their use in local cooking.

Storage and preparation

True spinach has a very short shelf life. Keep it in a plastic bag in the fridge and eat it within a couple of days. I would eat it stalks and all, unless they are very large, in which case it may be worth trimming them.

Perpetual spinach and chard will keep for longer. Don't be put off by some wilting, which is not necessarily a sign of ageing and does not affect the flavour, provided it is not accompanied by yellowing. The stalks, or mid ribs, are best sliced or torn out and discarded, or, in the case of chard, cooked separately – put them on a few minutes before the leaf. Once cut, the stalks brown, so if you are not going to use them immediately, put them in water acidulated with lemon juice. In Mediterranean cooking, the stalks are used as a vehicle for various strong sauces. The green leaves of chard, cooked without their stalks, can be substituted for spinach in most recipes. They tend to be less bitter (lower in oxalic acid) and more succulent than perpetual spinach, but are never as succulent as true spinach.

Gnocchi Verde

These spinach and ricotta gnocchi make a delicious light alternative to the more usual potato or semolina ones. Use true spinach, if you can get it; it gives a better result than the perpetual variety (and is easier to prepare!).

Serves 4 as a starter

1 tablespoon butter
1 small onion, finely chopped
450g spinach, tough stalks removed
75g plain flour
150g ricotta cheese
2 egg yolks
100g Parmesan cheese, freshly grated, plus extra to serve
freshly grated nutmeg
sea salt and freshly ground black pepper
Sage Butter (see page 217), to serve

Heat the butter in a small frying pan, add the onion and cook gently for 8–10 minutes, until soft but not coloured.

Blanch the spinach in a large pan of boiling salted water for 1 minute, then drain and refresh in cold water. Drain again, squeeze out the excess water and chop the spinach roughly. Add to the onion, seasoning well, and cook for about 8 minutes, making sure they are thoroughly combined. Tip the mixture into a large bowl and sift in the flour. Add the ricotta and mix well. Then stir in the egg yolks, Parmesan and some nutmeg and mix again. Season to taste.

Using 2 dessertspoons, shape the mixture into quenelles: take a spoonful of the mixture and then scoop it off with the second spoon, passing it from one spoon to the other until it is a neat oval shape. Place on a lightly floured tray and chill for 1 hour.

To cook the gnocchi, bring a large pan of salted water to the boil and add them in batches, being careful not to overcrowd the pan. When the gnocchi rise to the surface, give them about 3 minutes more, then scoop out with a slotted spoon and place in a warm serving dish. Serve sprinkled with Parmesan and drizzled with Sage Butter.

Spinach and Crab Frittata

Ideal for brunch or a light lunch. You could include diced roasted red peppers. For an Asian version, omit the Parmesan and nutmeg and add spring onions and chilli. Serve drizzled with oyster sauce.

Serves 4–6

400g spinach
3 tablespoons olive oil
1 onion, finely chopped
1 garlic clove, crushed
freshly grated nutmeg
6 eggs
1 tablespoon chopped herbs, such as coriander, parsley or chives,
    or a mixture
2 tablespoons freshly grated Parmesan cheese
200g fresh white crab meat
sea salt and freshly ground black pepper

Remove and discard the stalks from the spinach. Blanch the leaves in a large pan of boiling salted water for 1 minute, then drain and refresh in cold water. Squeeze out the excess water, chop the spinach roughly and set aside.

Heat 1 tablespoon of the olive oil in a pan, add the onion and garlic and cook over a moderate heat for 5–10 minutes, until soft. Stir in the spinach and season well with salt, pepper and nutmeg, then remove from the heat.

Lightly beat the eggs in a bowl. Mix in the spinach and onion, plus the herbs, Parmesan, crab meat and some seasoning.

Heat the remaining olive oil in a non-stick frying pan over a high heat for 2 minutes. Add the frittata mixture and reduce the heat to medium. Cook until the frittata is set underneath and still slightly runny on top, running a spatula around the sides to make sure it is not sticking. Place the pan under a hot grill for 1 minute to cook the top. Slide the frittata out of the pan and leave to cool for about 10 minutes, then cut it into wedges to serve.

Sesame Coconut Fish (or Chicken) with Chilli Spinach

Firm white fish such as halibut work best in this quick, light dish.

Serves 4

4 x 175g pieces of white fish fillet, skinned (or 4 chicken breasts, skinned)
3 tablespoons sunflower oil
1–2 red chillies, deseeded and finely chopped
2.5cm piece of fresh ginger, finely grated
300g spinach, stalks removed
sea salt and freshly ground black pepper

For the sesame coconut crust:
1 teaspoon brown sugar
2 teaspoons oyster sauce
1 egg, lightly beaten
2 tablespoons sesame seeds
2 tablespoons desiccated coconut
1 garlic clove, crushed
2 tablespoons chopped coriander

Mix all the ingredients for the crust together and spread them over the fish fillets. Chill for a few hours to firm up.

Heat 2 tablespoons of the sunflower oil in a large, ovenproof frying pan. Place the fish in the hot oil, crust-side down, and cook over a medium heat for about 5 minutes, until the crust is golden brown. Carefully turn the fish over with a spatula, transfer the pan to an oven preheated to 200°C/Gas Mark 6 and bake for 4–5 minutes (10 minutes for chicken), until cooked through.

Meanwhile, heat the remaining sunflower oil in a frying pan, add the chilli and ginger and cook for 2 minutes. Turn up the heat, add the spinach and cook, stirring vigorously, until wilted. Season to taste. Serve the fish on the spinach.

Grilled Leg of Lamb with Swiss Chard and Anchovy Gratin

This is a dish we often serve in the Field Kitchen. The gratin is based on one in the lovely book *A Table in Provence*, by Lesley Forbes (Webb & Bower, 1987). Jane doesn't need much persuasion to add anchovies to anything, but the chard and anchovy work particularly well together.

Serves 6

6 garlic cloves, crushed
2 tablespoons chopped rosemary
a good pinch of freshly ground black pepper
3 tablespoons lemon juice
4 tablespoons olive oil
1 leg of lamb, weighing about 2kg, skinned, boned and butterflied
   (you could ask your butcher to do this)

For the stock:
juice of ½ lemon
a splash of white wine
1 teaspoon sugar
1 bay leaf
a sprig of thyme

For the gratin:
2 bunches of Swiss chard (about 500–600g)
a large knob of butter
1 onion, chopped
3 garlic cloves, crushed
6 anchovies
1 tablespoon plain flour
1 tablespoon freshly grated Parmesan cheese
freshly ground black pepper

Mix together the garlic, rosemary, pepper, lemon juice and olive oil to make a marinade. Place the lamb in a large dish, pour over the marinade and leave at room temperature for 8 hours or overnight, turning the meat occasionally.

To make the stock, put all the ingredients in a pan with 500ml of water, bring to the boil and simmer for 20 minutes. Strain and set aside.

To make the gratin, separate the chard leaves from the stalks and blanch them in a large pan of boiling salted water for 1 minute. Drain well, refresh under cold running water, then squeeze out excess water. Set aside.

Cut the chard stalks across into 5mm strips. Bring the stock to the boil, add the chard stalks and simmer gently for 5 minutes. Drain the stalks and set aside, saving the stock for later.

Heat the butter in a pan, add the onion and cook gently for 15 minutes, until soft. Add the garlic and cook for a few more minutes. Remove from the heat and add the anchovies, stirring until they dissolve into the mixture. Return to the heat and stir in the flour to make a roux. Cook very gently for 5 minutes. Slowly stir in the reserved chard stock until you have a thick sauce. Simmer for about 5 minutes.

Stir the chard stalks and leaves into the sauce, together with the grated Parmesan and some black pepper. Transfer the mixture to a gratin dish and bake in an oven preheated to 160°C/Gas Mark 3 for about 20 minutes, until golden.

Remove the lamb from the marinade. Preheat a ridged griddle pan or a large, heavy-based frying pan and cook the lamb for 2 minutes on each side, until browned. Transfer to a roasting tray and finish off in the oven at 200°C/Gas Mark 6 for a few minutes, depending on how pink you like your lamb. Leave to rest for about 10 minutes, then serve with the gratin.

Swiss Chard and Onion Tart

We started serving this as a vegetarian option in the Field Kitchen and it is so popular that we try to make sure everyone gets a slice now. The recipe is not set in stone. Consider the base as a canvas: you can add what you like (within reason). Try a few chopped anchovies or some mushrooms sautéed with thyme. You could even crack a couple of eggs on before baking.

Serves 4

1 quantity of Shortcrust Pastry (see page 275)
50g butter
3 small onions, finely sliced
leaves from 1 sprig of thyme
300g Swiss chard
10 olives, chopped
½ tablespoon freshly grated Parmesan cheese
3–4 tablespoons crème fraîche
sea salt and freshly ground black pepper

Roll out the pastry on a lightly floured surface into a rough circle (or actually any shape – this tart is very rustic, so the less uniform, the better). Place on a baking sheet, prick with a fork in several places and chill for 15 minutes. Place in an oven preheated to 200°C/Gas Mark 6 and bake for 10–15 minutes, until golden brown.

Heat the butter in a pan, add the onions and thyme and cook gently for about 10 minutes, until soft but not coloured.

Meanwhile, separate the chard stalks from the leaves and chop both leaves and stalks roughly, keeping them separate. Add the stalks to a pan of boiling salted water and cook for 2–3 minutes, until tender. Remove the stalks with a slotted spoon and set aside. Add the leaves to the boiling water and blanch briefly. Drain well, refresh under a cold tap and then squeeze to remove as much water as possible.

Add the chard stalks and leaves to the onions and reheat gently. Season to taste and mix well. Spread the mixture over the pastry base and sprinkle with the chopped olives, Parmesan and a few blobs of crème fraîche. Bake in an oven preheated to 190°C/Gas Mark 5 for about 15 minutes, until lightly browned.

Easy ideas for spinach and chard

✦ Cook spinach or chard leaves in boiling water for 1 minute, then drain, refresh in cold water and drain again. Squeeze out all the liquid. Fry some sliced garlic in olive oil until soft, add the spinach or chard and toss with raisins or toasted pine nuts. Season and serve.

✦ Mix 200g cooked chopped spinach or chard with 1 egg, 200ml double cream, 1 tablespoon of grated Parmesan and some seasoning. Bake in a gratin dish or in a pastry case (see Sorrel Tart, page 212) at 150°C/Gas Mark 2 for about 25 minutes, until just set.

✦ Dress cold cooked spinach with pomegranate juice and seeds. Serve as part of a mezze or with grilled fish.

✦ For a quick soup, cook sliced spinach in a little butter, then add just enough milk and stock to cover and bring to the boil. Season well with salt, pepper and nutmeg, sprinkle with grated Parmesan and serve over toasted bread in a bowl.

See also:
Chickpeas with Carrots and Swiss Chard (page 98)
Braised Sweetcorn with Spinach (page 368)

Spring Greens

These hardy cabbages are sown late in the season (late July or August) and survive the winter as young, leafy plants. It is always a struggle to keep the pigeons off them in a hard winter, but if we succeed they grow away in the spring to produce small, loose-leaved hearts in March and April, when we are desperately short of home-grown greens. At this time the ground is still cold and, with no bacterial action to release nutrients, the plants are often starved of nitrogen, sometimes giving them a purplish colour and slightly tatty appearance. A bit of hardship and slow growth often helps develop the flavour; provided the hardship has not been too extreme, spring greens can provide a supply of deliciously sweet leaves when there is very little else around, doing away with the need to truck tired and expensive cabbages from Spain and Italy.

Don't be put off by appearances: when truly fresh, in season (from January to April) and grown without being pushed on with sacks of nitrogen, spring greens are bursting with flavour and vitality, making them one of our most underrated vegetables. It is a tragedy that so many of today's cooks are more at home with a trucked pepper or air-freighted mangetout on their chopping board than these humble, affordable, environmentally friendly and wonderfully nutritious little cabbages.

Storage and preparation

For a cabbage, spring greens have a relatively short shelf life, especially later in the winter when they are hungry for nitrogen. They should go straight into your fridge in a plastic bag and be eaten within four days. As the days lengthen in the spring, the plants desperately try to push out new leaves. Most modern vegetable crops have been bred to expect regular applications of ammonium nitrate at this time to keep them going. In the absence of this shot in the arm, our crops adopt a strategy of sacrificing the old to feed the young: scarce nutrients mobilised and withdrawn from the outer leaves and used for new growth. Don't always condemn an organic cabbage or lettuce on the grounds of yellowing of the outer leaves; it is part of a strategy to survive adversity and, with a bit of trimming, the centre may be fine.

If your spring greens have had a hard life (as indicated by smaller plants and tinges of purple), the flavour will be stronger and they may be better boiled;

always use plenty of salted water at a rolling boil. Lusher, softer greens are best steamed, and can also be stir-fried. The leaf ribs can be very sweet and tender right down to where they join the stalk, especially if sliced thinly. My wife always insists on a knob of butter with steamed or boiled greens but, as a purist greens lover, I like them just as they are. As with all greens, you should get them on to the table as fast as possible.

Spring Greens with Coconut and Chilli

In Samoa, one of the national dishes is palusami, which consists of a foil-wrapped parcel of young taro leaves, coconut cream and garlic placed in a stone oven, or umu, and cooked slowly for several hours. Jane has tried to emulate it using spring greens, which do look a bit like taro leaves. It is quite a rich dish and makes a lovely accompaniment to spicy grilled chicken or fish.

Serves 4

1 bunch of spring greens, thinly sliced
1 dessertspoon sunflower oil
3 garlic cloves, crushed to a paste with a pinch of salt
2 dried chillies, chopped
400ml coconut milk
juice of ½ lemon

Blanch the greens in boiling water for 2 minutes, then drain, refresh in cold water and squeeze out the excess. Set aside.

Heat the sunflower oil in a pan, add the garlic and chillies and fry over a low heat for a minute or so. Add the coconut milk and simmer over a high heat for 10 minutes, until reduced by about half. Stir in the spring greens and cook over a medium heat for about 10 minutes, until the coconut milk is just coating the greens. Finish with the lemon juice.

Spring Greens with Garlic and Soy Sauce

Spring greens are tender, full of flavour and packed with vitamins. This is a good way to get the best of their sweet, zesty, unadulterated spring flavour. You may be tempted to add chilli, ginger or lemon.

Serves 6

2 small bunches of spring greens
2–4 tablespoons sunflower oil
2 garlic cloves
soy sauce

Chop the greens crossways into strips of 1cm or less, cutting almost down to the stump. The stems and leaf ribs are the sweetest bits.

Heat the oil over a high heat in a wok or a large, heavy-bottomed frying pan. Peel the garlic and crush lightly with the back of a knife (keeping the cloves whole will help prevent them burning). Cook in the oil for about 20 seconds, adding the greens before the garlic browns. Cook for about 2 minutes, turning the greens constantly in the oil. Add 2 or 3 shakes of soy sauce, cook for a further 15 seconds and serve immediately.

Spring Greens with Wet and Wild Garlic

This recipe was born of complete desperation, when the fields were yielding spring greens and not much else, but the feedback we had from customers in the Field Kitchen was very positive.

Serves 6

1 tablespoon butter
1 tablespoon olive oil
2 wet garlic bulbs, chopped (or 1 garlic clove, sliced)
2 bunches of spring greens, shredded crossways into 1cm strips
1 bunch of wild garlic leaves, shredded
1 tablespoon freshly grated Parmesan cheese
sea salt and freshly ground black pepper

Melt the butter with the oil in a large saucepan. Add the garlic and cook for a few minutes without browning. Add the spring greens, turn up the heat and stir vigorously for about 4–5 minutes, until wilted. Stir in the shredded wild garlic leaves and cook for 1 minute. Add the grated Parmesan, season to taste and serve.

Easy ideas for spring greens

✦ Add lightly steamed spring greens to an omelette with a sprinkling of goat's cheese.

✦ Gently cook shredded spring greens in a little butter with chopped bacon and caraway seeds.

✦ Substitute spring greens for cabbage in Cabbage with Lentils, Chilli and Coriander (see page 80).

Squash and Pumpkins

Winter squash and pumpkins, along with other *Cucurbitaceae*, are native to America, where their ancestors grew wild as climbers. They are distinguished from summer squash, courgettes, marrows and other relatives by the fact that their fruits are harvested mature and can be stored for several weeks, or in some cases months. Pumpkins are really just a group of winter squashes, normally distinguished by their colour and generally with a lower dry matter, which means they don't keep as well.

With maize and beans, squash formed a staple of the Native American diet. People seem to be more conservative about their staple starch than they are about exotic fruit, and though squash have made huge strides in popularity, with butternut becoming a year-round feature on supermarket shelves, the nation remains divided on their culinary virtues.

Not many would deny their decorative qualities, and they are one of the few vegetables (they are, in fact, a fruit) that enjoy being stored in the warm, so even if you don't want to eat them, collect all shapes and sizes and enjoy them in a bowl or on a shelf throughout the winter.

All squashes are intolerant of frost and like a lot of heat and sun, so we don't plant until May or even June, and choose warm, protected fields to give the crop a fair chance of reaching maturity before the first autumn frost. Unfortunately our climate has put pressure on breeders to select fast-growing, early-maturing hybrid varieties at the expense of flavour. I hate to admit it, but squash imported from more southern climates often taste better than our home-produced versions.

For a while I tried copying the Native American practice of intercropping squash with corn and green beans. It was very rewarding, with all three crops producing virtually a full yield, seemingly without competing with one another. The beans and squash seemed to thrive in the protection afforded by the corn, even though there must have been some shading, and the trio appeared to share water amicably and collectively tolerated drought remarkably well. Sadly, field workers were less enthusiastic about having to tiptoe over the web of squash stems to pick the corn and beans and I was reluctantly obliged to return to conventional mono-cropping to maintain peace and keep a workforce. In a garden, where it may be more important to use land efficiently than time, I would recommend the practice.

Apart from miserable summers and early frosts, the main threat to pumpkins and squash (as with sweetcorn) is badgers. They occasionally punch a hole and scoop out the seeds but more frequently they just roll them around. The scratches their claws make on the skin develop into calloused, cankerous growth as the fruit heal themselves. I used to assume the badgers were just frolicking by moonlight until, returning from the pub one moonlit night, I caught them grubbing intently around in the pumpkin patch and realised they were searching for the worms and slugs that take refuge under the fruit.

There are numerous varieties of squash and the nomenclature gets thoroughly confusing, with the same types sometimes having more than one name even in the UK, and often different names around the globe. We keep experimenting but the varieties below are the ones that seem to perform consistently in our fields and the kitchen.

Pumpkins

In the UK the larger pumpkins are good only for making Jack-o-lanterns, their flesh generally being watery, bland and soapy. Some of the smaller 'sugar pumpkins' have firmer flesh and are good roasted or made into soup. Elsewhere in the world I have found large, firm-fleshed varieties that are often sold from markets and shops in segments for cooking. I suspect these varieties need a better summer than we get in the UK.

Pumpkins generally do not store well. The small ones may keep until December if they have had a really good summer to harden their skins but the large ones sometimes struggle to make it to Halloween before collapsing in a smelly mess.

Crown Prince

These satsuma-shaped, pale blue-grey squash (also known as Blue Hubbard or Queensland Blue) are very dense, with deep-orange flesh, and can grow to five kilos. They are the best-tasting, best-keeping, most reliable and highest-yielding squash we have grown. Unfortunately they tend to be too large for the UK market and very hard to peel; you sometimes need an axe to get into them.

Butternut

The best-known squash in the UK, these are buff coloured and elongated, with dense flesh and very few seeds. They are one of the few squash that can be peeled with a vegetable peeler and are therefore the easiest to prepare. Although they can sometimes taste very good, their popularity has attracted the attentions of the plant breeders, who have selected for yield, consistent fruit size and shape, and early maturity. These attributes have come at the expense of flavour, and some of the new varieties look the part but can have watery, soapy flesh. The older and better varieties struggle, in cool years, to ripen in our climate. We do grow a few ourselves, but buy most from a farmer in Provence, whose crop, I reluctantly have to admit, generally tastes much better than ours.

Green onion

Delicious small, green fruits that are either squat or onion-shaped. For all but the largest specimens, peeling is impractical, so they are best roasted in segments and then you can either scoop out the flesh with a spoon or leave your guests to deal with the problem.

Golden (or green) acorn

These yellow/gold, medium-to-small squash are good keepers. Roast in segments, unpeeled, as for green onion squash, above.

Red onion/Uchiki kuri

Small, orange, onion-shaped fruits with a great flavour. Best roasted in segments.

Turk's Turban

You'll know it when you see it. Looks great, but not that good to eat. Leave it on the shelf until desperate, or just enjoy its decorative qualities.

Storage and preparation

In the UK climate, the challenge is always to get the fruit fully ripe, with a hard, protective skin, before bringing them into store. We usually find ourselves nervously watching the weather forecast and then bringing them in in a mad rush when the first frost threatens. They must be handled like eggs to avoid damaging the skins and providing an entry point for rots.

Once inside, squash and pumpkin need to be kept somewhere warm and dry, ideally where the temperature never drops below 14°C. The harder-skinned varieties, such as Crown Prince, can sometimes last right through to the following autumn. Once the skin is cut, they should be put in the fridge and used within a week; hence the problem with the larger varieties. Wrapping in cling film is no benefit, in my experience.

With the exception of the thin-skinned butternut squash, peeling is a nightmare. The risk of serious injury can be reduced by cutting the squash in half first, so that at least you can lay it flat and prevent it rolling around whilst you set about the task with a sharp knife. Alternatively, if simply roasting, you can cook them in sections, with the skin on, and leave the problem to your diners. I have to say, this does not go down well in my family. If the recipe requires cooked flesh (e.g. for a risotto), you can roast them in halves and then scoop the flesh out when soft. Never roast a whole squash; it will explode, and if you and your oven survive you will be left with a long cleaning job.

Having halved your squash, which itself is not a job for the fainthearted (I recommend a really heavy knife or a meat cleaver), you can remove the seeds and pulp with a spoon. If the seeds are large and you have the time and inclination, you can sort them from the fibrous pulp and roast them in a moderate oven (about 180°C/Gas Mark 4) in a shallow layer with a little oil and soy sauce to eat as a snack.

Squash and Lentil Soup with Chilli and Fennel Seeds

A simple, satisfying soup for a chilly autumn evening.

Serves 6

2 tablespoons olive oil
1 onion, finely chopped
2 garlic cloves, finely chopped
2 dried chillies, finely chopped
1 tablespoon ground fennel seeds
200g green lentils
1 medium squash, peeled, deseeded and cut into 1cm cubes
sea salt and freshly ground black pepper

Heat the olive oil in a large pan, add the onion, garlic, chillies and ground fennel seeds and sweat gently for about 5 minutes. Then add the lentils and the diced squash. Cover with water and simmer for about 40 minutes, until both the squash and lentils are tender. Season to taste. The soup can be served like this, or you can blend a cupful of the soup and stir it back into the pan.

Dev-Mex Pumpkin Soup

We hold an annual Pumpkin Day at the farm, when we have up to 2,000 visitors. When we tried this pumpkin soup last year, Russell and Emily, who work in the Field Kitchen, succeeded in turning a random idea into something fabulous. The ingredients list may look long but it is delicious and easy to make. Roasting the pumpkin gives a better result but is not absolutely necessary.

Serves 6–8

1 pumpkin or squash (about 1.5 kg), peeled, deseeded and cut into 2cm
   cubes
3 tablespoons olive oil
2 onions, finely chopped
½ teaspoon smoked paprika
3 garlic cloves, crushed
2 red chillies, deseeded and finely chopped
400g can of tomatoes
1 litre chicken or vegetable stock
425g can of red kidney beans, drained
2 cooked corn cobs (see page 367)
1 tablespoon sweet chilli sauce
juice of 1 lime
sea salt and freshly ground black pepper

To garnish:
100g tortilla chips, crushed
75g Jarlsberg cheese, grated
2 tablespoons chopped coriander
1 ripe avocado, peeled, diced and tossed with the juice of 2 limes

Place the pumpkin cubes on a roasting tray and toss them with 1 tablespoon of the olive oil and some salt and pepper. Place in an oven preheated to 180°C/Gas Mark 4 and roast for 40 minutes, until slightly coloured.

Meanwhile, heat the rest of the olive oil in a large pan, add the onions and cook for 20 minutes, until tender and slightly caramelised. Stir in the paprika, garlic and chillies and cook for 3 minutes. Add the tomatoes, simmer for 15 minutes or until reduced and thick, then stir in the roast pumpkin. Purée with a hand blender, slowly adding the stock until well combined. Bring to the boil

and add the kidney beans and the kernels from the corn cobs. Season well, adding chilli sauce and lime juice to taste, and simmer for 10 minutes.

Before serving, add half the garnish ingredients and fold them through the soup, then scatter the rest on top.

Roasted Butternut Squash with Garlic and Chilli

We serve many variations on this salad throughout the year and we always receive requests for it. Sometimes early in the squash season, the flesh tends to be a little dry. Darren, our tour guide, suggested roasting the squash with oiled sliced onions and it seemed to work. Maybe the onions prevented the squash drying out, or perhaps we just used a little more oil!

Serves 6 as a side dish

1 butternut squash
olive oil for drizzling
2 garlic cloves, very finely chopped
1 red chilli, very finely chopped
leaves from 1 sprig of rosemary, very finely chopped

Cut the squash in half lengthways, remove the seeds, then peel and slice it across into pieces about 1cm thick. Place on a roasting tray and drizzle with olive oil. Bake in an oven preheated to 200°C/Gas Mark 6 for about 30 minutes, until the squash is tender. Sprinkle the garlic, red chilli and rosemary over the squash and return it to the oven for 10 minutes, until the garlic and chilli are cooked but not browned.

✦ The roasted squash is delicious used in a salad with dressed salad leaves, cooked Puy lentils and a sprinkling of feta cheese.

Squash Risotto with Fried Sage Leaves

When cooking this risotto, we have found a great method of using all the squash or pumpkin waste – make it into stock. Just put the scooped-out seeds and fibres into a pan, cover with water and bring to the boil. Simmer for 30 minutes, then strain. This stock can also be used in squash soups for a better colour and flavour.

Serves 6

1 medium squash (about 500g), peeled, deseeded and cut into 1cm
   cubes
1 tablespoon olive oil
1.5 litres vegetable stock or squash stock (see above)
100g butter
1 onion, finely chopped
360g Arborio rice
a splash of white wine or vermouth
2 tablespoons freshly grated Parmesan cheese, plus extra to serve
sea salt and freshly ground black pepper
Sage Butter (see page 217), to serve

Toss the squash cubes with the olive oil and some seasoning, spread on a baking tray and roast in an oven preheated to 200°C/Gas Mark 6 for about 20 minutes, until tender and lightly coloured. Remove from the oven and set aside.

Heat up the stock to simmering point in a pan. In a separate large, heavy-based pan, heat 50g of the butter, then add the onion and cook gently for about 5 minutes, until softened. Add the rice and a pinch of salt, stir until well coated in the butter and cook gently for a few minutes. Add half the roast squash and stir gently for 2 minutes. Pour in the white wine or vermouth and simmer until it has been absorbed. Add just enough of the simmering stock to cover the rice and stir well. Keep gradually adding stock, a ladleful at a time, stirring constantly. It's important to keep the rice at a gentle simmer and allow each addition of stock to be absorbed before adding more. After about 15–18 minutes, when the rice is tender but still has a little bite, remove from the heat and mix in the remaining squash plus the remaining butter and the cheese. Cover and leave to rest for 5 minutes. Then season the risotto to taste and serve with a sprinkling of Parmesan and the Sage Butter.

Easy ideas for squash and pumpkins

✦ Substitute sliced squash for potatoes in the gratin on page 284.

✦ Cut pumpkin or squash into wedges, toss with salt, pepper, ground cumin and olive oil and roast at 200°C/Gas Mark 6 for about 20 minutes, until tender. Scatter with chopped chilli and garlic, return to the oven for 5 minutes, then drizzle with hummus and scatter with toasted pumpkin seeds and fresh coriander.

✦ Make the shortcrust pastry on page 275 (or substitute bought shortcrust or puff pastry) and roll it out into a circle. Mix 200g roasted squash cubes with a handful of toasted pecans, a little chopped sage, 150g ricotta cheese and some salt and pepper. Spread over the pastry, sprinkle with grated Parmesan and bake at 200°C/Gas Mark 6 for 10–15 minutes.

✦ For a quick sweet and sour pumpkin dish, fry 1cm-thick slices of peeled pumpkin in olive oil until tender and lightly browned. Heat 1 tablespoon of red wine vinegar with 1 tablespoon of sugar until the sugar has dissolved, then season with salt and pepper. Pour this over the pumpkin slices and serve sprinkled with chopped mint or coriander.

Strawberries and Cane Fruit

Plastic tunnels and modern pesticides have revolutionised soft fruit production. The prevailing view in the industry is that you can't do without one or the other, and to be sure of a crop you really need both. We have obstinately persisted with outdoor fruit production and have developed systems that give us some good, if erratic, crops. I very much doubt if the farm has ever made a penny out of fruit and I have yet to persuade any of our co-op members to join in the madness. However, we have produced some fine fruit and progressively reduced the frequency of disasters over the years, so I remain optimistic that we shall one day turn a profit.

Strawberries

Strawberries were the first crop I grew on any scale. We made several mistakes, the most fundamental proving to be using an iron bar to make planting holes, and I can now tell you that if a bar is necessary to make the hole, the seedbed is too tight (closely packed). I lost a lot of money and when, after three years, I finally ploughed them in, I was singing with joy on the tractor seat. I swore I would never grow them again.

Twenty years later we are doing much better, though I suspect we still have a lot to learn. Strawberries are an essential part of the English summer and a key crop for our box scheme, especially as they crop early in the season, when we are still short of home-grown variety for the boxes. Over the years we have experimented with many systems and have moved in the opposite direction from most of the industry: while they have been intensifying and moving the crop indoors, often abandoning soil in favour of hydroponic growing, we have stayed outdoors, abandoned irrigation and widened the spacing between plants to reduce disease pressure.

Given the chance to behave naturally, strawberries will ripen from late May to mid July in the south, early June to late July in the north. By then I have normally had enough and am ready to move on to raspberries, currants, plums and all the subsequent joys of an English summer. But I am a freak, however, and this is not how retailing works. The shelves of our supermarkets have strawberries all year round, whatever the price and whatever the flavour. When I supplied supermarkets, Waitrose used to tell me that I should be grateful for this because customers would be 'in the habit' of buying

strawberries when the UK season started. Apparently statistics show that more fruit is bought in season if customers have been primed with fruit air-freighted in from Israel, Jordan, Egypt, South Africa or Florida during the winter and trucked from Spain throughout the spring.

Over the last 20 years the British strawberry industry has been very success-ful at stretching the season and displacing imports. Fruit can be produced earlier if it is covered with tunnels (for picking in early May) or grown under glass (late April), and can be extended into the late summer and autumn using waiting beds planted with cold stored runners, which crop 60 days later. Nonetheless, strawberries are best and cheapest in their natural season. I would strongly recommend against buying fruit earlier than mid April or later than August; either it will have travelled long distances or it will have been grown under glass in poor light conditions, resulting in disappointing flavour.

Raspberries

Raspberries come in two guises: the more common summer fruiting varieties (such as Glen Ample, Glen Magna and Glen Moy) grow their cane one year and flower and bear fruit the next, allowing them to crop in July, whereas autumn fruiting varieties (such as Autumn Bliss and Joan) send up cane, flower and fruit in the same season and hence fruit later (August to October). As a grower, I am torn between the autumn types – which can, without skill or finesse, be slashed to the ground in winter, removing the inter-seasonal bridge for disease that standing cane provides – and the summer raspberries, which require some very fiddly selective pruning and training but do generally have a slightly better flavour.

Growing raspberries is difficult enough but getting them to market in good condition is the real challenge. Whereas strawberries are picked with the calyx attached to the fruit, it is traditional in this country (though not in France) to pick raspberries naked. In the act of removing the calyx, the fruit is inevitably damaged, leaving it more susceptible to botrytis. Largely for this reason, rasp-berries have the shortest shelf life of any fruit. The plus side is that at their best they taste truly sublime.

Blackberries

After seven years of cultivating blackberries, we have given up and grubbed the crop out. The uncomfortable truth was that the wild fruit, which can be gathered for free from our hedgerows, invariably tasted much better. Breeding and cultivation may have increased the size but they have ruined the flavour. Having said that, I have eaten Himalayan varieties from my father's garden that have tasted very good.

Currants

By comparison to raspberries and strawberries, black and red currants are a doddle to grow. Vigorous enough to shade out most of the weeds, they suffer no serious pests and diseases and are far less prone to melting into a pool of juice covered in fungal fur. The down side is that they take a long time to pick, and sadly the market for the fresh fruit is tiny – which is a shame, because blackcurrants are a wonderful fruit. The vast majority of the UK crop is picked mechanically and goes into processing, largely to make Ribena.

Redcurrants look pretty and are easy to grow, but taste bitter and can be pretty nasty on their own – though they are a vital ingredient in a good summer pudding, combined with raspberries. In my view, their main virtue is decorative and for jelly.

Storage and preparation

Unless your fruit is underripe or you are planning to eat it straight away, all soft fruit is best kept in the fridge. If you get two days out of raspberries and three out of strawberries, you should be happy. Soft fruit bruises very easily if handled when damp, and can be picked only in dry weather. Disease levels build up during prolonged damp spells, when it can be very difficult to get fruit to customers with even this shelf life. Currants are normally good for a week. As with all fruit, take soft fruit out of the fridge a few hours before eating to get the best flavour.

I hope I am not dragged into court for saying so but I would never wash soft fruit, and certainly not the softer berries such as raspberries and strawberries. However, if you feel the need, make it brief, getting them on the towel to dry a.s.a.p. I never bother removing the hull from strawberries but some people like to. If they are fully ripe, you can just pull it out; otherwise ease it out with a small, sharp knife. Currants are often sold still on their stalks and can be quickly stripped off by running a fork down the stalk.

Strawberry Shortcake

The quintessential summer dessert. A little later in the season, try it with raspberries and poached peaches for a Melba-style shortcake.

Serves 4

350g strawberries
1 tablespoon icing sugar
juice of 1 orange
200ml crème fraîche
icing sugar for dusting

For the shortcake:
120g plain flour
60g cornflour
1 teaspoon baking powder
100g caster sugar
100g softened butter, diced
2 egg yolks
a drop of vanilla extract

First make the shortcake. Sift the flour, cornflour and baking powder into a bowl and stir in the sugar. Rub in the butter with your fingertips until the mixture resembles breadcrumbs. Stir in the egg yolks and vanilla and bring the mixture together into a dough. On a lightly floured surface, roll out the dough to 5mm thick and cut it into eight 9cm rounds. Place on a baking tray lined with baking parchment and bake in an oven preheated to 160°C/Gas Mark 3 for 10–12 minutes, until lightly browned. Remove from the oven and leave to cool.

Purée 150g of the strawberries with the sugar and orange juice. Pass the purée through a fine sieve if you prefer a smoother finish.

Slice the remaining strawberries. Put a shortcake biscuit on each of 4 plates, put a dollop of crème fraîche on top, then add the sliced strawberries and some strawberry sauce. Place the remaining biscuits on top, sift over a little icing sugar and serve.

Quick Strawberry Ice Cream

This is very easy to make at home as it doesn't require an ice cream machine. The addition of alcohol helps the freezing process and here we use a little red wine. Choose very ripe strawberries for the best flavour.

Serves 4

500g strawberries
1 tablespoon orange juice
2 tablespoons honey
50ml red wine
200ml double cream
150g plain yoghurt

Whiz the strawberries, orange juice, honey and red wine in a food processor, then strain through a fine sieve to remove the seeds.

Whip the double cream and yoghurt together until they form soft peaks, then fold them into the strawberry purée. Freeze until firm. About 20 minutes before serving, transfer to the fridge to soften slightly.

Chocolate Pavlova with Raspberries

One of the most popular desserts in the Field Kitchen, this is well worth the effort involved. Just remember, it will serve about 15 people, so make it for a crowd. If the berries are very tart, mix with extra icing sugar.

250ml crème fraîche
250ml double cream
200g raspberries
1 teaspoon icing sugar

For the meringue:
5 egg whites
300g caster sugar
3 drops of vanilla extract
1 teaspoon wine vinegar
1 teaspoon cornflour
2 teaspoons cocoa powder

For the chocolate layer:
450g dark chocolate
300ml double cream

First make the meringue. With an electric beater, whisk the egg whites until just stiff, then gradually add the sugar, a tablespoon at a time, whisking after each addition until stiff peaks are formed. Fold in the rest of the ingredients until the cocoa is mixed through the egg white.

Line a large baking sheet with baking parchment. Shape the meringue into 2 circles on the parchment, each about 25cm in diameter and 2cm deep. Place in an oven preheated to 120°C/Gas Mark ¼ and leave for 1½ hours, until the meringue is firm to the touch. Turn the oven off and leave the meringue in it for 30 minutes.

Using a heavy knife, cut the dark chocolate into very small pieces and place in a bowl. Heat the cream to boiling point and pour it over the chocolate. Stir together, being careful not to over mix or the mixture will split. If the chocolate doesn't combine with the cream and there are still a few lumps, place the bowl over a pan of simmering water and stir carefully until smooth. When the chocolate mix is ready, spread it over the 2 meringue discs and chill until set.

Whip the crème fraîche and cream together until they are just thick enough to hold their shape. Spread them over the chocolate meringue discs. Put the raspberries in a bowl, sift in the icing sugar and toss well. Arrange them over the 2 discs and place one on top of the other for a magnificent dessert.

Raspberry Trifle

Making trifle is very satisfying. Perhaps it's the challenge of getting each part perfect – though Jane says it's the look on Sam's face (her colleague in the Field Kitchen) as she devours it.

Serves 8

300g sponge cake, cut into 2cm cubes
3 tablespoons caster sugar
2 tablespoons raspberry liqueur or any berry liqueur, or sherry
400g raspberries, plus a few extra to decorate
½ gelatine leaf
a few toasted flaked almonds, to decorate

For the custard:
4 egg yolks
1 dessertspoon caster sugar
1 teaspoon cornflour
300ml single cream
4 drops of vanilla extract

For the syllabub:
100ml sherry
50ml brandy
juice and grated zest of 2 lemons
75g caster sugar
½ teaspoon freshly grated nutmeg
350ml double cream

Scatter the cubes of sponge cake over the bottom of a trifle bowl. Put 2 tablespoons of the sugar in a small pan with 2 tablespoons of water and heat gently until the sugar has dissolved. Remove from the heat and stir in the liqueur. Pour this mixture over the cake to soak it.

Put 250g of the raspberries in a pan with the remaining tablespoon of sugar and 1 tablespoon of water and heat until the mixture starts to bubble and the juices run. Liquidise in a blender or food processor and then strain through a sieve. Soak the gelatine in a little cold water for about 5 minutes, until soft, then remove from the water and squeeze out the excess. Add the gelatine to the hot raspberry purée and stir until dissolved. Pour the mixture over the sponge cake while still warm. Sprinkle with the rest of the raspberries and then chill.

Meanwhile, make the custard. In a bowl, mix the egg yolks with the sugar and cornflour. Put the cream in a pan with the vanilla and heat until it is about to boil. Pour it over the egg yolk mixture, stirring well, then return it to the pan. Cook over a low heat, stirring constantly, until thickened – don't let it boil or it will curdle. Strain the custard into a bowl, allow to cool a little, then pour it over the raspberry layer and chill well.

To make the syllabub, put all the ingredients in a large bowl and whip until soft peaks are formed. Top the trifle with the syllabub and decorate with toasted flaked almonds and raspberries.

Raspberry Brown Butter Tart

This is an absolutely stunning tart, and a good way of turning a small amount of raspberries into a dessert to feed 8. It works equally well with blackberries, blueberries or even figs.

Serves 8

3 eggs
300g caster sugar
1 tablespoon finely grated orange zest
60g plain flour
175g unsalted butter
1 vanilla pod, split and scraped
200g raspberries
icing sugar, for dusting

For the sweet pastry:
175g plain flour
60g icing sugar
125g unsalted butter, cut up
2 medium egg yolks

First make the pastry. Put the flour and icing sugar in a food processor and mix briefly. Add the butter and pulse until the consistency resembles breadcrumbs. Add the egg yolks and pulse until the pastry comes together. Wrap in cling film and leave in the fridge for at least 30 minutes.

Roll out the pastry on a lightly floured surface to about 2mm thick, then use to line a 28cm loose-bottomed flan tin, pushing the pastry up the sides so it comes slightly above the top of the tin. Chill for 30 minutes, then line the base and sides with a piece of baking parchment and fill with baking beans or rice. Bake in an oven preheated to 180°C/Gas Mark 4 for 10 minutes, then remove the paper and beans and bake for another 5 minutes or until golden brown. Remove from the oven and set aside.

To make the filling, put the eggs, sugar and orange zest in a bowl and whisk until well combined. Sift in the flour and whisk to combine. Heat the butter and vanilla in a pan until the butter foams and goes dark brown. Whisk it into the egg mixture. Remove the vanilla pod.

Sprinkle the raspberries over the base of the pastry case, pour the butter mixture over the fruit and bake at 180°C/Gas Mark 4 for about 40 minutes, until the top is golden brown and the filling is just set. Leave to cool to room temperature, then dust with icing sugar and serve.

Berry Gratin

This is a good dessert to prepare in advance: you can keep the sabayon mixture in the fridge for up to 8 hours and have the berries ready in their dishes. We tend to make it with raspberries but any type of berry will work well. For a slightly more substantial pud, put the berries on a layer of sponge before topping with the sabayon.

Serves 4

110g caster sugar
4 large egg yolks
3 tablespoons berry liqueur, such as cassis or framboise
365ml whipping cream
250g berries

Put the sugar, egg yolks, 2 tablespoons of the liqueur and 1 tablespoon of the cream in a large, heatproof bowl and whisk together with a handheld electric beater. Place the bowl over a pan of simmering water, making sure the water does not touch the base of the bowl. Continue whisking for about 10 minutes, until the mixture has increased in volume and thickened enough to leave a trail on the surface for a few seconds when drizzled from the whisk. Take the bowl off the heat and whisk for another 5 minutes.

Whip the rest of the cream with the remaining liqueur until it forms soft peaks. Fold into the cooled sabayon.

Divide the berries between 4 individual gratin dishes or just one large one. Top with the sabayon mixture and place under a hot grill for about 3 minutes, until lightly browned. Serve immediately.

Blackberry and Apple Plate Pie

This pie was traditionally made on an enamel plate. They can still be found but a shallow pie dish will do.

Serves 6

a double quantity of Sweet Pastry (see page 360)
about 1.5kg Bramley apples
3 tablespoons caster sugar
100g blackberries
a little milk, for glazing
icing sugar, for dusting

Divide the pastry in half and roll out one piece on a lightly floured surface. Use to line the base of a 25cm enamel plate or shallow pie dish.

Peel and core the apples, then cut them into slices about 5mm thick. Mix them with the sugar and blackberries in a bowl and then pile on to the pastry base.

Roll out the remaining pastry and lay it on top of the pie, pressing down at the edge to seal and trimming off the excess. Crimp the edges. Make a few cuts in a shape on top of the pastry, so the steam can escape, then decorate with leaves, apples etc made out of the excess pastry – go crazy! Brush the top of the pie with a little milk, then place in an oven preheated to 190°C/Gas Mark 5 and bake for about 40 minutes, until the apples are tender and the pastry is browned. Dust with icing sugar and serve.

Baked Custard with Macerated Blackcurrants

This is based on a Richard Corrigan dish and is sublime. Customers often tell us it's the best thing they have ever eaten. It would probably work with raspberries as well, but would not be as sharp.

Serves 6

200g blackcurrants
2 dessertspoons caster sugar
crème de cassis or brandy (we sometimes use Suzanne's
    blackcurrant fruit vinegar essence, which is produced
    locally – www.suzannesvinegars.co.uk)

For the custard:
400ml double cream
200ml milk
a dash of vanilla extract, or ½ vanilla pod
6 egg yolks
70g caster sugar

To make the custard, put the cream, milk and vanilla in a pan and bring almost to boiling point. Remove from the heat and leave to infuse for half an hour.

Whisk the egg yolks and sugar together until pale and creamy. Pour the cream mixture over the eggs and sugar and mix well. Strain the mixture into a 23cm gratin dish or other shallow ovenproof dish. Place the dish in a roasting tin containing about 3cm of hot water and bake in an oven preheated to 140°C/Gas Mark 1 for about 50 minutes, until the custard is just set. Remove from the bain marie and leave to cool to room temperature.

While the custard is baking, place half the blackcurrants in a bowl with half the sugar and the cassis or brandy. Mix well and leave to macerate. Put the rest of the fruit in a pan with the remaining sugar and 1 dessertspoon of water. Heat, stirring, until the sugar has dissolved, then remove from the heat. When cool, mix with the other blackcurrants.

Drizzle the blackcurrants over the cooled baked custard before serving.

Blackcurrant and Beetroot Relish

A quick relish to serve with terrines, duck, lamb or game.

Serves 4

1 tablespoon blackcurrant jelly
1 tablespoon raspberry vinegar (or red wine vinegar)
1 tablespoon crème de cassis
125g cooked beetroot (see page 21), finely diced
55g blackcurrants
a handful of chopped mint
sea salt and freshly ground black pepper

Put the blackcurrant jelly, vinegar and crème de cassis in a pan and heat gently until smooth. Add the beetroot, blackcurrants and some seasoning and heat through. Stir in the mint and check the seasoning. Serve either warm or chilled.

Easy ideas for strawberries and cane fruit

✦ Toss strawberries with a drizzle of good balsamic vinegar and a little black pepper to bring out the flavour.

✦ Mix crushed berries with a little sugar and use to fill a sponge cake, adding a layer of mascarpone cheese, too.

✦ Mix puréed berries with an equal quantity of plain yoghurt and orange juice, sweetening with a little sugar. Freeze in moulds for an easy dessert.

✦ Add a handful of blackberries or raspberries to the crumble on page 9, omitting the dried fruit.

✦ To make a fruit compote, warm some mixed berries with a little sugar until the juices run. Use as a topping for vanilla ice cream or as a sauce for pancakes.

See also:
Rhubarb and Strawberry Crumble (page 302)

Sweetcorn

The arrival of sweetcorn, one of the very few ergonomically designed vegetables, is a welcome relief to the back after a summer bent double picking lettuces and courgettes; corn bears its cobs at the perfect height. Unfortunately the local badger population shares our enthusiasm for the crop. During our first year of growing corn, I returned from a few days away in August to find the field devastated, with only a narrow perimeter strip left standing. My paranoid mind raced through a list of possible ill-wishers with scores to settle: had Peter Melchett mistaken it for a GM trial? Had the local rave crew staged an all-nighter in my field? In the end the corn-laden poo and the teeth marks identified the culprits.

Badgers have a sweet tooth, with a taste for strawberries and other fruit, but sweetcorn is their favourite. It would not be so bad if they worked methodically and finished the cobs they started, but surveying the destruction in the morning is like being the first one to regain consciousness after a wild party. It is as if the entire county's badger population had gathered to make merry: rolling around in groups, grabbing a mouthful here and there, but mostly just enjoying the wanton destruction. We have found that several hundred volts through an electric fence, erected before they get their first taste, can keep them at bay. Even then, they outsmarted us one year by tunnelling a full 20 metres under the fence, emerging well inside the field. By leaving the perimeter intact, they managed to destroy most of the field before we found the tunnel.

Maize, which is native to Mexico and Guatemala, has become as important a staple crop as wheat or rice, particularly in poorer tropical areas, where local varieties are often the basis of subsistence farming. In these areas the corn is almost always allowed to mature, then dried and ground into flour to be used in tortillas or porridge. In the UK we are on the climatic extreme for the crop. It is a sun and heat lover and struggles in a cool summer, even though we choose warm, protected, south-facing fields. Our sweetcorn varieties have been selected for a very slow conversion of sugars to starch, which leaves a window of about ten days between the grains turning yellow, becoming fully filled and sweet and then turning starchy and chewy. Over the years the plant breeders have got better and better at this selection, to the extent where (I think) some of the 'super-sweet' varieties are now almost too sweet.

Maize has a slightly particular photosynthetic process that is extremely efficient at high temperatures. In a hot summer, once this kicks in, the growth

rate is staggering. The male flowers appear at the top of the plants, normally in late July or early August, and release so much pollen that it comes off in clouds as you walk through the shoulder-high crop, sometimes turning the ground yellow. By this stage the tassels are emerging from the developing cobs lower down to trap the windborne pollen. A pollen grain must land on each tassel, which is actually a small, flexible tube leading to a grain waiting to be fertilised inside the wrapper leaves. In a good summer we can be picking sweetcorn by mid August but more often it is late August or even September before the first cobs are ready. The pickers could do with X-ray perception, as they have to judge whether a cob is fully filled and ripe just by the feel (once you start peeling back the leaves and peering inside, it will quickly deteriorate). Normally they get it right, but we ask our customers to let us know if more than the occasional cob is not up to scratch and we will replace them.

Each plant usually produces at least two cobs but it is rare for more than one to be fully filled and saleable. When we have finished picking, we leave the rest standing, and the stubble provides a wonderful food source for wildlife. It also has the virtue of attracting pheasants from miles around, which can provide a few additional meals in December.

Storage and preparation

A lot of fuss is made about 'getting the water boiling before you pick the cob', in order to get the sweetest corn. This is based on the fact that the sugar supply (photosynthesis) is cut off when you pick the corn and the sugars will then quickly be converted to starch. With the new super-sweet varieties, this is less the case but it is still worth keeping the cobs in the fridge and using them as soon as possible. They come in their own packaging, and will always keep better if the sheathing leaves are left intact. It is the height of supermarket madness to strip these off the cobs in order to wrap them in less effective, more polluting plastic.

Before boiling corn cobs, you need to pull off the green husks and the silky threads. The time for boiling varies from about 4 minutes (for very fresh corn, and if you want a good crunch) to 10 minutes or more – in UNSALTED water. If you add salt, the kernels will take longer to cook.

In seasons when the corn arrives before you pack the barbecue away for the winter, the cobs can be very good grilled outdoors. Soak the entire (unpeeled) cob in water for at least an hour before cooking slowly on the barbecue over a lowish heat, turning periodically. When the outer leaves brown, the cob is normally just right (this can take 25 to 45 minutes). The peeled-back leaves make a natural handle for holding the hot cobs. You need a fair amount of space on the barbecue, and they take a while to cook, so either start them early or satisfy the normal carnivorous meat lust first. You can also adapt this method to roasting: prepare the cobs in the same way and cook for a similar time at around 200°C/Gas Mark 6.

I once soaked a whole batch in the river for a staff barbecue, unknowingly upsetting a proprietorial fisherman, who tried to stir up trouble by reporting us to the Environmental Health Department. They mounted a raid in response to reports that we were washing our vegetables in the river.

Braised Sweetcorn with Spinach

This is a lovely dish to cook using fresh corn. Try to get a slightly brown colour on the corn kernels, as this imparts a faintly caramelised, smoky flavour.

Serves 4

2 corn cobs
50g butter
1 garlic clove, crushed
300g fresh spinach
sea salt and freshly ground black pepper

Stand each cob upright on a board and cut downwards with a sharp knife in a sawing action to remove the kernels.

Melt the butter in a pan, add the corn, then cover and cook gently for 10 minutes, until just tender and lightly coloured. Add the garlic and mix well. Meanwhile, blanch the spinach in boiling salted water for 30 seconds, then drain and refresh in cold water. Squeeze out excess water, chop the spinach roughly and add to the corn. Cook for 3 minutes or so, until heated through, then season with salt and pepper and serve.

Chicken, Leek and Corn Soup

Soup day in the Riverford staff canteen was not very popular (it has since been binned) but it gave us the chance to experiment. This chicken chowder was a big success.

Serves 4

2 corn cobs
50g butter
2 red chillies, deseeded and diced
2 streaky bacon rashers, diced
1 onion, chopped
1 garlic clove, chopped
2 leeks, halved and sliced
2 floury potatoes, peeled and diced
the meat from 4 chicken thighs, skinned and diced
1 litre chicken stock
200ml single cream
1 tablespoon chopped chives or parsley
sea salt and freshly ground black pepper

Cut the kernels from the sweetcorn cobs – the easiest way to do this is to stand each cob upright on a board and cut downwards with a sharp knife in a sawing action.

Heat the butter in a large pan, add the chillies, bacon, onion, garlic and leeks and fry for about 10 minutes, without browning. Add the potatoes, chicken, corn and stock and simmer for 15–20 minutes, until the potatoes are tender and the chicken is cooked. Stir in the cream and herbs, season well and serve.

Sweetcorn Fritters

Jane has made literally hundreds of these over the years and is still cooking them today. I think that is recommendation enough. They make a great canapé topped with guacamole and soured cream. Or serve them as they do in Australia – as a brunch dish, with rocket, avocado, bacon and some tomato salsa.

Serves 6

3 corn cobs
125g plain flour
1 teaspoon baking powder
2 tablespoons polenta
1 teaspoon sugar
2 eggs
1 egg yolk
2 tablespoons crème fraîche
125ml milk
2 tablespoons butter
1 red chilli, finely chopped
½ red onion, finely chopped
1 tablespoon chopped coriander and/or chives
2 teaspoons olive oil
sea salt and freshly ground black pepper

Peel the husks off the corn cobs, then cook them in boiling water for about 10 minutes, until just tender. Drain well and cut off the kernels.

Put the flour, baking powder, polenta and sugar in a bowl. Add the eggs and yolk and beat together. Gradually beat in the crème fraîche and milk until you get a thick, smooth batter. Heat half the butter in a pan until brown and add it to the batter. Add the chilli, onion, corn and herbs and season well.

Heat the oil and the remaining butter in a frying pan until quite hot. Drop tablespoonfuls of the mixture into the pan and fry over a medium heat for about 2 minutes on each side, until golden brown. Serve immediately.

Corn on the Cob with Red Pepper and Chive Butter

Instead of roasting and skinning fresh red peppers for this, you could buy a jar of peeled peppers. We recommend the Spanish ones, as they usually have a good smoky flavour.

Serves 8

2 red peppers
125g softened butter
1 garlic clove, crushed
1 chilli, chopped
1 teaspoon sweet chilli sauce
1 tablespoon chopped chives
8 corn cobs
sea salt and freshly ground black pepper

Roast the red peppers in a hot oven until the skin is lightly blackened or blistered (or do this under a hot grill). Place in a bowl, cover with cling film and leave for 20 minutes – this helps loosen the skin. Peel the peppers, discarding all of the skin and seeds. Place the butter, peppers, garlic, chilli and chilli sauce in a food processor and process until well combined. Stir in the chopped chives and some salt and pepper.

Boil or barbecue the corn cobs (see page 367), then smear the butter on them while they are still hot.

Easy ideas for sweetcorn

✦ Cut the kernels off some ears of fresh corn and spread them out on an oven tray. Dry-roast in an oven preheated to 160°C/Gas Mark 3 for about 20 minutes, to give a slightly smoky taste. Add to kidney beans and chopped tomato with an oil and vinegar dressing to make a salsa to serve with grilled meats or fish.

✦ Use cooked corn in a frittata (see page 328), together with kidney beans, grated cheese and diced red onion.

✦ For a simple sweetcorn soup, cook 1 chopped onion and 2 crushed garlic cloves in a little butter until soft, then add the kernels from 3 cobs of corn and cover with a mixture of half water and half milk. Simmer for about 10 minutes, until the corn is tender, then purée and pass through a sieve. Reheat and adjust the seasoning. Stir in a little Red Pepper and Chive Butter (see page 373) or sprinkle with the toppings from Dev-Mex Pumpkin Soup (page 344).

See also:
Dev-Mex Pumpkin Soup (page 344)
Pak Choi with Chicken Broth (page 318)

Tomatoes

There can be few foods more environmentally damaging or disappointing to eat than a Dutch or English hothouse tomato picked in the winter. Despite this, they have become as much a staple part of our diet as that other member of the *Solanaceae* family, the potato. Unlike the potato, though, they struggle in our damp, cool climate and will never be at their best here. Without the benefit of protection, their natural season would be about five minutes at the end of September, and even then they would lack the intensity of flavour of an Italian tomato. As a grower, I can't help thinking life would be much simpler if Cortes had left them in Mexico, but they are here to stay, so we must rise to the challenge and make the most of the climate we have.

Using cold tunnels, we can extend the season from June to mid October, which is as far as we go at Riverford. Under heated glass, tomatoes can be picked from March to Christmas but the energy cost is insane, resulting in about 2 kilos of carbon dioxide being pumped into the atmosphere for every kilo of tomatoes produced. Where waste or low-grade heat is used from combined heat and power electricity generation or other sources, it can make sense, but generally, if we must eat tomatoes earlier than July or later than October, from a taste and environmental perspective it would be better to import them. Better still, just give them a miss in their fresh form from November to April.

Plant breeding is a bit like post-Thatcherite Britain: in the rush to maximise whatever can be measured, less quantifiable qualities are lost. With such intense pressure on the more easily quantified factors, most notably yield, flavour has suffered particularly badly with tomatoes. The problem of poor-tasting varieties is compounded by the way they are grown: the roots of most non-organic tomatoes never touch the soil. They are drip-fed a lifeless, computer-controlled solution of nutrients through an inert medium of glass fibres (like the Rockwool in your attic). Everything is controlled, right down to the level of carbon dioxide they breathe to maximise the harvest. This sort of production gives huge yields but will never create the depth and subtlety of flavour that results from interaction with the living soil.

Given the abuses suffered by tomatoes, it is amazing that they ever taste of anything, but there are signs of a revival. The public has become so disenchanted with them (tomatoes have become symbolic of poor flavour resulting from industrialised production methods) that it is demanding something better. The industry is responding with some superior-tasting varieties. I am sceptical about vine-ripened tomatoes; they are grown in the same way as all the rest and there is no intrinsic reason for them to taste any better than the standard types, but they have become a means of differentiation to show that there has been at least some consideration of flavour. To produce a trellis of red fruit, they must be left on the plant until the ones lower down have at least partially ripened. Perhaps more significantly, the vine is included in the pack; it is the vine that contributes more flavour and aroma of ripe tomato than the fruit itself. Since getting the idea from Heston Blumenthal, I include some vine when making tomato sauce and it does seem to give a more intense flavour (hook it out and discard before serving).

At Riverford, we have tried virtually every variety of tomato, from commercial and gardeners' catalogues, including many heritage/heirloom ones. The best we have ever grown, and the one I would always recommend to gardeners, is the cherry tomato, Gardener's Delight. The flavour is consistently superb, even in gloomy summers. Sadly, its thin skin, which is one of the things that make it so good to eat, means it is very prone to splitting. After a rash of complaints, we have retreated to Favorita, which tastes very nearly as good and normally survives the trip from the farm without bursting out of itself. Of all the standard-sized tomatoes, Douglas has proved the best for us, though it does not compare in flavour to Favorita. Disappointingly, none of the weird and wacky varieties has produced exceptional taste in our tunnels. We had a brief flirtation with beefsteak/Marmande types but, again, found that in our climate they didn't really produce the flavour we had hoped for.

We have also played around with various plum tomato varieties for cooking but I have reached the conclusion that, after a lot of work in the polytunnels and the kitchen, the result is no better than a good canned tomato.

Storage and preparation

Tomatoes don't like being kept below 10°C (it affects the texture as well as the taste) so unless they are getting overripe, it is best to keep them out of the fridge in a cool vegetable rack. Ideally they would be picked ripe and eaten immediately, but the veg trade is risk averse and if they have had to face the long trip from Spain or even Morocco they will almost certainly have been picked virtually green.

To skin tomatoes, cut a little cross in the base of each one, then place in boiling water. Leave for 30 seconds, then drain and refresh in cold water; the skin should peel off easily. To deseed, cut the tomatoes into quarters and scoop out the seeds with a small knife, or just with your thumb.

Gazpacho

This was the very first dish we served in the Field Kitchen and it is based on an excellent version made by a friend of Jane's, Mazz Piotrowski, a chef in Sydney. Yes, not very Torremolinos, but a highly refreshing dish that can be produced without much fuss. Apparently the Spanish always have some gazpacho in their fridge so they can have a swig when they come in after a night on the town.

Serves 6

500g cherry tomatoes, roughly chopped
½ cucumber, peeled and roughly chopped
1 red pepper, roughly chopped
4 garlic cloves, crushed
a bunch of basil
1 red onion, chopped
1 red chilli, chopped
1 tablespoon chopped coriander
1 tablespoon sugar
2 tablespoons good-quality red wine vinegar
1 teaspoon salt
150ml olive oil

Mix together all the ingredients except the oil and leave to stand for 10 minutes. Blend in a food processor or liquidiser, gradually adding the olive oil. Pass through the finest plate of a mouli-légumes or through a very fine sieve. Check the seasoning and then chill thoroughly before serving.

Toasted Bread Salad with Basil and Tomatoes

This was devised as a crunchy alternative to the Italian bread salad, panzanella, which if made badly can be a bit slimy. The dressing is very good with grilled fish or French beans, too.

Serves 6

1 ciabatta loaf, ripped into chunks
600g well-flavoured tomatoes, cut in halves or quarters
120ml extra virgin olive oil
2 tablespoons red wine vinegar
1 garlic clove, crushed
2 teaspoons capers, soaked in cold water for 20 minutes,
   then squeezed dry
3 anchovies
leaves from a small bunch of basil
sea salt and freshly ground black pepper
good olive oil for drizzling

Bake the ciabatta chunks in an oven preheated to 200°C/Gas Mark 6 for about 5 minutes, until toasted but still soft in the middle. Squeeze the juice from about a third of the tomatoes into a food processor, along with any juice that escaped when you cut them up. Add the oil, vinegar, garlic, capers and anchovies and blitz to make a dressing. Check the seasoning.

Put the toasted ciabatta in a bowl with the remaining tomatoes, the shredded basil and the dressing and toss well. Drizzle with good olive oil and serve.

Basic Tomato Sauce

A versatile sauce that makes a good base for salsas and pasta dishes. If serving it with penne, add some chilli and rosemary with the garlic, then finish it off with a little cream. Alternatively, add the basic tomato sauce to any type of pasta with a couple of knobs of butter, a splash of balsamic vinegar, fresh basil and grated pecorino cheese.

Serves 4

2 tablespoons olive oil
4 garlic cloves, finely chopped
450g good, ripe tomatoes, skinned, deseeded and chopped
1 teaspoon sugar
sea salt and freshly ground black pepper

Heat the olive oil in a heavy-based pan, add the garlic and cook gently for a few minutes, until softened but not coloured. Stir in the tomatoes and sugar and raise the heat until the tomatoes are simmering. Lower the heat again and cook gently for about 1 hour, until reduced and thickened. Season well.

Home-dried Tomatoes

A simple way of producing your own equivalent to sun-dried tomatoes. They are excellent tossed in a salad, used in tarts or mixed with pasta. Dry as many tomatoes as you like; they keep well.

4 tablespoons olive oil
16 tomatoes
1 tablespoon caster sugar
sea salt

Drizzle about half the olive oil over 2 baking trays. Cut the tomatoes lengthways in half, then slide the knife around the inside of each one and remove the pulp and pips. Arrange the tomato halves on the trays so that they are close but not touching. Drizzle the remaining oil over the top and sprinkle with the sugar and a little salt.

Put the trays in an oven preheated to 150°C/Gas Mark 2 and cook for about 45 minutes; the tomatoes should look shrunken and slightly coloured when they are done. Remove from the oven and leave to cool.

To store, pack the tomatoes into jars and cover completely with good-quality olive oil. They will keep for about 6 months without refrigeration.

Fried Green Tomatoes

On a road trip across the States, Jane ate these for the first time at a bustling restaurant in that eccentric town, Savannah. This version is based on the Jane Grigson recipe and if you can eat then without thinking about Kathy Bates squatting over a mirror, do try them; they are delicious.

Serves 4

450g green tomatoes, cut into slices 5mm thick
1 egg, lightly beaten
cornmeal or polenta for coating
8 rashers of smoked streaky bacon or pancetta
1 tablespoon sunflower oil
1 tablespoon butter
a little chopped parsley and/or basil, to garnish
sea salt and freshly ground black pepper

Season the tomato slices with salt and pepper. Put the beaten egg in a shallow dish and spread the cornmeal out on a plate. Coat each tomato slice in the egg, letting any excess run off, and then coat them in the cornmeal.

Fry the bacon in the sunflower oil until it is crisp and all the fat has run out. Remove the bacon from the pan and crumble it, then set aside.

Add the butter to the bacon fat in the pan and fry the tomatoes until golden on both sides. Place on a serving dish and scatter the crumbled bacon over them. Sprinkle with the chopped herbs and serve.

Easy ideas for tomatoes

✦ To make tomato bruschetta, grill some ciabatta or sourdough bread on both sides. Rub one side with a peeled clove of garlic and drizzle with good olive oil, then top with diced cherry tomatoes, a little finely sliced red onion, shredded basil, crushed garlic and a drizzle of balsamic vinegar.

✦ For a fresh summer pasta dish, halve some extra-sweet cherry tomatoes and toss with crushed garlic, shredded basil and cooked linguine. Season, then finish with olive oil and a little good red wine vinegar. Capers and anchovies can be added too, as well as crisp fried breadcrumbs.

✦ You can make a quick relish by mixing together 200g diced tomatoes, 1 diced onion and 4 tablespoons of chopped coriander, parsley or mint, then seasoning with ½ teaspoon of cayenne pepper, ½ teaspoon of roasted and ground cumin seeds, ¾ teaspoon of salt and 2 tablespoons of balsamic vinegar. Serve with spicy fish dishes, Indian food or just on toast for a delicious healthy snack.

✦ Drizzle cherry tomatoes on the vine with olive oil and roast at 200°C/Gas Mark 6 for about 15 minutes, until their skins are beginning to burst. Serve as a garnish for summer chicken or fish dishes.

See also:
Fattoush with Broad Beans (page 48)
Ceviche (page 130)
Braised Shoulder of Lamb Stuffed with Salsa Rossa (page 132)
Grilled Courgette, Tomato and Bean Salad with Basil Dressing (page 139)
Mexican One-pot Courgettes (page 141)
Chunky Avocado and Tomato Salad with Coriander and Sweet Chilli Dressing (page 210)
Baked Turnips with Tomatoes (page 387)

Turnips and Swedes

Much as I enjoyed *Monty Python* and more recently *Blackadder*, I have never fully forgiven them their derision of the humble turnip. This much-maligned vegetable deserves better.

There are essentially two very different types of turnip – summer and winter – and they need different treatments in the kitchen. The frost-hardy winter turnip is sown in mid to late summer for use throughout the winter months. It is slower growing and very similar to swede (in fact, in Scotland both swedes and turnips are known as neeps). This turnip was one of the first vegetables to be cultivated in northern Europe and hence is the one that Michael Palin and his mates fought over with clubs. In my opinion, it has no virtue over the swede and can taste quite rank later in the season. It should really be left to the cattle – the conclusion reached by most of northern Europe. At Riverford, we used to grow a variety called Golden Balls, mainly for amusement value as it is supposedly Posh's term of endearment for Becks. We dropped it when he went to Real Madrid.

Summer turnips are another matter. Purple Top Milan, the most common variety, is fast growing, sweet and tender. It is more like a radish than a swede and has the same rapid, vigorous growth, which, together with good frost tolerance when young, makes it one of the first crops to be ready from a spring sowing.

I love swede in the winter (nothing goes better with roast beef than mashed swede with plenty of pepper and butter) but it defeats me why anyone would want to eat it in the summer. Such is the enslavement of our industry to continuity of supply that some bizarre trading has developed to plug the summer gap. Through late April, swede might be kept in cold store, then they are imported from as far away as Canada, New Zealand and Tasmania until the spring-sown new-season crop, hurried on with crop covers, is ready in July.

In Devon it is traditional to sow swede on Midsummer's Day, in which case the first ones will reach the target one-kilo weight in early autumn and the stragglers will be ready in March. Our growers live in fear of the voracious flea beetle, which seems to be able to live on nothing in a fallow, sun-baked field, ready to devastate the emerging seedlings, sometimes before they even get above ground. They are immune to all organically acceptable sprays and thrive in hot, dry weather. The traditional treatment was to drive a flock of sheep around the field just before emergence, stirring up a cloud of dust,

which is said to choke the beetle's spiracles (breathing apertures). Apart from choking, they are also susceptible to drowning, so we always pray for a thunderstorm after sowing.

By late March the remaining roots are sensing spring, and quality deteriorates rapidly as they go tough and woody in preparation for sending up a seed-head. We have a grower on the east coast of Scotland who often sends a lorry load down in April, but even there by the end of the month they are inedible, and even the sheep find them hard, regularly leaving teeth in the stumps. My brother studied agriculture at Edinburgh, where they had a research project fitting false teeth to aging ewes.

Storage and preparation

Both types of turnip are the plant's natural starch store, enabling the plant to hold energy as starch from one season to the next. Winter turnips can be kept for months, though it is hard to imagine anyone fighting over them after that time. Summer turnips will keep without much deterioration for at least two weeks in the bottom of the fridge, as long as you remove the leafy tops so they do not draw moisture from the turnip. If you plan to eat the tops, however, they should be left attached to the turnip and used as soon as possible, as they have a very short life. They can be cooked in the same way as other greens.

Winter turnips are best kept as a component of soups and stocks, or used as a mash (with a lot of help from butter). The best way to cook summer turnips is to braise them (see Braised Carrots and Turnips with Honey, page 92). They are also wonderful with other spring vegetables in light stews such as Navarin of Lamb (page 401), and can be roasted (they go particularly well with beef), alone or in a mixture of summer vegetables. All but the smallest turnips will need peeling. If you are not using them immediately, put them in acidulated water to prevent browning.

Swedes should keep for a month or more in the fridge, if fresh, though there will be some deterioration in flavour. Besides the dreaded flea beetle mentioned above, the biggest problem for growers is attack from the maggots of cabbage root fly. Damage is normally restricted to surface layers at the base of the swede. You will often find organic swedes have been heavily trimmed around the base to remove damaged flesh, but if you see the telltale holes it is worth trimming more to remove this.

Turnips, Brussels Sprouts and Beetroot with Hazelnuts

The success of this dish relies on cooking the different components well and finishing them off with a really good wine vinegar. You can use the same technique with other cooked vegetables.

Serves 6

4 beetroot, trimmed
400g Brussels sprouts, halved
400g turnips, peeled and cut into wedges 2cm thick
3 tablespoons butter
1 small red onion, finely chopped
50g hazelnuts, finely chopped
2 teaspoons chopped thyme
3 garlic cloves, crushed
1 tablespoon Muscat vinegar
sea salt and freshly ground black pepper

Put the beetroot in a dish, add a splash of water, then cover with foil and bake in an oven preheated to 200°C/Gas Mark 6 until tender – about 45 minutes, depending on size. Meanwhile, add the sprouts to a large pan of boiling salted water and cook for about 5 minutes, until just tender. Remove with a slotted spoon, refresh in cold water, then drain and set aside. In the same water, cook the turnips for about 6 minutes, until just tender, then drain and refresh in cold water. Drain again and set aside.

Melt the butter in a large frying pan, add the onion and hazelnuts and fry for about 3 minutes, until the nuts start to brown. Add the thyme and garlic and mix well. Add the beetroot, sprouts and turnips and cover the pan. Cook gently for about 5 minutes to heat the vegetables through. Sprinkle with the vinegar, season to taste and mix well.

Baked Turnips with Tomatoes

Turnips have always been treated with more respect in Europe than in the UK. This Sicilian-inspired dish is best served with grilled fish and Salsa Verde (see page 216).

Serves 4

4 medium turnips, peeled and thinly sliced
1 red onion, thinly sliced
7 plum tomatoes, cut into rounds 5mm thick
1 tablespoon olive oil
1 garlic clove, crushed to a paste with a little salt
1 teaspoon dried oregano (or 1 tablespoon fresh oregano)
sea salt and freshly ground black pepper

Choose an ovenproof dish about 23 x 33cm and arrange half the turnips in it in an overlapping layer. Scatter with half the onion and arrange half the tomatoes on top. Mix the olive oil and garlic together and drizzle half of it over the tomatoes. Sprinkle with half the oregano and season with salt and pepper. Repeat with a second layer of everything.

Cover with foil and bake in an oven preheated to 160°C/Gas Mark 3 for about 1 hour, until the turnips are tender. Remove the foil and place under a hot grill for a few minutes before serving.

Creamed Turnips with Smoked Haddock

A kind of turnip brandade. Serve with a crisp green salad and crusty bread.

Serves 4

1 tablespoon butter
1 onion, finely chopped
2 garlic cloves, crushed
500g turnips, peeled and cut into 1cm dice
300ml milk
300g undyed smoked haddock
2 tablespoons double cream
2 tablespoons chopped parsley
1 tablespoon capers, soaked in cold water for 20 minutes, then squeezed
  dry and chopped
1 egg
sea salt and freshly ground black pepper

Melt the butter in a large pan, add the onion, garlic and turnips and cook gently, covered, for about 10 minutes, until softened. Add the milk and simmer for 10 minutes. Lay the smoked haddock over the vegetables (in pieces, if necessary) and cook for 5 minutes, until the fish is just done. Remove the haddock from the pan, taking out any bones or skin, and set aside.

Drain off the milk from the turnips. Put the onion and turnips in a food processor and blitz until smooth, adding a little of the milk if necessary. Add the haddock, cream, parsley, capers and egg and blitz together quickly, then season to taste. Transfer to a shallow ovenproof dish and bake in an oven preheated to 180°C/Gas Mark 4 for 20 minutes, or until set.

Middle Eastern Pickled Turnips

The addition of beetroot here gives the turnips a pink tinge. Serve them as part of a mezze, or in pitta bread with salad, falafel and hummus, or simply on their own.

1kg turnips, peeled and quartered
2 beetroots, peeled and sliced
275ml white wine vinegar
3 garlic cloves, peeled
4 tablespoons salt

In a couple of Kilner jars, layer the turnips with the beetroot slices. Put 1 litre water, vinegar, garlic and salt in a pan and heat gently until the salt has dissolved. Pour the mixture over the turnips and beetroot so they are completely covered, then seal the jars. The pickle will be ready for eating after about a week.

Ham Hock Soup with Swede

Jane says her Mum makes this for her every time she goes home. It's a hearty, nutritious northern soup that makes a single ham hock go a long way.

Serves 6

1 ham hock
1 onion, roughly chopped
1 celery stalk, roughly chopped
4 carrots, finely chopped, plus 1 roughly chopped carrot
1 tablespoon olive oil
1 swede, finely chopped
4 leeks, finely chopped
100g split peas
100g red lentils
1 tablespoon chopped parsley
sea salt and freshly ground black pepper

Put the ham hock in a large pan, cover with water, then add the onion, celery and roughly chopped carrot. Bring to the boil and simmer for 2–3 hours, until the meat is falling off the bone. Drain off the stock and set aside.

Heat the olive oil in a separate pan, add the finely chopped carrots, swede and leeks, then cover and sweat for 5 minutes, until softened. Add the split peas and lentils and cook for 1 minute. Add 1 litre of the reserved cooking liquid, bring to the boil and simmer for 1 hour, adding some water or more of the stock from the ham if it goes dry. When the pulses and vegetables are tender, add enough water or stock to thin the soup to the desired consistency. Shred the meat off the ham hock and add to the soup. Season to taste, stir in the chopped parsley and serve.

Easy ideas for turnips and swedes

✦ Boil or steam peeled chopped turnips, then mash them with butter and seasoning. Pass through a mouli-légumes or blitz in a food processor until smooth.

✦ When roasting beef, chicken or lamb, place peeled turnips around the meat about an hour before the end of the cooking time. Or toss them in olive oil and roast with other root vegetables with some garlic and herbs (see page 404).

✦ Turnip leaves are fantastic to eat if they are in good condition. Blanch them briefly and then braise in a little oil with anchovy and chilli. Alternatively, shred the leaves and add them to braised turnips (see Braised Carrots and Turnips with Honey on page 92) in the last few minutes of cooking.

✦ Substitute turnips for half the potatoes in the gratin on page 284. A little shredded proscuitto can be added to the layers and some grated Gruyère sprinkled on top.

✦ If you are boiling swede to serve with a roast, save the cooking liquid to make a flavoursome gravy.

✦ Mash equal quantities of boiled swede and carrot with plenty of butter and black pepper. Fantastic with roast beef.

See also:
Braised Carrots and Turnips with Honey (page 92)

Food miles: why local
is not always best

When Professor Tim Lang first coined the phrase 'food miles', he had no idea what an emotive focus of consumer discontent his term would become. I suspect even he would acknowledge that the time has come to assess what we mean by it and when it matters. As with almost all environmental and ethical debates, the answers are not simple.

Here are a couple of examples. Due to the huge amounts of heat required to grow long-season tomatoes in northern Europe, each kilo of tomatoes typically results in approximately 2–3 kilos of CO_2 emissions. They may be local but they are certainly not good for the environment. If we must eat tomatoes outside June to October, when they can be produced without heat, it is undoubtedly more benign to truck them from southern Europe, where little or no heat is required and the emissions from transport will be less than 300g of CO_2 per kilo.

If you drove more than two miles to buy your vegetables from a farm shop, this would result in more emissions than getting a veg box delivered, even assuming the farm shop grew the same proportion of vegetables themselves as we and our co-op do – something that is extremely unlikely.

After almost two years of studying Riverford's carbon footprint in conjunction with Exeter University, we have reached the uncomfortable conclusion that local is often not best for the environment. It may offer socio-economic benefits, but then so can imports, especially those from the developing countries of West Africa, South America and the Caribbean, when shipping rather than air-freight is a realistic possibility.

The truth is that ships and, to a much lesser extent, lorries are incredibly efficient at moving our food around compared to our own shopping habits, which are almost always car based. Driving around to individual specialist producers, even if they are fairly local, is an environmental disaster. Getting their produce delivered individually by courier is unlikely to be much better. Such shopping may support small producers, fill us with a warm glow and give us access to some wonderful food but it is not going to save the planet. Energy consumption in food distribution is heavily skewed to the final step of getting the stuff to your home. In our case, around 26 per cent of emissions result from the delivery vans, compared to 20 per cent for lorries, even after including imports by road of produce that cannot be grown in this country.

As far as I am aware, all the attempts to calculate supermarket carbon footprints have excluded what I would assume to be the two largest elements in any genuine assessment: the journey home from the store and the packaging. Bizarrely, the supermarkets don't feel responsible for these.

The conclusion must be that any environmentally sensible system of food distribution requires consolidation, so that the final trip to your house not only carries as much produce as possible but is also as short and infrequent as possible. This (plus avoiding the madness of hothouse production, airfreight and excessive packaging) is likely to be more of an influence on the carbon footprint of your food than the distance separating producer and consumer, as measured in the overly simplistic concept of 'food miles'. While the promotion of small, local producers by food journalists, the Slow Food movement and various food awards is commendable for quality, cultural and social reasons, if we are going to consider the environment it must go hand in hand with sensible consolidation of distribution.

This realisation came as a shock to us, especially when it occurred to me that the supermarkets I have devoted so much of my life to damning are in fact very good at consolidation. However, while they pursue a policy of huge, out-of-town stores, ridiculously excessive and poorly thought-out packaging, overly centralised distribution, reliance on air-freight, promotion of global trade at the expense of seasonality, and staggeringly damaging emissions of refrigerant gas losses, all combined with their routine abuse of suppliers, I will continue the crusade. Were they to put their greenwash aside and quietly address these issues, it is possible that I would have to find another cause.

At Riverford, we are experimenting with electric and even pedal-powered vehicles but I am sceptical of their practical contribution outside city centres. During 15 years of running the box scheme, my inclination has always been to stick to what we do well, namely vegetables. Our study has forced me to acknowledge that in the long run, whatever our policies on packaging and local production, the only way we can make sense of the emissions associated with the final journey to the door is through consolidation – i.e. by selling a broader range, thereby reducing the need for our customers to make other shopping trips. We are slowly doing this by working with other producers with similar values to our own. I feel sure someone will let me know if we get to look too much like the supermarkets.

Mixed Vegetable Dishes

Soupe au Pistou

When we served this at the Organic Food Festival in Bristol one year, it was so popular there was virtually a stampede.

Serves 6–8

100g dried haricot beans, soaked in cold water overnight, then drained
2 heads of garlic, cut horizontally in half
olive oil
1 onion, 3 celery stalks and 3 leeks, finely chopped
3 garlic cloves, finely sliced
400g can of tomatoes
5 new potatoes, 3 carrots, 2 turnips and 3 courgettes, finely diced
100g French beans, cut into 5mm lengths
100g runner beans, finely sliced
sea salt and freshly ground black pepper

For the pistou:
a bunch of basil
2 garlic cloves, crushed to a paste with a little salt
100g Parmesan cheese, freshly grated
150ml olive oil

Put the drained beans in a pan, cover with fresh water and add the halved garlic heads. Bring to the boil and simmer for an hour or until tender. Add a splash of olive oil, season and then remove from the heat. When the mixture has cooled, squeeze the garlic cloves out of their skins into the beans.

Heat 2 tablespoons of olive oil in a large pan, add the onion, celery and leeks and cook slowly for about 15 minutes, until soft but not coloured. Add the sliced garlic and cook for 1 minute. Stir in the tomatoes, turn up the heat and add the potatoes, carrot and turnips. Cook over a high heat for 1 minute, stirring constantly, then reduce the heat and cook for 10 minutes. Add the courgettes and beans, plus enough water just to cover. Bring to the boil and simmer for 5 minutes. Add the cooked haricot beans with enough of their cooking liquor to give a soupy consistency. Season to taste. Whiz the pistou ingredients together in a food processor, then stir into the soup.

Winter Minestrone with Farro and Beans

Farro is an ancient form of wheat that reputedly kept the Roman legions going. It has a firm, chewy texture and is used in Italy in vegetable soups or combined with summer vegetables in salads. Italian delis stock it but if you can't find it, you could substitute barley.

Serves 6–8

2 tablespoons olive oil
1 onion, finely chopped
1 leek, finely chopped
1 celery stalk, finely chopped
2 carrots, finely chopped
2 turnips, finely chopped
3 garlic cloves, finely chopped
a pinch of dried oregano
400g can of tomatoes
425g can of borlotti, haricot or cannellini beans, drained
200g farro, soaked in cold water for 1 hour and then drained
500g cavolo nero or kale, shredded
good-quality extra virgin olive oil, for drizzling
sea salt and freshly ground black pepper
freshly grated Parmesan cheese, to serve

Heat the olive oil in a large pan, add the finely chopped vegetables, then cover and cook slowly for 30 minutes, until very soft and slightly caramelised. Add the garlic and oregano and cook for 2 more minutes. Stir in the tomatoes and simmer for 10 minutes, until reduced and thickened. Add the beans and the farro, cover with water (or stock) and simmer for 30 minutes or until the farro is tender. Add the shredded cavolo nero and cook for 15 minutes. Season to taste and add extra water or stock if the soup is too thick for your liking. Drizzle with olive oil and serve with Parmesan cheese.

Moroccan Lamb Soup

This is a version of harira – a traditional North African soup made with chick peas, lentils, lamb and warm, fragrant spices such as cinnamon and coriander. If you don't have the vegetables listed below, just substitute whatever is available.

Serves 6–8

1 tablespoon butter
1 tablespoon olive oil
2 onions, chopped
3 carrots, diced
3 celery stalks, diced
1 leek, diced
4 turnips, diced
a pinch of saffron
250g shoulder of lamb, cut into 1cm dice
3 garlic cloves, crushed
½ teaspoon ground cinnamon
1 teaspoon ground turmeric
1 teaspoon ground coriander
200g red lentils (and/or yellow split peas)
400g can of tomatoes
1 litre chicken stock
425g can of chick peas, drained
1 tablespoon chopped coriander or mint
sea salt and freshly ground black pepper

Heat the butter and oil in a large pan, add the vegetables and saffron and cook for 5 minutes. Stir in the diced lamb, garlic and spices and cook slowly for about 20 minutes, until the vegetables and meat are lightly browned.

Add the lentils and/or split peas and cook for 5 minutes. Add the canned tomatoes and simmer for 15 minutes over a low heat. Pour in the chicken stock, bring to the boil, then reduce the heat and simmer for about 30 minutes or until the lentils are soft and the meat is tender. Stir in the drained chickpeas and season well. Sprinkle with the herbs and serve.

Navarin of Lamb and Spring Vegetables

This late spring (or early summer, depending on the weather) stew contains so many vegetables that it is a meal in itself. Serve with a green salad and some decent bread to mop up the juices.

Serves 8

1kg boneless shoulder of lamb, cut into 2cm dice
25g butter
1 tablespoon plain flour
1 tablespoon tomato purée
about 1 litre chicken or lamb stock
1 garlic clove, crushed
1 teaspoon sugar
1 bouquet garni (a sprig of rosemary, a sprig of thyme and a bay leaf,
    tied together)
8 new potatoes, scrubbed and halved
8 carrots, scrubbed, halved if large
8 small onions or shallots, or 2 large onions cut into quarters
5 turnips, peeled and cut into quarters (or left whole if they are
    very small)
200g peas (frozen are acceptable)
200g broad beans (optional)
1 tablespoon chopped parsley
sea salt and freshly ground black pepper

Sprinkle the lamb with salt and pepper and leave for 1 hour. Heat the butter in a large, heavy-based pan, add the lamb (in batches if necessary) and cook over a medium heat for about 10 minutes, until browned all over. Add the flour and cook, stirring, over a low heat for about 4 minutes. Add the tomato purée and then gradually stir in half the stock until you have a smooth sauce. Add the garlic, sugar and bouquet garni, plus enough of the remaining stock just to cover the lamb. Bring to the boil, cover and simmer for 1 hour. Add the root vegetables and onions and cook, uncovered, for 45 minutes, until tender. Skim off any surface fat, season to taste and add the peas, and the broad beans, if using. Simmer for 5 minutes, then scatter with the parsley and serve.

Shin of Beef, Noodle and Vegetable Soup

Jane used to make this soup for Tokelauan dignitaries in Samoa. Essentially a reworking of the classic Vietnamese noodle dish, pho, it is a great way of making the most of a cheap cut of beef and any spare vegetables that are lurking in the fridge. If you already have some good stock to hand, there is no reason why you can't use other types of meat or fish, reducing the cooking time accordingly.

Serves 6–8

1kg shin of beef (on the bone, if possible), in 2 or 3 large chunks
2 onions, sliced
4cm piece of fresh ginger, peeled and thinly sliced
1 red chilli, thinly sliced
3 star anise
1 tablespoon soy sauce
1 beef stock cube
1 head of garlic, cut horizontally in half
100g rice noodles, soaked in hot water for 10 minutes, then drained
1 tablespoon chopped coriander or basil
about 400g mixed vegetables – choose from:
   carrot and/or celery batons
   cauliflower and/or broccoli florets
   purple sprouting broccoli florets
   peppers, sliced
   spinach, chard and/or pak choi
   mushrooms, sliced

Place the beef in a pan with the onions, ginger, chilli, star anise, soy sauce, stock cube and garlic. Add enough water to cover by 3cm and bring to the boil. Reduce the heat, cover and simmer for 2 hours or until the beef is tender.

Add the prepared vegetables to the pan and cook for 10 minutes. Turn off the heat and add the rice noodles. Thin with a little hot water, if necessary, to give a soup consistency, then sprinkle with the herbs. To serve, you can either leave the beef in chunks or take it out of the pan and break it up into smaller pieces, removing the bone.

Indonesian Green Vegetable Salad with Coconut Dressing

Jane first ate this at a hotel buffet in Bali. The blachan in the coconut dressing has quite a strong, fishy taste and can be omitted if you prefer, but it is important to keep tasting the dressing to check that it has the right balance of sweet and sour.

Serves 4

450g mixed green vegetables, such as French beans, Chinese cabbage,
   Hispi cabbage or spinach
¼–½ cucumber
shredded mint leaves, to garnish

For the coconut dressing:
100g desiccated coconut
1 garlic clove, peeled
1 green chilli, deseeded and chopped
1cm piece of blachan (dried shrimp paste), if available
juice of 1 lemon or 2 limes
sugar, to taste
sea salt

Blanch French beans in boiling water for 2–3 minutes, until just cooked. Drain and then rinse immediately in cold water to retain the colour. Shred cabbage and spinach, but not too finely, blanch in boiling water for 1 minute, then drain. Refresh in cold water and drain again. Cut the cucumber into 2.5cm lengths and then cut each chunk into 10 pieces.

For the dressing, put the coconut and 150ml water in a pan, bring to the boil and simmer for 5 minutes. Remove from the heat and leave to cool. In a pestle and mortar, pound the garlic and chilli to a paste with the blachan, if using, then mix in the coconut. Add the lemon or lime juice, plus sugar and salt to taste.

Transfer the dressing to a large bowl, then add the prepared vegetables. Toss well and serve sprinkled with the shredded mint.

Roasted Root Vegetables

We serve this in various guises throughout the autumn and winter, depending on what is available. Roasting root vegetables caramelises them slightly and intensifies their natural flavours. We occasionally drizzle them with a little honey before cooking and then finish the dish off with a splash of balsamic vinegar.

Serves 4

about 1kg mixed vegetables – choose from:
  baking potatoes
  beetroot
  carrots
  celeriac
  Jerusalem artichokes
  squash
  parsnips
  red onions or shallots
  kohlrabi
  turnip/swede
4 garlic cloves, unpeeled
olive oil for drizzling
1 teaspoon thyme leaves and/or chopped rosemary
sea salt and freshly ground black pepper

Peel the vegetables and cut them into 3cm chunks; if you are using beetroot and carrot, cut them slightly smaller, as they take longer to cook. If using onions, simply cut them into quarters, leaving the root on to hold them together; leave shallots whole.

Parboil the potatoes for 2 minutes, then drain. Put all the vegetables in a roasting tray in a single layer, add the garlic and drizzle with olive oil. Sprinkle with the thyme and/or chopped rosemary and season with salt and pepper. Place in an oven preheated to 180°C/Gas Mark 4 and roast for about 1 hour, turning halfway through, until all the vegetables are tender and browned.

✦ You could cook a selection of vegetables, prepared as above, in parchment parcels, following the recipe on page 223.

Spring Vegetable Risotto

This risotto can be made with one, two or a mixture of vegetables but is also a very good way of using up bits from your box. If you are including spinach, you might need a little less stock, as it gives off liquid during cooking.

Serves 4

1.15 litres good-quality chicken or vegetable stock, preferably
  homemade
1 tablespoon olive oil
2 tablespoons butter
1 onion, finely chopped
1 leek, finely chopped
1 celery stalk, finely chopped
1 garlic clove, crushed
220g Arborio rice
150ml vermouth or white wine
1 tablespoon freshly grated Parmesan cheese, plus extra to serve
1 tablespoon chopped parsley, chives or spring onions
sea salt and freshly ground black pepper
500–600g mixed vegetables – choose from:
  courgettes, diced
  French beans, chopped
  asparagus spears, sliced
  shelled fresh peas
  broad beans, blanched briefly in boiling water
  spinach leaves

Bring the stock to simmering point in a pan. Heat the olive oil and half the butter in a large, deep frying pan and add the onion, leek and celery. Cook gently for about 5 minutes, until soft, then stir in the garlic. Add the rice and turn up the heat a little. Season well and cook for a minute, stirring so the rice is coated with the fat. Add the vermouth or white wine and cook, stirring, until it has evaporated. Start adding the hot stock a ladleful at a time, keeping the mixture at a simmer and adding more stock when each addition has been absorbed. Add the vegetables according to how long they take to cook: courgettes, French beans and asparagus should go in 5 minutes after starting to add the stock; peas 10 minutes (add them at the end if using frozen ones); and broad beans and spinach 15 minutes. After the rice has been cooking for

15–18 minutes, check it: when it is done, it should be tender but still slightly chewy. The whole dish should have a creamy appearance.

Take the pan off the heat and stir in the remaining butter and the Parmesan. Season to taste, then cover and let it sit for 5 minutes. Sprinkle with the herbs or spring onions and extra Parmesan, then serve straight away.

Vegetables à la Grecque

A light, refreshing way of preparing summer vegetables. It can be served hot or cold, on its own or as an accompaniment to pâtés and cold meats. It will keep happily in the fridge for a week, making it a good dish to dip into.

Serves 8 as a side dish

600g vegetables – use just one type or a combination, for example:
    fennel, cut into quarters
    cauliflower, cut into florets
    leeks, cut into 3cm lengths
    celery hearts, split into sixths
    button mushrooms, halved
1 tablespoon olive oil
juice and grated zest of 2 lemons
1 onion, sliced
3 garlic cloves, crushed
8 coriander seeds
½ teaspoon fennel seeds
1 bay leaf
a sprig of thyme
a sprig of rosemary
½ teaspoon salt
chopped parsley, to garnish (optional)

Place the prepared vegetables in a large pan with all the rest of the ingredients except the parsley. Add enough boiling water just to cover, then cover the pan and simmer for about 5 minutes, until the vegetables are just tender. Transfer to a serving dish and leave to cool. Sprinkle with chopped parsley before serving, if liked.

Malaysian Vegetable Pickle

Variations on this can be found throughout Southeast Asia. It is generally served as an accompaniment, bringing a different texture and a sharpness to all sorts of dishes.

Makes about 1kg

100g plain, unroasted peanuts
6 almonds
3 small onions, chopped
2 garlic cloves, chopped
5 tablespoons sunflower oil
1½ tablespoons ground turmeric
300ml white vinegar
3 tablespoons light soft brown sugar
sea salt
500g mixed vegetables – choose from:
  carrots, sliced
  cauliflower florets
  cabbage, sliced
  cucumber, sliced
  French beans, sliced
  green and/or red chillies, sliced

Put the peanuts on a baking tray and roast in an oven preheated to 200°C/Gas Mark 6 for 10–15 minutes, until browned. Rub off the skins and pound the nuts lightly in a pestle and mortar, then set aside.

In a food processor, grind together the almonds, onions and garlic. Heat the oil in a pan, add the onion, garlic and almond mixture and fry for 3 minutes, until lightly browned. Stir in the turmeric, followed by the vinegar, sugar and salt. Add the sliced vegetables and cook for 5 minutes. Finally add the peanuts. Leave to cool, then transfer to a sterilised Kilner jar or a jar with a screwtop lid. Keep for 2 weeks before using. Once opened, the pickle should keep for about 6 weeks in the fridge.

Mexican Dressing

This dressing can be used to liven up an assortment of vegetables at any time of year. Try it tossed with a combination of early-summer salad vegetables (e.g. French beans, sugarsnaps, tomatoes, cucumber and avocado), or with a mixture of blanched late-summer vegetables (squash, corn, tomatoes and runner beans), or with roasted or boiled winter root vegetables.

Serves 6–8

50ml lemon or lime juice
150ml olive oil
½ red onion, finely chopped
2 chillies, finely chopped
2 garlic cloves, crushed
1 tablespoon chopped coriander
½ teaspoon ground cumin
sea salt and freshly ground black pepper

Put all the ingredients in a food processor and blend until smooth. Can be kept in the fridge in a jar with a screwtop lid for several weeks.

The last leek: using up the odds and ends in your veg box

Sometimes when you're down to the last leek, plus perhaps a couple of carrots and half a cabbage, inspiration runs dry. We asked everyone involved in Riverford how they use up box ends. Below are some of our favourite suggestions which you can adapt to suit what vegetables you have left over.

✦ To use up any greens, blanch them for a minute or two in boiling water, then cook gently in olive oil with sliced garlic and chilli. Stir in some drained canned pulses (such as cannellini, borlotti or flageolet beans), season well and drizzle with good olive oil.

✦ Stir-fry shredded cabbage, chard or spring greens in a little oil for a few minutes and serve sprinkled with soy sauce.

✦ Try different vegetables in the risotto recipes on page 178 and page 406. Add a few dried porcini mushrooms (soaked in hot water for about 20 minutes first) if using earthy root vegetables.

✦ Almost any raw or cooked vegetables are good served with the Mexican Dressing on page 409.

✦ Buy a bottle (or five!) of sweet chilli sauce. It can lift most vegetables from being a plain boiled or steamed accompaniment to the main attraction.

✦ Make a frittata, substituting vegetables for the spinach and crab in the recipe on page 328. Add different cheeses and herbs, if you like.

✦ Most vegetables can be turned into soup: sweat some onions and/or leeks in butter or oil, add your chopped vegetables, plus any seasonings (thyme, rosemary, ginger, cumin, chilli), then cover with stock or water and simmer until tender. Blend until smooth and season to taste.

✦ Chargrill one or a mixture of vegetables such as fennel, courgettes, peppers and tomatoes, then dress with oil and vinegar and serve on toast.

◆ Make stock: chop up the woody outer stalks of celery, the odd carrot and other vegetable scraps (but not starchy vegetables such as potatoes and parsnips), then cover with water in a pan, add a few aromatics, if you have them (bay leaves, thyme sprigs, parsley stalks) and simmer for about 30 minutes. Strain and keep in the fridge for a few days, or in the freezer. If you don't have the time or the inclination to make stock, simply chop up the vegetables and freeze them for later.

◆ Just about anything can be juiced with a good-quality juice extractor and you can use odd bits of fruit and veg to make delicious mixed juices. Try beetroot, apple and ginger; apple, celery, cucumber and mint; carrot, apple and ginger; or carrot, celery and pear.

Riverford Bread

Not a vegetable dish, but it makes a meal of any of the soups and stews in this book. This is the bread we serve in the Field Kitchen, and we have had so many requests for the recipe that we felt we had to include it.

Makes 2 loaves

2 teaspoons dried yeast (fast action yeast is fine)
2 dessertspoons brown sugar or honey
3 dessertspoons olive oil
600ml tepid water
450g malted flour (or wholemeal flour)
450g white bread flour
150g rye flour
2 teaspoons salt
2 tablespoons polenta

Stir the yeast, sugar or honey and olive oil into the tepid water in a large bowl and leave for 5 minutes. Gradually add the flour and salt, mixing to form a dough – you can do this either by hand or in a mixer fitted with a dough hook. You may have to add more flour or water, depending on the consistency. However, it is better for the dough to be wetter rather than dry.

Turn out on to a work surface and knead for 10 minutes or until smooth and elastic. Place in a large bowl, cover and leave for about 1 hour, until doubled in size.

Knock back the dough, cut it in half and shape into 2 loaves (we do this by hand to make long sausage shapes but you could put each piece in a greased loaf tin, if you prefer). Roll the loaves in the polenta and place on greased baking trays, then cover and leave to rise again for about 40 minutes.

Bake in an oven preheated to 220°C/Gas Mark 7 for 15 minutes. Turn the loaves over and cook for a further 5–10 minutes, until they sound hollow when tapped on the base. Leave on a wire rack to cool.

Index

Recipes in lower case type refer to easy ideas or recipe variations.